SERIOUS
BARBECUE

Smoke, Char,
Baste, and Brush
Your Way to
Great Outdoor
Cooking

HYPERION
NEW YORK

SERIOUS BARBECUE

Adam Perry Lang

WITH **JJ GOODE** AND **AMY VOGLER**

PHOTOGRAPHS BY **DAVID LOFTUS**

Copyright © 2009 Adam Perry Lang

Photography by David Loftus

Library of Congress Cataloging-in-Publication Data

Perry Lang, Adam.
    Serious barbecue : smoke, char, baste, and brush your way to great outdoor cooking /
Adam Perry Lang, with JJ Goode and Amy Vogler.
        p.   cm.
    ISBN 978-1-4013-2306-6
1. Barbecue cookery. I. Goode, JJ. II. Vogler, Amy. III. Title.
    TX840.B3P48 2009
    641.5'784--dc22
        2009001765

Hyperion books are available for special promotions and premiums. For details contact the
HarperCollins Special Markets Department in the New York office at 212-207-7528, fax 212-207-7222,
or email spsales@harpercollins.com.

BOOK DESIGN BY SHUBHANI SARKAR

First Edition

10 9 8 7 6 5 4 3 2 1

TO MY WIFE,

FLEUR

AND TO MY CHILDREN,

MAX AND **NOA**

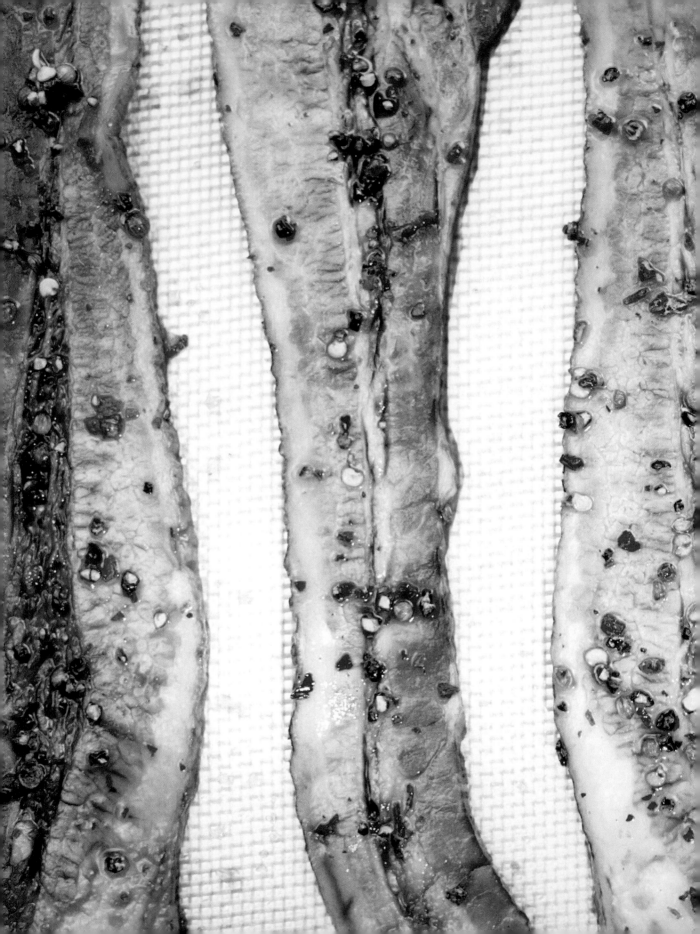

Contents

SERIOUS
BARBECUE

Introduction

What struck me was the sky, the endless expanse of blue that stretched over the New Mexico ranch where I first became obsessed with barbecue. I had been slaving away in restaurant kitchens for almost a decade, and hadn't seen nearly enough sky. But I wasn't complaining:

These were some of the best kitchens in the world. While attending the Culinary Institute of America, I began working at Le Cirque under Daniel Boulud, then as part of the select kitchen team that helped launch Boulud's first restaurant, Restaurant Daniel. I later moved to Paris to work with the legendary Guy Savoy, among others. Then I really hit the jackpot: I became a private chef, a job that took me all over the world and to that sprawling ranch in New Mexico.

In my downtime on the ranch, I'd hang out with the Texas-born ranch hands who worked on the property, mending fences, breaking horses, and otherwise keeping the place running. We had a blast. We shot arrows at Styrofoam deer, caught and cooked rattlesnake, and, best of all, made amazing barbecue with a 1,000-pound pit that my new buddies had fashioned using a welding torch and an old propane tank. At this pit, I found a new respect for the primal art of barbecue and the people who

cooked it. The food is elemental, at its core just meat and fire, and its appeal is obvious. One look at a slab of brisket, coated with its deep mahogany crust, or a mass of juicy pulled pork, and you get the sudden urge to tear into it with both hands. It was everything the complicated stuff I'd been cooking in restaurants was not. And yet my new friends were as passionate as any of the professionals I'd met in French kitchens. I saw a chance to explore something new, to learn about an entirely different culinary culture.

Of course, this insight didn't register right away. At the time, one of the ranch hands suggested I open a barbecue restaurant. "No way," I thought. I was familiar with that game—the investors, the sky-high rent, the reviews published just weeks after a place opens—and I wanted no part of it. But I got over that pretty quickly. I had an entrepreneurial itch and wanted to cook mind-blowing food that didn't come with a hefty price tag, and barbecue is one of those cuisines whose appeal is universal—at barbecue joints, I've seen truckers and oilmen, cashiers and bankers all eating side by side.

In 2003, after I'd spent time tasting barbecue with some of the best pitmasters in the world, I opened Daisy May's BBQ USA, a no-frills barbecue joint on the westernmost reaches of midtown Manhattan, and dispatched a small fleet of pulled-pork-and-chili-slinging street carts. To help fund this adventure, I took a gig as executive chef at Robert's Steakhouse, where I dry-aged carefully sourced prime beef for as long as sixteen weeks. In 2007, I left Robert's to become the meat maestro at Mario Batali and Joe Bastianich's fabulous Vegas steakhouse, Carnevino.

As for those reviews I dreaded, they came in a flood, and weren't so scary after all. Actually, they were glowing. All of a sudden, my restaurant (and often my face) was everywhere—in *The New York Times*, *New York* magazine, *Food & Wine*, *Vogue*, and more. I was on TV with Rachael Ray, catering parties for Jean-Georges Vongerichten and Daniel Boulud, and featured in the book *Perfection* by Heston Blumenthal, who called my dry-aged steaks the best in the world. I had proved myself to the food industry and the New Yorkers who packed Daisy May's, but I wasn't finished. I was determined to show the rest of the country what I could do, to dispel the ridiculous notion—nearly a religious truth among some Southerners—that great barbecue couldn't exist in New York, that a Yankee couldn't hold his own with the big boys of the South.

This was the same kind of talk I'd heard for years in French kitchens: If you're not French, you can't cook great French food. Now it was: If you're not from Kansas City or North Carolina or Texas, you can't cook great barbecue. To me, it was all nonsense. Cooking isn't genetic—it's about what you learn and how you apply it. So I set out on the barbecue competition trail with

just my knives and a tent. (At first, I had to borrow an offset smoker.) If the biggest pork competition was in Iowa, then I'd go to Iowa. If the best of the best were gathering to cook ribs in Kansas City, that's where I'd be.

And here's the thing—I won. In Kansas City, at the American Royal Invitational (aka the World Series of Barbecue), my pork shoulder won first place. In Des Moines, at the World Pork Expo, one of the most prestigious competitions in the country, I was named Grand Champion, plus my ribs got a perfect score. I finally had a grassroots sort of barbecue validation from some of the toughest critics around. And, man, was it sweet.

Even better, I fell in love with the culture. Like the ranch hands I'd met in New Mexico, the people on the competition circuit inspired me with their passion. Many had come from thousands of miles away, hauling smokers, coolers, spouses, and kids. There were pop-up 10-by-10 tents next to $300,000 trailers (and, believe me, the big guys didn't always win). I experienced firsthand that barbecue is a lifestyle, and those who choose to take part in it form a community: They share meals and beer, they swap advice and stories. Sure, everyone wanted to win, but the point of it all wasn't the competition, it was the camaraderie. For my first competition, I borrowed everything—the tables, chairs, smoker, and mobile trailer—from the friends I made in the barbecue community. One of my competitors even picked me up at the airport.

This spirit is alive at Daisy May's. If you come by, you'll see why I left those fancy French kitchens. Barbecue fanatics pack the three communal tables, some nibbling from racks of sweet, sticky Kansas City–style pork ribs and others are tearing into my blue-ribbon-winning pork shoulder. Then a whole pig comes out, and for a minute, everything stops. Heads turn, bodies shift, and people rise to see the animal in all

its glory—the juicy, pinkish flesh, the burnished skin. A few snap pictures. The lucky group that ordered it beams proudly as they slip on latex gloves and go at it. (They might even offer a bite to the onlookers.) This is the food I want to teach everyone to cook.

When I started writing this book, my first order of business was to take a stand: "Barbecue" does not just mean the slow-cooked, smoke perfumed meats of the South. It also means the charred, juicy direct-grilled meats, which I had become equally obsessed at perfecting. So let's dispense with the controversy that lurks around many a barbecue book. When I was growing up on Long Island, barbecuing meant going into someone's backyard and grilling. This is what it means for most people in the Northeast. Sure, cooking over high heat (what I'll call Yankee barbecue) and cooking slowly with indirect heat (Southern barbecue) are very different methods, but both have a right to the noble title. That means you'll find recipes in this book for Porterhouses and skirt steaks, pork chops and chicken breasts—not just pork ribs, pork shoulder, and brisket.

This is an exciting time to be talking about meat. It's becoming easier and easier to buy meat from animals that have been raised with animal welfare in mind, and so much of the time, this careful raising goes hand in hand with better-tasting meat. And as this book went to press, folks in the meat industry have been buzzing about the passage of the 2008 Farm Bill, which included a rule called Country

of Origin Labeling (COOL). It requires grocery stores of a certain size to display where the meat they sell comes from. This is good news for consumers.

While I was researching this book, I spent a lot of time in the supermarket, thinking about what kind of meat is available, what labels tell you, and what they don't. I was inspecting a particularly pretty rib eye when a man came up to me. He apologized for interrupting my romantic moment with the meat and asked what everyone should but few people have the nerve to. "I don't really know how to pick out steaks—could you help?" Without knowing it, he had come to the right guy. But answering him taught me something, too. It gave me a blueprint for this book. Because to answer him, I had to ask my own questions: Did he want a supremely beefy, fat-riddled steak, like a rib eye, or one that takes well to marinating, like a flank steak? Or did he want a cut that he could cook slowly to a meltingly tender texture? And how much was he willing to spend? Would he rather pay a bit more for an extra bump in flavor? Or would he sacrifice a little beefiness for a really tender steak?

These questions informed the book's structure. I didn't want to just offer recipes. I wanted to teach people how to identify exactly what they want, and how to find it at the market. I wanted to make them better, more demanding consumers, to teach them to be better cooks, not just recipe followers. My goal was to create instinct. I also wanted to give people options. It's easy to give a few great recipes for a ridiculously marbled prime strip steak, but not everyone is willing to pay the relatively high price. So in each chapter, I take you on a trip through the butcher case, providing one amazing recipe for almost every cut you can think of, a recipe that accentuates its best qualities.

I had another goal in writing this book: simplicity. The paradox of barbecue is that mak-ing this elemental food not just good but great can seem complicated until you know what you're doing. So I've tried hard not to over-whelm you with information. Instead of provid-ing everything there is to know about, say, charcoal or brining, I provided only what you need to know.

Then, of course, there's the matter of style. My style. You'll notice that many of the recipes have techniques in common. For instance, no matter what I'm grilling, I typically use season-ing blends *and* glazes *and* basting butters *and* sauces at strategic times during the cooking process. I don't just want to add flavor, I want to build it, brick by brick, layer by layer. And wait until you see what a difference this makes! I also do things like paint my cutting board with glazes or butters, so that when I'm slicing my barbecue, each piece picks up some added oomph. And instead of always using a basting brush to apply butter to my meat, I use a make-shift version made of a bunch of herbs tied to the handle of a wooden spoon, because it adds, yes, yet another layer of aroma and herbaceous-ness. I'm always asking myself: Where can I find flavor? Where is no one else looking? And fi-nally, I like to debunk barbecue myths: In my world, flare-ups are good (as long as you control them, and I'll show you how to do it by jockey-ing, flipping, and stacking), wrapping your Southern barbecue in foil is *not* sacrilege, and recipes don't call for room-temperature meat. In fact, I've written just about every recipe for meat that has come straight out of the fridge.

Yet while I often diverge from the expected, I'm not out to be flashy or creative. Rather, my goal was to create a book that you'll turn to again and again. A book that any novice could pick up and use to make a killer pork shoulder or rib eye. A book that any old hand can use to bring his food to the next level, to achieve that holy grail of barbecuing: bragging rights with a side order of good times.

BARBECUE
BASICS

TOOLS AND EQUIPMENT

Whether you're a novice or expert, whether you're planning to grill a few steaks or barbecue a brisket, this is what I think you should have on hand. Of course, I know it sounds like a lot, so for you part-timers, I've provided a just-enough-stuff list, too.

Just-Enough-Stuff List

Tongs, oil towel, grill brush, fire extinguisher, firebricks, instant-read thermometer, spatula, lighter, cutting board.

TONGS: Heavyweight restaurant tongs. Avoid the fancy ones, because they just tire your hands.

OIL TOWEL: Soaked but not dripping in canola oil (which is cheap and has a higher smoke point than, say, olive oil). Just don't use a towel that you'd ever use to wash your face.

GRILL BRUSH: Invest in the sturdiest you can, one with heavy tines that won't fall out. It's better to replace it often rather than invest in a fancy one, and price doesn't always indicate quality.

HEAVYWEIGHT GRATES: Preferably cast iron. Use them even if you have to lay them on top of the flimsy ones that come with your grill.

ENOUGH FUEL: Do not get caught with half a tank of propane or too little charcoal. Always, always have more than you think you need, just in case—you'll notice I haven't mentioned lighter fluid.

SAFETY ASH BUCKET AND SHOVEL: You'd be surprised how long ashes stay lit. Have a safe place to put them. The shovel makes it easy to move them.

FRESH SPICES: Don't ruin a great meat with dull spices. Buy small amounts. Keep replacing them.

PLATTERS READY FOR YOUR BARBECUE: Don't get caught without a big enough platter. And have it ready for your food, because a hot cooker is not a safe resting place for finished meat.

FIRE EXTINGUISHER: Hey, you never know.

THREE TYPES OF THERMOMETERS:

- An instant-read thermometer gives you a quick, accurate temperature reading.
- A remote thermometer: Great for large cuts, it lets you monitor the temperature in real time without opening and closing the cooker door.
- A laser thermometer: For calibrating your cooker's temperature. (See Calibrating Your Grill page 15.)

NOTEPAD AND PEN: Write down everything— what works, what doesn't, and ideas for next time. When it comes to barbecue, school's never over.

WATER AND SUNBLOCK: You'll be having so much fun you might not notice that accidents with the barbecue are not the only way to get burned outside.

SPRAY BOTTLE: Not for taming the flame, but for spraying the meat with liquids like watered-down apple juice to add color and flavor.

BAKING DISHES AND ALUMINUM PANS: Handy for everything from shuffling meat around to adding pastes during cooking to (when it has seen better days) using as a drip pan. The disposable ones are cheap, reusable, stackable, and easy to clean.

PLASTIC QUART CONTAINERS OR MASON JARS: Great for mixing sauces, glazes, spices, and everything else.

IMMERSION BLENDER: One of the greatest inventions: Why haul your ingredients to a blender when you can bring the blender to them?

MICROPLANE GRATER: Grates the finest garlic, shallots, apples, chiles, and citrus zest, all of which are awesome for adding last-minute flavor boosts.

TWO CUTTING BOARDS: One for raw meat (not wood for this one, please), one for cooked meat. I sometimes drizzle sauce or glaze, or even butter, salt, pepper, and fresh herbs, on this second board, so when I'm slicing, the meat picks up some extra flavor.

FIREBRICKS: Wrapped in heavy-duty aluminum foil, they can weigh meat down, block heat and serve as a safe resting place for meat, and if placed on a sheet pan they can create super-hot spots on the grill grates. They're more resistant to heat than regular bricks.

HEAVY-DUTY ALUMINUM FOIL: For wrapping, for keeping things warm, for creating an effective makeshift griddle on a grill, for cleaning your grill (just crumple it up!).

HEAVY-DUTY PLASTIC WRAP: For keeping things moist throughout cooking. Just have it. You'll understand why.

HEAT-PROOF GLOVES: For moving grill racks, or for handling hot meat or coals.

BEAR PAWS (BEAR CLAWS): They make pulling pork shoulder a snap.

SPICE GRINDER: Do I have to tell you why? A coffee grinder works well, especially if you use it exclusively for spice grinding.

LARGE RESEALABLE BAGS OR GARBAGE BAGS: For marinating meat.

A SHARP KNIFE: So you can slice your barbecue the way you like it.

A GRIDDLE: Enables flare-up-free browning—particularly useful for fattier items like burgers or rib eyes.

SYRINGE (INJECTING NEEDLE): For injecting brines.

GRILL PRESS: For weighing down meats and vegetables. It keeps items in contact with heat source, which helps them brown evenly and exceptionally, and helps them keep their integrity of shape.

GRILL BASKET: Lets you apply direct heat to cuts that are too tender to handle without them falling apart—think pork belly, trotters, and my picnic ham.

MEAT POUNDER: For flattening meat and whacking in flavorful ingredients. You can use a rolling pin, if you'd like.

DIRECT GRILLS:
GAS GRILLS, CHARCOAL GRILLS, KETTLE GRILLS

What Direct Means

Direct grilling means hitting meat, fruits, or vegetables with heat that hasn't been deflected or significantly diffused. This is especially useful for cuts that have lots of fat and low amounts of collagen. Contrary to popular opinion, it does not always involve high heat (which can make really leaner cuts like chicken breasts tough and dry), though the temperature used for direct grilling tends to be higher than those used for indirect cooking. You want to use that direct heat to get grill marks, which are cool-looking but, even more important, also carry a lot of the flavor characteristic of outdoor cooking. That's why we typically put relatively thin cuts like steaks, chops, and loins directly over the heat: By the time the interior is cooked to perfection, the outside has had the chance to become all brown and delicious.

Who Is It For?

If you love steaks, chops, and chicken with beautiful brown crusts and grill marks, a direct-heat cooker is for you, though you can also close the lid and use it like an oven. This is the cooker that provides grilled flavor with stunning char.

Where the Flavor Comes From

When you're direct grilling, there are two sources of flavor to keep in mind—besides that of the meat and whatever you put on the meat, of course:

- Caramelization: The heat changes the composition of the proteins and sugars in the meat and forms all sorts of new and tasty flavor compounds.
- Flavor bombs: As fat and moisture leave the meat, they drip onto the heat source and vaporize, transforming and rising back up to the meat and bringing tons of flavor with them. Nothing delivers more flavor of this sort than a charcoal fire, though many gas grills now come with a lava rock diffuser that comes pretty close.

Heat

Many grills rely on gas or electricity for heat. Others rely on natural fuels like wood and charcoal. Some grills even let you switch between gas and charcoal. Choose whatever makes you most excited about cooking, whether that's the ease of turning a switch to control the heat, as with a gas grill (which I almost always prefer to electric), or the rustic feeling of grilling over charcoal.

Natural Fuel Versus Gas

Don't get me wrong—I love gas grills, but nothing beats cooking over wood or charcoal. It might take a bit of patience and skill to master, but it delivers the hottest heat and the ultimate in "grilled" flavor.

Using Wood on Your Gas-Powered Cooker

Even if your grill doesn't have a smoke box, you can use wood smoke to give your meat color and flavor. Make an envelope out of a piece of aluminum foil, fill it with chips, pellets, or sawdust, close it up, and poke a bunch of holes in it (about ten in a 5-inch × 5-inch packet). Put this directly on top of the coals or on the heat deflector plate, and cook away.

Managing Flare-Ups

It's an almost inevitable result of direct grilling. Any time you have fat or oil dripping onto coals, wood, or gas flame, you can get a "flare-up," when the flames suddenly rise up and engulf your meat. I'm not as averse to flare-ups as some outdoor cooks. In fact, I embrace them, though there's a fine line between this burning your meat and giving it a flavor boost. (You'll have to decide for yourself where you stand, but either way, when you do get a big flare-up, please don't try to extinguish it with water! You wouldn't put out a grease fire with water, would you?) Flare-ups are not such a great thing, however, when sugar or delicate spices are involved.

To make sure you have the right amount of flame assisting the development of tasty caramelization without moving into the no-fly zone of carbonization, I do three things:

- Jockey: When you see an unwanted flare-up, don't panic. Just move your meat to another hot part of the grill. If you're still getting flare-ups and are afraid that your meat might burn, retreat to the lower-temperature zone.
- Stack: If your grill doesn't have a zone of lower temperature, try stacking, putting any meat that needs a break from the flame on top of one that doesn't. It will continue cooking because of the residual heat but it will be protected from direct flame.

• Flip: Yet another way to make sure a flare-up doesn't burn your meat.

Grates

Some people think picking a grill is just about finding the one with the most BTUs. But remember, your heat is coming from two different places: The flames and from the grates that have absorbed heat from those flames. That means you should take care choosing the material for these grates. I go for heavyweight steel or cast-iron grates. They take a bit longer to heat up, but once they do, they hold on tight to that heat, giving you the ability to create serious caramelization in the form of grill marks and making it less likely that your meat will stick to them.

Keep those grates clean! Get the best brush you can find and replace it often.

And as you're cooking, use your tongs to rub the grates with a dedicated towel dipped in (but not dripping with) canola oil. This forms a slick surface and prevents meat and char from sticking. Duck skin works, too, just don't use olive oil. It has a lower smoke point and doesn't form as effective a barrier.

The Griddle

This inexpensive cast-iron device that you place right on your grill grates helps you gather an intense heat and render fat, without that fat dripping onto the fire. That way, you can caramelize without having to deal with flare-ups. It's particularly useful for fattier cuts, like prime or choice steaks, or my hamburger, which has a bunch of beautiful fat to keep it juicy. After some of the fat has rendered, moisture has evaporated, and caramelization has begun, I'll often transfer the meat to the grill grates, so the flavor bombing can begin.

INDIRECT COOKERS

What Does Indirect Mean?

Indirect cooking means that your heat source is either in a chamber far from your meat (as in an offset cooker) or that the heat source is blocked or deflected by a metal plate (as in a stacked cooker). While direct grilling is like cooking on your stovetop—the flames or burner heats your pan, which cooks whatever's in it—indirect cooking is more like roasting in your oven. Because the heat—whether it's produced by charcoal, wood, gas, or electricity—is deflected, by the time it reaches the meat, it's a gentle sort of heat that envelops it rather than hits it from just one side.

Who Are They For?

If you're into ribs, pulled pork, brisket, and meats that you'd roast—items that develop dark, tasty crusts on the outside—then you want the oven-like heat provided by an indirect cooker.

The downside is that most of these give you no option to direct grill, to apply concentrated heat to one specific area. Plus you don't get the flavor bombs that happen when meat juices and fat hit the coals and vaporize.

Sizes vary wildly: You can get a gigantic cooker or a tiny one. Just be sure you pick the one that actually matches your cooking habits: You might buy a giant cooker, because it looks awesome, but if you don't fill it up, it won't have the natural moisture inside that's so great for barbecue.

What to Use It For

Nothing beats indirect cooking for thick cuts, like the brisket and the shoulder. The relatively mellow heat can penetrate deep into the meat before the outside of the meat has overcooked, plus it can break down collagen into gelatin, turning tough cuts into meat you could cut with a spoon.

Barbecue and Indirect Cooking

There are exceptions, but when people talk about Southern barbecue, they're typically referring to a type of cooking that can be classified as indirect. Charcoal or wood provides heat as well as flavor.

You can cook indirectly on any barbecue. With ceramic and indirect cookers, sure, but even direct grilling can provide indirect heat: All you have to do is put meat somewhere other than directly over the fire, or far enough above the fire.

Gas Versus Natural Fuel

Gas barbecues let you turn a dial to set the temperature, while those powered by natural fuels require a more hands-on approach. I actually prefer the latter. First off, gas-powered units typically have an opening to keep gas from building up inside (otherwise, uh oh!). The problem is, this lets out natural humidity, which is a cook's friend. Plus, I really like the challenge of mastering the dampers, of adapting to different external conditions. Think about it like this: You can go up a mountain two ways—you can take a helicopter or you can climb. It's your choice.

My Ideal Heat Source

I love combining charcoal (for heat) and wood chunks (for some more heat, but mostly for controlled smoke flavor).

Your Goal

Consistent temperature, just enough smoke.

Trick

Just as there are hot spots on your grates when you're direct grilling, different areas in your indirect cooker will be hotter than others. Use this to your advantage, moving meat that could use a bit more color to a hotter area or vice versa.

Seasoning

I once saw a guy take out just about every spice in his cupboard and head outside. I asked what he was up to and he said that he was going to season his grill! In this context, seasoning means something different. As you cook on your indirect cookers, you get this healthy buildup of creosote and resin (by-products of cooking with coal and wood) that will insulate your barbecue—that is, it will make its internal temperature less vulnerable to external temperature fluctuations. To get this buildup, all you have to do is cook, but you can encourage it by occasionally wiping down the inside of your cooker (when it's off, please) with a towel dipped in (but not dripping with) canola oil. If the "seasoning" starts to flake, scrape it off; otherwise, it'll flake onto your food. Nowadays, smokers are so well insulated that seasoning has become less of an issue.

NOTE: Always, always look at the operating manual first. Some cookers should not be seasoned.

CERAMIC COOKERS

Who Are They For?

Ceramic cookers can be used for direct grilling, radiant oven-like heat, *and* indirect cooking. So if you want just one cooker that will let you grill some beefy skirt steak with intense char one day and slow-cook pork shoulder the next, this is for you. I recommend this for novice barbecuers, but I use it all the time in competition, so it's great for cooks of any experience level.

Here's why they're great: First of all, you don't have to keep feeding them fuel. You can maintain a temperature of 250° F for 17 hours with just five pounds of charcoal. Second, because they have great insulation and really hold on to heat, you won't spend much time fiddling with the dampers, even in challenging weather. (Just remember that they also take a while to heat up, and it's tougher to bring their temperature down if you need to.) Finally, if your deck or yard is space-challenged, you'll love the compactness of these cookers. Yet the area of their cooking surface is also small, which means that if you're looking to cook, say, a whole brisket, you'll need to trim it to fit.

My Ideal Heat Source

Charcoal for heat, wood for smoke flavor. Because these cookers are slightly more vulnerable to clogging caused by stray ash, I typically use lump charcoal rather than briquets.

Inside the Cooker

These barbecues give you a very moist cooking environment—and when you're barbecuing, moisture is your friend. The only downside is that they also create a low-oxygen environment, which means you get slightly less smoke penetration.

Hot Tip

Unlike most direct grills, you can't create lower-heat zones on ceramic cookers using coals. But you can create them with fire bricks, laying them on the grates and putting a griddle or foil on top. Some companies offer a ceramic plate as an accessory, for this very purpose.

Be Aware

Occasionally, when you're direct grilling and the cooker gets really hot, you get a big burst of heat and smoke followed by flame when you open the lid. To limit the chance of this, close the bottom damper before opening the lid, or burp your cooker, opening it just a little to let some of the heat and smoke out. Then open it all the way. (Still, be very careful when you do.)

TEMPERATURE CONTROL

Calibrating Your Grill

Take two different grills, turn their dials to High, and you get two different temperatures. So how do you know what I mean when I suggest that you grill something over high heat? Easy! I figured it out for you. I bought an inexpensive laser thermometer, and pointed it at my grill grates. Now you can be sure that my definition of, say, high heat is the same as yours. And if it's not, you can adjust accordingly.

Here are the temperatures the thermometer registered:

> low=300°F
> medium=450°F
> high=525°F
> sear=750-plus°F

I suggest you do the same with your grill. Turn the knob to each setting, let the grates preheat, and then slowly run the laser thermometer across the surface to measure the temperature of the grates. (The temperature you record will probably vary slightly, so take the average.) This works with natural-fuel grills, too, though instead of turning a knob, you can test by using different woods or different distances between the grates and the coals. Not only will you know whether your Medium is the same as mine, but you'll also identify your grill's hot spots, which will help you use them to your advantage. You can do the same for the inside of your indirect cooker.

Hot Tip

If your grill's high setting brings you to only 500°F, you're not out of luck. Try putting a metal sheet pan on top of the grates and topping it with a few bricks wrapped in aluminum foil. After 10 minutes of trapping the heat, your grates will see a boost in temperature.

Using Those Hot and Cool Spots

Perfectly even heat is a great thing, especially on a grill with a small surface area. But on a unit with lots of space, I welcome hot spots. When you need to add some extra char or crisp some skin, transfer your meat to a hot spot. Meat getting a little too dark? Move it to a cooler one. Find out which spots are which by using a laser thermometer to test the temperature of the grill grates or by laying pieces of white bread on the grates to see if any char slower or faster than the others.

To create areas with different levels of heat on a gas grill, you can typically just turn a few knobs. On a grill without mechanical temperature control, it's all about piling coals. The higher the pile, the more heat you'll get.

Dampers: Controlling Heat by Controlling Oxygen Flow

Temperature control in an indirect cooker is a bit different. The amount of fuel and the quality of insulation will affect how *long* your fire burns, not how hot it gets. That's what the dampers are for. Because each barbecue is different, there are no hard-and-fast rules to damper control. You'll quickly get to know the quirks of your cooker. Developing a feel for it is part of the fun.

THE BASICS: Opening the dampers allows oxygen in, stoking the fire and thereby raising the temperature inside the cooker. Closing them means just the opposite.

GET GOING: When you start the fire, you'll need

the heat to build up momentum, so keep the dampers wide open. When you're approaching your goal temperature, close your dampers by half. (There's no rule for exactly when you should start closing your dampers, but after a few tries, you'll get the hang of it.) As the temperature continues to rise, close the dampers a little more, then a little more. Once you've hit your goal temperature, leave those dampers where they are.

MONITORING: Be vigilant and watch the temperature for any movement. Going a few degrees up or down is natural, but if you notice a steady rise in temperature, close your dampers a smidgen. If your cooker's temperature drops steadily, open your dampers a little. If this doesn't work, you might need to add more coals or wood. Or even carefully clean out some ash.

Weather

You can barbecue in any weather—you just have to know how to adapt to different conditions.

WINDY: In this case, an open damper will bring in more air than usual, so you don't need to open the dampers quite as much as you typically would.

HIGH HUMIDITY: If the outside air is heavy with water and stagnant, you may need to compensate by opening the dampers a bit more than you typically would.

LOW HUMIDITY: If the air outside is especially dry, then it's especially loose and free-flowing, so you may not need to open the dampers quite as much as you typically would.

VERY COLD: If it's cold, you might need more fuel to reach and maintain your goal temperature, unless your cooker is really well insulated.

VERY HOT: Even a really, really hot day won't bring temperatures even half as hot as those inside your cooker, so it won't affect you much. But you will use less fuel.

MAINTENANCE

Maintaining your outdoor cooker is easier than you may think. And though every one is different (so do follow the instructions that come with yours), there are some basic principles that you should always be aware of.

- I'll say it again: Keep that grill surface clean! Get a good, sturdy grill brush and replace it often.
- Seek out a heavy-duty grill surface, like stainless steel or cast iron, and oil it as you cook. Use tongs to wipe the grates down with a cloth or rag soaked, but not dripping, with canola oil.
- Each time you finish cooking, clean your grill grates and add a coat of oil so it's ready to go next time.
- You can clean your grates with Simple Green, a great degreaser that's nontoxic. Of course, if you have cast-iron grates, only use degreasers or soap in the most desperate of circumstances.
- Cleaning the outside of your cooker is nice to do, but it's mostly cosmetic.
- A crust on the inside of your indirect cooker is great because it insulates the walls from the temperature outside. But when it gets flaky, you must clean or scrape it, or else those flakes can end up on your food.
- You can use a no-fume oven cleaner for the deep-down dirt inside your cooker, but make sure to rinse it really, really well afterward.
- The deflectors in gas cookers typically have little holes that can get clogged with the by-products of vigorous cooking. Make sure you clean them to ensure free-flowing fuel.

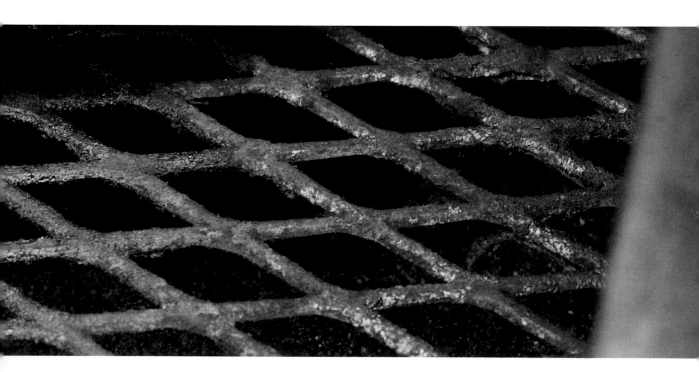

CHARCOAL

Wood becomes charcoal when it's heated in an environment where there's no oxygen. Moisture and all sorts of other stuff burns off, leaving mainly carbon. Charcoal usually burns longer than wood, and it's much lighter and more efficient, but it doesn't offer the same flavor to your food when you're cooking long. That's why I like to use it as a primary heat source in the indirect cooker and while adding wood for flavor.

The Two Types

Lump Charcoal (Pure Charcoal)

THE GOOD: It produces less ash than briquets, and it doesn't have any additives.

THE BAD: It can get crushed easily, and the resulting powdery coal and uneven pieces only hurt your cause.

Especially good for the ceramic cooker, because ceramics are slightly more susceptible to airflow blockage that results from residual ash buildup.

Charcoal Briquets

Briquets are charcoal that's been formed into uniform pieces and combined with other ingredients, including borax and cornstarch, that help approximate the burn of pure charcoal.

THE GOOD: I love the consistent size.

THE BAD: These don't smell as good as lump charcoal and some people rag on them for containing less-than-natural binders. But I've never noticed a major difference in flavor.

TIP: Scoop out coal rather than pouring it from the bag to keep the loose stuff out of your cooker.

Avoid

Lighter fluid or charcoal treated with lighter fluid. It's too easy to build a natural fire to settle for this chemical-tasting stuff. The only exception is if the coal vapor or fumes never come in contact with the food, like when you're cooking with the Caja China.

Igniting Charcoal

Whatever method you choose, once your coals have turned white (or "ashed over"), you're ready to go.

- Chimney starter: Put some crumpled newspaper into a chimney starter and top it with charcoal. Ignite the newspaper, and watch your coals follow suit.
- Parrafin starter: Scatter a few of these little squares of compressed sawdust and wax throughout your coal pile (the number depends on the size of your pile) and ignite each one. These are great for ceramic cookers, and are my overall favorite.
- Propane torch: Just hit the coals with the flame of your torch. A very effective, if not very efficient, brute-force sort of way to get your coals started. It looks cool, too.
- Electric coil: Like the coil on an electric stovetop, this gets plugged in and buried in the coals. It heats up and ignites the coals.

Temperature Control

- Direct: Your cooking temperature is determined by how far your coals are from the grates. A higher pile means higher heat. A lower one means lower heat.
- Indirect: The amount of coal determines how long the fire will burn. Manipulation of

the dampers (see page 15) determines the temperature. Because opening the fire box lets oxygen in, and oxygen can cause temperature spikes, add extra charcoal only when you must.

Temperature Drops

If your temperature falls, it can mean that your coals are going out or that they've ashed over too much. Just add more coals. But be careful—you don't want to disturb too much of the ash (which can end up on your food), and don't add too much at once because your goal is a steady fire. Too much ash buildup might also be the culprit. In that case, carefully scoop it out.

Combining with Wood

I love this: If you just use wood, you risk too much smoke (particularly if the wood is too wet); if you just use charcoal, you miss that wood-smoke flavor. When you combine the two, the coals take care of the heat, and the wood adds amazing flavor and color. All you have to do is put wood chunks (or chips, if you must) on top of smoldering coals.

NOTE: For recommendations and reviews on specific brands of charcoal, check out this amazing Web site: nakedwhiz.com.

WOOD

Is there anything more basic than cooking with wood? It makes me feel like I'm a cook in an age long ago, before bottled barbecue sauces and plastic-wrapped meat.

Whether you're cooking lamb chops over a wood fire or using wood smoke to add color and flavor to brisket, you have to know how to achieve that perfect smolder. You need to get slow, steady wisps of smoke that lay lightly on your meat, rather than some big, thick stream, like you'd see billowing from the stack of a locomotive. The key is choosing wood with the right level of moisture. But first you have to decide what kind of wood to use.

Dispelling a Myth

Picking a certain type of wood is not about choosing between different flavors that you'd like to impart to your meat—cherry and apple might smell very different, but the flavor difference is very, very subtle. Rather, different woods bring different levels of smoky assertiveness and some burn hotter than others.

Types

Don't overthink. I prefer to use particular woods with certain kinds of meat, but it really comes down to whatever wood—the store closest to you only sells hickory, your dad always used cherry, you've won competitions with oak—gets you cooking. The type of wood you use isn't the be-all-end-all factor for great barbecue. There are hundreds of woods to cook with, but for me, they all fall into these four categories.

- Mild woods (alder):
WHAT THEY OFFER: Offer sweetness and mild smoke flavor, bring a sweet perfume but not a real smoky depth of flavor, add a lot of color.
BEST WITH: Ideal for salmon and other fish, but I will use it for meat if I can't get something else.
- Fruitwoods (cherry, apple):
WHAT THEY OFFER: Like alder, but a touch more assertive; fragrant, but the delicious smell doesn't always translate to flavor. They also add a nice color to the finished meat.
BEST WITH: The mild smoke works best with relatively mild-flavored meats, like chicken and pork, or in combination with more assertive woods that need to be toned down.
- Oak and hickory
WHAT THEY OFFER: Generate solid heat, medium to strong flavor.
BEST WITH: If my barbecue and I were being transferred to a desert island and I *had* to pick one wood to use for everything, it would be oak.
NOTE: Avoid green (aka young) hickory, because it can impart excessive acidity and bitterness. How do you know it's young? If it feels very heavy for its size.
- Mesquite
WHAT IT OFFERS: Aggressive flavor, which makes it too strong for long cooking in the indirect cooker; burns wicked hot, which makes it great for direct grilling.
BEST WITH: Game meats. Mesquite smoke can overwhelm the delicate flavor of pork or chicken. It's also great for direct-grilled beef and lamb.

Shape: The Garlic Analogy

You can cook with whole, crushed, sliced, chopped, and pureed garlic—it's all garlic, but you get a different intensity of garlic flavor from each form. It's the same with wood.

LOGS: Burn for a long time, burn hot. Great for large-scale cooking because they minimize how often you have to feed the cooker; plus, if you have easy access to logs, it'll save you from having to go to the store to get bags of charcoal.

Be aware: If the wood is water-logged, it'll give off too much smoke.

Great for direct grilling, but you really have to burn them down.

CHUNKS: Consistent smoke, mild flavor. I love chunks because you get mild smoke flavor and you have more control than you do with logs (once you put a whole log on, you're committed to it, whereas you can remove and add chunks during cooking). Using chunks in conjunction with charcoal gives you great control of smoke, too, because you can adjust the amount of smoke gradually by adding or removing chunks.

Great for direct grilling.

CHIPS: Even more smoke, moderate flavor. I use chips when I want to use smoke for flavor and color rather than as a heat source, like when I'm cooking on a gas grill. They never give you a really deep smoke flavor.

SAWDUST: Maximum smoke, minimal heat, adds a lot of color in a short amount of time. Great for small or thinner items, like fish, sausages, or beef jerky, that need a quick blast of smoke. Just be careful: Too much of this smoke creates a numbing, aggressive flavor.

PELLETS: These are basically just compressed sawdust, and do a good job of providing heat and flavor, though you typically won't use them unless you have a cooker designed to take pellets, like a Fast Eddy or a Traeger. But hey, these win a lot of competitions, and I own a few.

LIQUID SMOKE: I rarely touch the stuff. If you do, use it in moderation, because it can easily overpower your meat and reveal its artificial-tasting quality.

Selection

When you're choosing wood at the store, you want to pick wood that feels neither too heavy for its size (that means it's waterlogged and will give off too much smoke) nor too light for its size (it won't give off enough smoke). Also avoid green wood (wood that's too young), which is typically damp to the touch, because it can impart a bitter taste to your meat.

Soaking: The Remedy for Too-Light Wood

Wood with the ideal moisture content doesn't go up in flames as quickly as dry wood, which means you maintain a smoldering temperature for longer. And that means more smoke.

SAWDUST: Add just enough water so that it feels like wet sand.

CHIPS: At least 15 minutes.

CHUNKS: 30 minutes to four hours.

LOGS: Two to six hours, though the water won't reach the center even after long soaking. So try to select logs that have been properly aged (that feel neither too heavy nor too light for their size).

Igniting Wood

Once you've picked your wood type and shape and soaked it, you're ready to ignite it. You can do this the same way you light charcoal: in a chimney starter with some crumpled newspaper or another type of starter. Or do like I do and start with a pile of smoldering coals and put the wood on top.

A Friendly Reminder

This might seem obvious to you old hands, but to novices, I have to say it: Don't cook while wood is flaming. Instead, wait until the wood burns to ashed-over, glowing embers.

ALDER

APPLE

CHERRY

PECAN

RED OAK

WHITE OAK

HICKORY

MESQUITE

DONENESS

Don't cut into the meat to check the temperature. Despite the common wisdom, all the juices won't spill out (hey, it's meat, not a water balloon), but the area you cut will dry out a bit and your presentation will suffer.

Instead, buy an instant-read thermometer. Nothing gives you an easier, more precise reading for the price.

The metal prong that you insert into the meat has a little dimple on it. That's where it reads temperature, so be sure this dimple goes where you want the temperature read.

Be sure to wipe down your thermometer each time that you test the temperature, especially if the temperature seems to have stopped climbing without good cause. Otherwise, fat from the meat can build up and cause an inaccurate reading. And always clean your thermometer with warm soapy water after you stick it into meat that's not fully cooked.

Training Your Touch

To determine whether burgers and steaks are done to your liking, some people suggest a trick: Poke the meat with your finger and compare the feeling to various spots on your hand. But I say, What's so bad about a thermometer? I much prefer its precision. If you'd like, each time you stick it in your meat, take a finger and prod the meat's surface. That way, you train yourself to associate the feel of the meat with the *actual internal temperature* (rather than something arbitrary, like your hand). And you'll graduate from your thermometer training wheels in no time. For larger cuts of meat, always use your thermometer.

Know When to Pull Your Meat

If you take a steak off the grill when it's medium rare, by the time it gets to the table, its rosy pink center will have faded. That's because meat, which has absorbed a lot of heat energy, continues to cook after it leaves the grill. (This is one reason my recipes tell you how long to let meat rest before serving it.) This is true of all cuts, though it has an even greater effect on thin and bone-in cuts (the bone conducts a lot of heat). Luckily, compensating is easy. Here are some general guidelines:

- Thin cuts (those an inch thick or less) and bone-in cuts: Pull them from the barbecue when their internal temperature is about 10 degrees below your target temperature.
- Thicker cuts (an inch or greater): Pull them from the barbecue about 5 degrees below your target temperature.

The Plateau (AKA Where Most Slow-Cooked Barbecue Gets Ruined)

When you're cooking a brisket, pork shoulder, or any other cut that relies on long, slow cooking to turn its collagen into gooey, rich gelatin, you'll notice the temperature of your meat rise and rise and then screech to a halt around 160°F. It stays there for awhile, and makes cooks who aren't expecting this temperature plateau freak out. They open the cooker door again and again in a frantic search for the cause. They turn up the heat. And they take all sorts of other measures (messing up their meat in the process) to solve what seems like a problem but is actually totally normal. This, my friends, is when the magic of barbecue happens. If you're a geek like me, see the Science section (page 374) for a more thorough explanation. For the rest of you, just expect it and ride it out.

The FDA and Doneness

In matters of meat, like a lot of things in life, you trade risk for reward. The FDA recommends cooking poultry to a minimum internal temperature of 165°F, steaks to 145°F, and pork to 160°F in order to prevent food-borne illnesses. For me, following this advice often leads to overcooked meat. My recipes reflect my preferences for temperature, though I've tried to give you options when possible. In the end, the choice is yours.

BUILDING FLAVOR

Let's talk a bit about marinades, brines, sauces, and other ways to build flavor.

MARINADE

The right marinade improves almost any cut, whether you want to add a jolt of flavor or make something that's chewy seem tender. I say "seem tender" because marinades don't actually tenderize meat to the degree once thought. Rather, all that flavor, especially the perky acid, makes you salivate, and that makes even chewy cuts a pleasure to sink your teeth into.

Blueprint

Marinade = Acid + Oil + Salt + Sugar + Flavor

ACID: This is the key to a great marinade—it can be fruit juice, vinegar, Worcestershire, or anything else with enough acidity. When tart ingredients hit the grill and vaporize, they give the meat this irresistible lip-smacking quality. Ideas include orange, grapefruit, lemon, lime, or pineapple juice; white wine, red wine, sherry, cider, or balsamic vinegar. Note that your choice of acid will impact the color of your finished product.

OIL: You can use infused oils, but I tend to stick

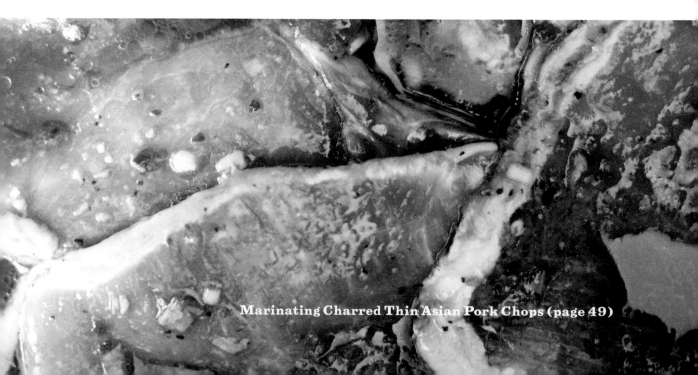

Marinating Charred Thin Asian Pork Chops (page 49)

with plain old canola. The oil doesn't really impact the flavor (plus, since you wipe off the marinade before you start cooking, you might as well wipe off something inexpensive). I like to think the oil's main purpose is to act as a sort of buffer that tempers the acid while still letting it do its tasty work without making the outside of the meat chewy, as it starts to break down proteins.

TIP: One of the best marinades out there is Italian-style salad dressing. I typically make it from scratch, but in a pinch, I'll use the bottled stuff (see page 279 for a recipe using Italian dressing).

SALT AND SUGAR: Aside from adding their elemental flavors, they create movement on a molecular level, guiding the other ingredients in your marinade into the meat.

FLAVOR: This is where you get to add just about anything that you think will taste great with your meat. I'm talking about ginger, garlic, herbs, chile peppers (fresh or dried, though the dried ones should be soaked in hot water first or else they don't communicate their flavors as well). These ingredients can also add color. Note that green ingredients tend to turn brown when they're exposed to the acid in a marinade, though the flavor is typically not affected.

HOW MUCH: Marinate your meat in a container or resealable bag with just enough of your marinade to immerse the meat. Before you close the bag, push out as much of the air inside as you can.

HOW LONG: Be careful when marinating very thick cuts of meat, like pork shoulder or whole turkey. By the time the flavors have reached the center, the acid will have made the outside of the meat very dry and chewy. If you're intent on using a particular marinade on a thick cut, try diluting it with a simple brine. Leaner cuts should spend less time in a marinade or should be immersed in one with slightly less acid than normal.

BRINE

Rubs, glazes, and sauces are great for adding flavor and texture to meat's surface. But sometimes you want to get flavor *inside* the meat. That's what brines are for. All you do is submerge your meat in a brine (a mixture of water, salt, and whatever other tasty ingredients you'd like), and because of osmosis (see Science page 374), which I bet you haven't thought about since sixth-grade science class, the brine's components enter into the cells of the meat. The result: a seemingly magical infusion of flavor and juiciness.

The Brine Continuum

Brines of different intensities have very different effects on meat.

A light brine (that is, one with a low ratio of salt to water) can be so subtle that your guests will simply taste juicy, flavorful meat. They won't even suspect that you've used a brine. As the ratio of salt to water increases, you get even more flavor, saltiness, and an extra wallop of juiciness; meat that's been properly brined can reach higher internal temperatures without drying out. You also get a denser texture that's juicy, but it's not the same free-flowing juiciness you get when you bite into a burger. As the salt-to-water ratio climbs, you start to get stronger seasoning and an even denser, firmer texture that's great for items, like ham and pork loin, that you're planning to serve sliced at room temperature or cold. At the extreme, your meat can become overly salty and develop an almost rubbery texture.

Blueprint

Basic: Water + Salt

Next level: Water + Salt + Sugar + Flavor

SALT: Always use Kosher salt.

SUGAR: You can use refined sugar, brown sugar, honey, or juice.

FLAVOR: Fresh garlic, herbs, spices, juices, apple

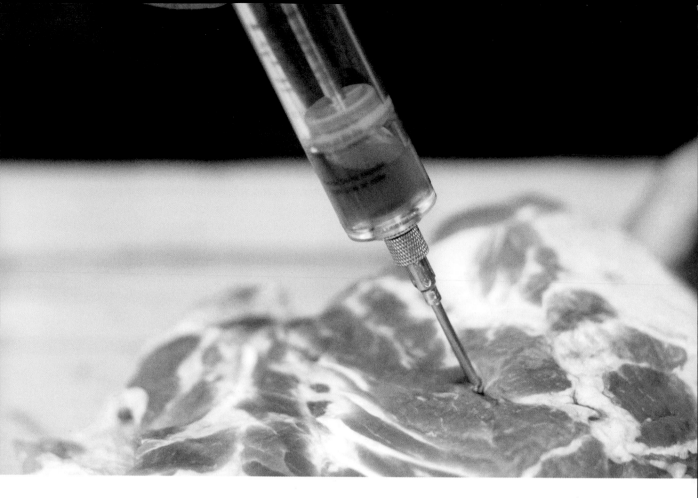

cider, annatto seeds (which are found in some of the Goya seasoning mixes I use), and other colorful ingredients will contribute to the color of your finished product.

NOTE: You'll need a container large enough to hold what you're brining and enough brine to just cover the meat.

Injecting a Brine

For many cuts, immersing the meat in the brine works beautifully. But for larger, thicker cuts, like whole turkey or pork shoulder, I like to inject. Here's why: By the time the brine has penetrated the innermost meat, the outer layer has been exposed to the brine for so long that it is too dense and strongly flavored. So, instead of waiting for the brine to reach the center, I bring

it there myself and jump-start the brining process. After you've injected, you typically need to wait only a minimum of two hours, but sometimes as long as 24 hours, before cooking. It really depends on the thickness of the meat.

When to Inject

Typically when the cut is more than three inches thick.

What to Use

Stainless steel syringe or plastic syringe with a large chamber and a thin tip.

How to Do It

Before injecting, make sure you strain the brine in a fine strainer or cheesecloth to extract any bits that could clog the syringe.

Starting from the upper left of your meat, insert the tip of a syringe filled with brine into the flesh (for aesthetic reasons, I do what I can to avoid puncturing skin). Pull the tip out slightly and inject as you do, so the brine fills the gap created by the syringe. Insert into the same hole six to ten times (this will go quickly once you get the hang of it), each time angling the tip in a different direction, so you inject in the shape of an upside-down funnel. Remove the syringe and repeat the method so that every two inches or so has been injected—imagine a grid or a checkerboard.

SEASONING BLEND

A lot of people call these rubs. But I'm not a fan of actually rubbing ingredients onto meat: Too much just sticks to your hands. Instead, I scatter spice blends on the surface of the meat, patting it occasionally to be sure it adheres. So I'm going to call these seasoning blends. They come in two forms: dry and wet.

Dry

While marinades and brines help flavors penetrate your meat, dry seasoning blends give you an intensely flavored, heavenly looking crust. Its components are all dry, so expect the full, concentrated power of spices and chiles.

Blueprint

Dry seasoning blend = Color base + Salt + Sugar + Flavor + Heat

COLOR BASE: This can be something flavorful, but really, it's all about color. Use ingredients like bright red paprika, burgundy chile powder, and finger-staining yellow turmeric.

SALT: Plain works wonders, but I also like to go multidimensional with simple-to-make salts infused with dried mint, fresh thyme, or any number of other ingredients.

SUGAR: Not only does it bring a sweet note, but it also aids in caramelization. For a darker crust, look to brown sugar.

FLAVOR: OK, now it's time to add big, upfront, and aromatic flavors. Ingredients like black pepper, onion and garlic powders, cinnamon, cumin, ground cardamom, Old Bay, whatever! I don't make a habit of making dry blends in bulk, because the spices dull with time. Plus it's so easy to grind whole spices (which last longer in your cupboard, by the way) in a spice grinder every time you need them. Make just as much as you need, or if you must, store any leftover rub in an airtight container.

HEAT: Want a boost of heat? Look to chile powders such as cayenne or anything cool-looking labeled "hot."

TIP: If meat happens to be particularly dry and the seasoning blend is not adhering, I sometimes spray the surface with a little water before applying the spice mixture, which helps it stick. You don't want to let the blend sit on the meat too long, but you also want to give it enough time to sort of bond with the meat's natural moisture and form a crust. So add it at least 5 minutes before you start cooking.

TIP: Don't be shy with your blend, but don't cake it on either. Too thick a layer can block smoke penetration and limit natural caramelization. I like to add a second and even third layer of seasoning as meat cooks (especially toward the end) to reinvigorate the flavors of those spices—so the spark they bring never fizzles.

TIP: When using your own blend, be aware that one that tastes really good eaten off your finger won't always taste great coming out of the barbecue. I'm thinking specifically of sugar—if you use too much of it, it will burn.

Wet

The addition of some moisture means that a dry seasoning blend can penetrate the meat a bit more. Plus, your crust will have a slightly different texture: Instead of the lovable grittiness and pop-pop-pop of flavors of a dry blend alone, the wet blend will bring more of a glaze-like sheen and a texture like cooling lava. One's not better than the other—it just depends on what you're going for. And hey, no one says you can't do what I often do: spread on a wet one and then coat it with a dry one! Just keep each layer thin.

Blueprint

Paste = Something Tasty and Wet +
Dry Seasoning Blend

TASTY AND WET: I'm talking Worcestershire, beef base, prepared yellow mustard, juice, Coca-Cola, Sriracha, hot sauce, or any mixture of these kinds of flavor compounds.

DRY SEASONING BLEND: Mine or yours!

SAUCE

To look at the sea of sauce-soaked ribs and brisket out there, you'd think the condiment is more central to barbecue than the meat. It's not. Then again, to listen to some barbecue purists, you'd think the sauce is completely unnecessary. I can't agree with that either. Sauce is an important component that awakens your palate with a bolt of flavor and melds beautifully with smoky meat. Different regions in the South favor different types (a simple vinegar-based version in eastern North Carolina, a sweet and tangy sort in Kansas City, an awesome mayo-spiked white kind in Alabama). My sauce takes cues from all of them but mimics none. I make sure that it highlights but never overwhelms the barbecue's flavor, and gives you just the right relief from the meat's richness so you can keep on eating.

Blueprint

Fresh ingredients + Store-bought +
Suspended + Finishing

1. FRESH INGREDIENTS. I typically use ingredients like onions, garlic, and bell peppers as my flavor base, cooking them in a bit of canola oil to concentrate their flavors by helping their natural moisture evaporate. Avoid cooking fresh ingredients in fats like butter and bacon fat, because they'll solidify when they're cool.

2. STORE-BOUGHT INGREDIENTS. I'm talking about intensely flavored condiments like ketchup, prepared yellow mustard, honey, jams, brown sugar, Worcestershire sauce, and vinegars. Add acidic ingredients, like cider vinegar or lemon juice, toward the end of your sauce-making. Not only can they slow the breakdown of onions and garlic, but cooking them can affect their liveliness.

3. SUSPENDED INGREDIENTS. Imagine biting into a juicy drumstick slicked with sauce, and as you chew, all of a sudden you taste a rush of fresh thyme or the zip of green apple. These are items that aren't blended into the sauce, but instead are suspended throughout. This may sound basic, but try it and watch your sauces come alive!

4. FINISHING INGREDIENTS. This is when the sauce becomes 3-D. Adding things like grated garlic, lemon zest, and jalapeños into your sauce right before serving brings a whole other layer of flavor and fragrance and ensures that your sauce tastes bright and fresh.

TIP: The ideal texture for a sauce depends on what you're cooking. Pulled pork has a texture that can stand up to sauces that have grated apples, little pieces of fruit in peach preserves, onions, coarsely ground pepper, and even little segments of citrus. Strip steak and filet mignon, on the other hand, have a more delicate texture, so I'd suggest using a sauce or glaze without chunks.

Dressing up a Commercial Sauce

I've seen plenty of cooks win barbecue competitions by dressing up a commercial sauce. It's a quick way of bypassing the mixing of store-bought ingredients like honey, ketchup, and mustard, and it also brings a familiar flavor that your eating audience will relate to. Doctor it with any or all of my three other elements of sauce, and you're guaranteed something tasty.

GLAZES

Nope, these are definitely not just for show, though they do give food a beautiful sheen. But also, they hit your palate right up front with intense flavors that make your mouth water. And as we know, salivation has a huge impact not only on flavor but also on texture and tenderness. The glaze, which you apply to the surface of the meat as it cooks, enhances caramelization, grabs onto the flavors of the barbecue or grill, and, thanks to the sugars, prevents too much of the meat's natural juices from escaping as steam. That's why I also brush it onto the face of any slice of meat. I even paint my cutting board with it, so the meat glazes as I slice. Because you use less of it than you do sauce, the flavors should be in-your-face sweet and sour.

Blueprint

Glaze = Sugar + Acidity + Textural stuff

SUGAR: It gives the glaze its ability to create an amazing layer of caramelization and helps form a barrier that reduces the amount of steam that escapes from the meat. Try dark or light brown sugar, honey, corn syrup, jams, or preserves.

ACIDITY: Make sure to balance that sweetness with vinegars, lemon juice, or anything else with snappy acidity.

TEXTURE: Think chiles, chunky fruit preserves, and anything else you'd use in a sauce.

TIP: Because glazes contain a lot of sugar, I prefer to apply them near the end of cooking, so they're less likely to burn. You also want to give the meat's natural sugars time to caramelize—the glaze is a complement to, not a substitute for, this tasty transformation. And instead of adding it once, I apply several layers as the cooking continues. This really builds flavor.

TIP (MY RECIPES TAKE THIS INTO ACCOUNT, BUT WHEN YOU'RE MAKING YOUR OWN GLAZE): Thinner cuts of meat do well with glazes that contain more sugar—since the meat cooks relatively quickly, you want your glaze to caramelize quickly as well. For thicker cuts, you want this caramelization process to happen more slowly, because the cut will typically take longer to cook. So thin your glaze (that is, lower the sugar concentration) a bit with water, apple cider, or juice.

WRAPPING

To wrap or not to wrap—that is the question. Purists say nope, no way, definitely not. They call wrapping all sorts of names that in the realm of barbecue are extremely derogatory. "It's braising!" they sneer. "It's practically steaming!" they snarl. I hear them, but disagree with vigorous objection.

Look, if you pack your barbecue with meat, you get this beautiful humidity inside the cooker that will lead to insanely tender ribs, pork shoulder, and brisket. But what if you're just cooking a few racks of ribs? Or a single pork shoulder in a largely unfilled smoker (mind you, this is still enough to feed at least six people)? Sorry, purists—this means you need to wrap your meat in foil.

I find that wrapping creates a sort of microclimate inside the foil that approximates the environment of a full barbecue. What does this do? Well, to get the collagen in the meat to convert to gelatin—this is the magic of barbecue, the process that leads to its characteristic luscious texture—it needs to absorb moisture. So I just barely coat ribs, chicken thighs, pork shoulder, brisket, and any other collagen-rich cuts in a mixture of liquid with a little sugar (or honey), and a touch of liquid, wrap it in foil, and stick it back in the cooker. Later, I'll unwrap the meat and pop it back in the cooker, so it can get some more smoke flavor and the wrapping mixture can tighten up, becoming yet another delicious layer of flavor on the outside of the meat. Here are some things to keep in mind:

- Only wrap meat once it has developed some crust and color. If you wrap when it's too "blond," you'll get tender meat but a boiled look and less intense flavor.
- Wrap in two layers of foil: That way, the sugar in your wrapping mixture won't easily burn, and any bones won't poke through the foil.
- Make sure to wrap completely, so there's no way that moisture can escape.
- You don't have to wrap each item individually—if you're in a rush, you can, for instance, put a few racks of ribs in an aluminum pan and cover the top tightly with foil. It's not ideal but it works.

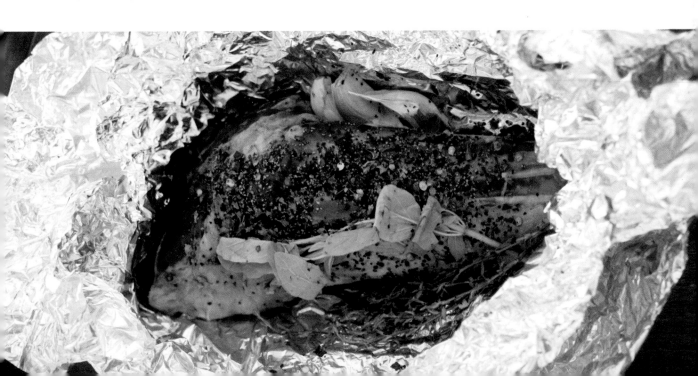

SOUTHERN VERSUS YANKEE BARBECUE

This question has sparked more arguments than I can count: Does grilling count as barbecue? The problem is the word "barbecue" means different things to different people. If you grew up in the Northeast, like I did, you probably remember charring sausages and steaks over high heat and calling that barbecue. If you're from the South, though, the word suggests slow cooking with lower heat. But even down South, people's opinions diverge on what constitutes the real thing. Some Texans will insist that only beef brisket cooked with the heat of post oak and served without embellishment is truly 'cue. Meanwhile, sauce-slicked ribs and burnt ends reign in Kansas City, mutton rules in western Kentucky, and folks in North Carolina argue whole hog or shoulder with spare vinegar sauce or ketchup-spiked. The lesson here is that, though you might have a favorite, it's all barbecue, and it all can be tremendously delicious. Still, for the sake of clarity (and sanity), here are the major differences in the two categories: Southern-style barbecue and Yankee barbecue.

1. • Southern-style barbecue generally relies on slow indirect cooking with temperatures typically around 225°F to 275°F.
   • Yankee barbecue is more about quick cooking over high heat—from 350°F up to, well, as high as the cooker can go.
2. • In Southern-style barbecue, smoke is an integral part of the flavor profile.
   • In Yankee barbecue, smoke is just an accent, a hint of the outdoors.
3. • Part of the magic of Southern-style barbecue is how its practitioners transform relatively cheap, tough cuts of meat into what tastes nothing short of luxurious.
   • Yankee barbecue gives you plenty of inexpensive options, but is especially awesome for premium cuts, like the rib eye and tenderloin, which respond very well to its direct heat.
4. • Southern-style barbecue is a way of life, a lifestyle backed by more than a century of tradition.
   • Yankee barbecue, though no less noble, is more of a pastime, mainly practiced by weekend warriors.
5. • Southern-style barbecue emphasizes tradition: Old-schoolers abound who wouldn't even think of changing the methods they've been using or the sauce they've been serving for decades. For good or bad, however, this landscape is beginning to change.
   • Yankee barbecue embraces innovation: Without the same traditional bounds of its Southern counterpart, outdoor cooks are eager to experiment, incorporating flavors and techniques from all over the world. (Sometimes for the better and sometimes for the worse.)

TWELVE MYTHS ABOUT BARBECUE

1. **PUTTING MEAT ON A HOT GRILL SEALS IN ITS JUICES.** It just ain't so, though a nice char or flavor-packed mahogany crust will make you salivate, making the meat *seem* more juicy.

2. **IN SOUTHERN BARBECUE, MORE SMOKE MEANS BETTER MEAT.** Too much smoke overpowers other flavors, numbs your tongue, and can even mess with your digestion. The ideal is even smoke evenly delivered over long period of time. (See page 20 for more on wood.)

3. **COOK PAST 160°F AND YOU'VE OVERCOOKED YOUR MEAT.** If you're grilling a rib eye, sure. But the magic of Southern barbecue typically takes place around 160°F and above. (See Science page 374.)

4. **MEAT THAT'S FALLING OFF THE BONE IS A GOOD THING.** Hey, if you're into it, but to me, it's overcooked. Rather, you should be able to bite through, say, a baby back rib with little resistance but the meat should never give up its delicate chew.

5. **SOUTHERN BARBECUE IS DANGEROUS, BECAUSE YOU COOK AT A LOW TEMPERATURE FOR A LONG TIME.** Trust me, you're safe. But if you need more reassurance, see Science page 374.

6. **SEASONING WITH SALT BEFORE COOKING MAKES MEAT DRY.** If you don't, you just won't get the same flavor. Just add your salt right before you throw the meat on the grill.

7. **REAL GRILLMASTERS USE ONLY SUPERHIGH HEAT.** Not if they know what they're doing. For thinner cuts, this is a good rule of thumb. But thicker cuts often need moderate heat, so the outside of the meat doesn't over-char before the inside is done.

8. **ALWAYS COOK WITH THE FAT SIDE UP.** I've heard so many times on the barbecue competition circuit that this helps keep meat moist, and I just don't buy it. It's not like the fat passes through the meat; rather, it just drips off. I actually prefer cooking with the fat side down, so it makes contact with the hot grates and renders more readily.

9. **NEVER PUT COLD MEAT ON A HOT GRILL.** I've heard all sorts of reasons for this rule, including that the grill will shock the meat, making it tough. I actually think grilling meat while it's cold can be quite useful. That way, the center takes a bit longer to cook past rare, and you're able to add an even darker, more beautiful crust. In fact, as I mentioned in the introduction, unless I've said otherwise, the details of every recipe rely on your starting with the meat cold.

10. **WRAPPING MEAT IN FOIL WITH A LITTLE LIQUID IS BRAISING, NOT BARBECUE.** Listen, I'm interested in great results, not purity for purity's sake. And when you're cooking in a barbecue that's not fully loaded (and therefore doesn't have a lot of natural humidity), wrapping is essential to getting that characteristic barbecue texture. Wonder why? See Wrapping page 31.

11. **WINNING BARBECUE COMPETITIONS TAKES A LITTLE BIT OF SKILL AND A LOT OF LUCK.** Come on, the same guys might not win every time, but they're usually up there in the top ten or the top five.

12. **A DIRTY GRILL MEANS BETTER FLAVOR.** Nope, dirt is dirt. The blackish gunk on your grill can contribute its bitter, off flavor to any meat that touches it. So please get a sturdy brush and clean your grill grates and racks obsessively.

Charred Thin Asian Pork Chops (page 49)

PORK

WHAT IS PORK?

Pork is built for barbecue. I'm reminded of this delicious fact every time I pull a mammoth shoulder from the smoker that's so tender it wobbles as I pull it into strands. My fingers break through the dark, glistening crust—a team of pork-friendly flavors that has become all caramelized—revealing lush, pinkish flesh. It has this delicate sweetness that's the perfect canvas for so many of the spices and seasonings in the barbecue repertoire: molasses, apple juice, vinegar, and mustard, just to name a few.

As usual, lovely fat is what accounts for a lot of pork's flavor, but the distinctive texture of slow-cooked pork comes from collagen. You see it in other meats, too, but pork packs a ton. Without getting too scientific, I'll just say that low, slow cooking turns collagen into gelatin, and every time a rib knocks your socks off with stick-to-your-ribs succulence, you're enjoying the contributions of that gelatin.

Though the shoulder, ribs, and whole hog are the cuts that rule Southern barbecue, outdoor cooking is friendly to just about every part of the pig. What I've done is given you my absolute favorite recipe for each cut, plus I've laid out what qualities matter when you're selecting and cooking pork, so you can take your own best pork recipes to a new level.

THE IMPORTANCE OF COLLAGEN

If you learn how to pick pork that's high in collagen, you'll see a serious improvement in your barbecue, stews, and chilis. Unlike fat, however, collagen is not easy to spot. So how do you maximize the collagen in the pork you buy? For one, certain cuts have more than others. Think about it this way: Work equals collagen. The more work a muscle does, the more collagen it typically has. That's why the shoulder is such a collagen powerhouse. So are the trotters and the hams. Even after you've decided on your cut, you can make sure you max out the collagen and increase your chances of unctuous success by picking the biggest shoulder or rack of spareribs you can find. Because typically, the larger the cut, the more overall collagen. And while bigger cuts require more patience from you, the cook, they pay off big-time.

THE IMPORTANCE OF FAT

Pork might not have a consumer-geared grading system, as beef does, that leads people like you and me toward exceptionally distributed fat. Still, fat plays a big part in flavor and makes pork seem juicy and tender, especially when you're applying high heat for a relatively short amount of time. I've noticed a sort of magic about pork fat: It carries flavor like almost no other type does. It also tempts like no other, melting into this super-savory liquid that cooks around the world use to add flavor to everything from greens to beans. Even vegetarians have been known to partake, claiming that bacon should somehow be an exception. I don't blame them.

But nowadays, a lot of the pork you see on supermarket shelves has very little fat. In the mid-1980s, the pork industry gave the public what it seemed to want: lean meat. The industry decided that pork would compete with the popular chicken (hence the slogan "The Other White Meat"), so it began supporting a system of breeding and raising that dramatically reduced the fat content in what was once a pretty fatty animal. This transformed pork from meat with character to meat that's mild-mannered, and it tidied up the image of an animal long known as a garbage eater. But during the past several years, old-school breeds have been resurrected by farmers who love the distinctive character, tenderness, and richness of their meat. Let me be clear: One is not better than the other; they're just different. You and I get to choose which one's best for whatever we feel like cooking.

So ask yourself: Do you want the mildly flavored meat of animals bred for volume and uniformity that typically has very little intramuscular fat (meat that people in the industry call commodity) or the rich, über-flavorful meat that comes from more old-fashioned breeding and raising? I haven't noticed a major difference in collagen between the two, so you can achieve that rich, unctuous texture that marks the best barbecue by cooking with commodity or heirloom. The big difference is in flavor and juiciness. And as I'll explain, there's a time and a place for each option.

COMMODITY PORK

I'll often go for the less expensive, more mildly flavored lean meat, which works well if you treat it as a canvas for big flavors. Plus, because cooking is about pleasing your audience, I always take other people's preferences into account. In competition, for instance, I'd rather use the kind of pork familiar to the folks doing the judging—heck, it's what I was familiar with as a young chef. But at its worst, the pork has a pale flavor and can easily become tough and cardboard-like even if it's just barely overcooked. The good news is you can nip this in the bud. The best way is to choose pork with flecks of fat evenly interspersed throughout the meat. And while I cringe to say it, if you're desperate, you can buy pork that's been injected with, or packed in, a solution that contains phosphates, which adds flavor and

moisture. But beware: Too much of this solution will make your pork dense, rubbery, and too salty—a state I call hammy. Plus, you're paying for this added liquid when you should be paying just for meat. And since there's no way to tell just by looking at the package how much has been injected, you end up playing Russian roulette with your dinner—sometimes you win, but when you lose, you lose big. Instead, I prefer to enhance the flavor and succulence myself with a supercharged brine, which is lower in sodium, higher in flavor, and gives you total control. Or I'll lay off the brine and just cook leaner cuts like the chop or the tenderloin with a short blast of high heat and serve them right away, so they don't have a chance to dry out.

HEIRLOOM

Lots of chefs have fallen for the more distinctive flavor and higher proportion of fat of this kind of pork, and I'm one of them. As the term "heirloom" suggests, these pigs represent a return to an older way of doing things—old-school breeds, like Berkshire and Red Wattle, that generally receive a more careful kind of raising. It tends to add up to better meat. But buyer beware: Now that "heirloom" has become a buzzword, some farmers and companies are jumping on the bandwagon, exploiting the marketing value of the old breeds without practicing the kind of animal husbandry that allows this promising pork to realize its potential.

I can't get enough of the bold flavor of heirloom pork. When you grill it or barbecue it, you'll notice its porky character and slightly sweeter flavor, but also its amazing mouthfeel, firmer texture, and the way it seems magically moist rather than waterlogged. It's more forgiving of overcooking, too. Yet just as not everyone

who likes fish likes mackerel, I've met plenty of pork lovers who find meat from heirloom breeds too intense. And, I'll admit, it's not what I'd call everyday pork. First of all, it's typically three times the price of the leaner, more commercial stuff. And it's often too rich for everyday eating.

SELECTION

NO GRADES. NO PROBLEM. The pork industry, unlike the beef industry, doesn't communicate to consumers the amount and distribution of marbling in particular cuts of pork. So you have to be able to spot great marbling yourself. Luckily, that's simple: Just look for flecks of fat like little snowflakes interspersed throughout the pinkish flesh.

This is a bit easier to spot when you're looking at the flat side of a chop or medallion. Yet you can still spot it when you need to find a shoulder, crown roast, or some other bulky cut. Look for microstriations of fat—and keep this rule in mind: Go for streaks, not clumps.

Once you know how to pick out great pork, you'll never have to rely blindly on price as an indicator of quality. And you can head to ethnic markets, where the labeling is minimal and the turnover is high. These markets are especially great for inexpensive cuts like shoulder, trotters, and spareribs—those that could feed a family without breaking the bank.

AVOID FROZEN All else equal, frozen meat is not as good as fresh. This is especially true with pork, because of its particularly delicate cell structure. Freezing, particularly if it's done too slowly, creates what I like to think of as microtears in the cell, and out comes moisture, which, as you can imagine, is bad news for your dinner. If you must buy frozen, look for meat with no traces of ice crystals or freezer burn (spots that look cooked), because they indicate it hasn't been frozen properly.

GO LARGE I go for the biggest examples of shoulders and ribs I can find, because the bigger the cut, the more collagen it typically contains. And more collagen means greater potential for silky, luscious mouthfeel when you're slow cooking. Larger cuts are also more forgiving of overcooking and give you more pieces to pick through in order to find the finest tangle of meat, the one that could earn you that perfect score in barbecue competition, if you're into that sort of thing, or that all-important compliment from your most hard-to-please buddy. Just bear in mind, of course, that bigger cuts take longer to cook.

SPOTTING SHINERS You're selecting racks of ribs and you've found several with marvelous fat flecking the meat. You know they'll be tasty, but how can you tell if they'll be nice and meaty? The answer: Find the ones with "shiners," and put them back in the meat case. Shiners are areas where bones show. They indicate that the butcher has cut too much meat from them—a grave sin, as far as I'm concerned.

BUYING HEIRLOOM PORK This is a no-brainer, right? You find beautiful, fatty, flavorful heirloom pork and you buy it. Think again. The reality is, it doesn't always sell as quickly and as readily as the typical supermarket pork, so you have to be on your toes to make sure that the carefully raised meat hasn't been ruined by an inefficient supply chain. For example, does the store sell a lot of this heirloom pork, and if not, do they freeze it? How often does the store get it? And when? Just a few questions can help you decide whether this particular supply of premium pork will be worth your money.

BEYOND LABELS At supermarkets, pork doesn't always measure up to the claims made on labels. But useful information is available—you just have to demand it. So ask the butcher, call the store manager, and check the sell-by date on each package so you know how often the meat is rotated.

CIDER-BRINED PORK CHOPS WITH APPLE JELLY GLAZE

SERVES 8

I love the combination of apples and pork so much that I immerse these thick chops in an apple cider–spiked brine for a few hours to keep them juicy, enhance their color, and start the apple avalanche. Then, I glaze them with even more apple—sweet jelly tarted up with some lemon juice. To add a bit of smoke, I used a bit of smoked paprika in my seasonings blend.

Brine
1 tablespoon crushed hot red pepper flakes
2 tablespoons boiling water
2 cups apple cider
2 cups water
½ cup kosher salt
½ cup honey
10 garlic cloves, peeled, halved, germ removed, and grated on a Microplane grater

Eight 1½-inch-thick pork rib chops, 8 to 10 ounces each

Seasoning Blend
2 tablespoons mild chile powder, preferably Chimayo (see Sources page 378), Ancho, or Hatch
1 tablespoon sweet paprika
1 tablespoon firmly packed dark brown sugar
¾ teaspoon dry mustard
¾ teaspoon pimentón (see Sources page 378), or other smoked paprika
½ teaspoon garlic salt

½ teaspoon coarsely ground fresh black pepper
½ teaspoon kosher salt
¼ teaspoon Old Bay Seasoning (see Sources page 378)

Glaze
½ cup apple jelly
1 tablespoon freshly squeezed lemon juice
½ Granny Smith apple, peeled, cored, and grated on a Microplane grater

About ¼ cup canola or vegetable oil

¼ cup finely chopped chives

1. Place the pepper flakes in a small bowl and pour the boiling water over them. Let sit for 1 to 2 minutes to rehydrate the flakes. Combine all the remaining brine ingredients in a blender or in a bowl, using an immersion/stick blender. Stir in the pepper flakes and the soaking water.

   Place the chops in an extra-large resealable plastic bag (or divide between two large bags). Pour over the brine, squeeze out any excess air from the bag, and close. Roll the bag to evenly coat all of the meat in the brine, and refrigerate for 2 to 3 hours.

2. Preheat one grate of a well-oiled charcoal or gas grill to high and another to low.

3. Combine all of the seasoning blend ingredients.

   Place all of the glaze ingredients in a jar with a tight-fitting lid and shake to combine. Set aside.

4. Remove the chops from the brine, letting any excess brine remain in the bag. Lightly pat dry with paper towels.

   Sprinkle the seasoning blend evenly on all sides of the chops.

   Using your hands or a brush, evenly, but lightly, coat with canola oil.

5. It is preferable that the chops be moved to a clean area of the grate when flipped during the initial charring. Depending on the grill size, they may need to be cooked in batches to ensure there is a clean portion of the grill to flip to.

   Place the chops on the high grate, and keeping the lid open, do not move the chops until they are well marked and lightly charred, about 3 minutes. Flip, still over high, with the lid open, and repeat on the second side, grilling for about 3 minutes.

   Move the chops to the low grate, and close the lid. Open the lid every few minutes, flipping, jockeying, and stacking throughout the remaining cooking time.

   Cook about 8 minutes for medium, about 10 minutes for medium well, and about 12 minutes for well-done. The chops will continue to cook as they are glazed.

   Give the glaze a quick shake to reincorporate any ingredients that may have settled. Brush with the glaze on the first side, flip, and brush on the second side.

6. Remove the chops from the heat and let rest for about 5 minutes.

   Sprinkle with chives and serve.

SPICE-CRUSTED THICK RIB PORK CHOPS

These are some seriously hefty chops, so thick that mouths will drop when they come off the grill. The key to cooking thick cuts since they take a bit longer than thinner ones is making sure that the exterior and interior are done at the same time. That's why I start them on high to get the caramelization going, then move them to lower heat, so you can be sure everything works out smashingly.

Brine

1 tablespoon crushed hot red pepper flakes
2 tablespoons boiling water
4 cups apple cider
2 cups water
¼ cup kosher salt
¼ cup firmly packed dark brown sugar
4 garlic cloves, peeled, halved, germ removed, and grated on a Microplane grater

Six 1½-inch-thick pork rib chops, 8 to 10 ounces each

Seasoning Blend

2 tablespoons mild chile powder, preferably Chimayo (see Sources page 378), Ancho, or Hatch
2 tablespoons dry mustard
1 tablespoon garlic salt
1 teaspoon finely ground fresh black pepper
1 teaspoon cayenne pepper

Finishing Dressing

About ½ cup extra virgin olive oil
Juice of 1 lemon
3 tablespoons coarsely chopped flat-leaf parsley
1 tablespoon honey
1 medium shallot, peeled and grated on a Microplane grater
1 small garlic clove, peeled, halved, germ removed, and grated on a Microplane grater

About ¼ cup canola or vegetable oil
8 tablespoons (4 ounces) unsalted butter, melted
1 bunch thyme sprigs, tied in an Herb Bundle (page 365)

Fleur de sel
Finely ground fresh black pepper

1. Place the pepper flakes in a small bowl and pour the boiling water over them. Let sit for 1 to 2 minutes to rehydrate the flakes. Combine all of the brine ingredients including the pepper flakes and the soaking water in a large bowl, stirring to dissolve the sugar.

   Place the chops in an extra-large resealable plastic bag (or divide between two large bags). Pour over the brine, squeeze out any excess air from the bag, and close. Refrigerate for at least 12 hours, or up to 1 day.

2. Preheat one grate of a well-oiled charcoal or gas grill to medium-high and another to medium-low.

3. Combine all of the seasoning blend ingredients.

   Place all of the dressing ingredients in a jar with a tight-fitting lid and shake to combine. Set aside.

4. Remove the pork chops from the brine, letting any excess brine remain in the bag, and lightly pat the chops dry with paper towels.

   Sprinkle the seasoning blend evenly on all sides of the chops.

   Using your hands or a brush, evenly, but lightly, coat the chops with canola oil.

5. It is preferable that the chops be moved to a clean area of the grate when flipped during the initial charring. Depending on the grill size, they may need to be cooked in batches to ensure there is a clean portion of the grill to flip to.

   Place the chops on the medium-high grate, and, keeping the lid open, do not move the chops until they are well marked and lightly charred, about 3 minutes. Flip, still over medium-high, with the lid open, and repeat on the second side for about 3 minutes.

   Brush the chops with butter using the herb bundle. Move to the medium-low grate, and close the lid. Open the lid every few minutes, flipping, jockeying, and stacking throughout the remaining cooking time.

   Cook about 9 minutes for medium, about 12 minutes for medium well, and about 15 minutes for well-done.

   Remove from the heat and brush with butter using the herb bundle.

6. Give the dressing a quick shake and drizzle about half on a cutting board. Top with the chops and let rest for about 5 minutes.

   Cut to separate the meat from the bone and slice the meat on a diagonal into ¼-inch slices, drizzling with the remaining dressing, and making sure all slices are coated.

   Sprinkle with fleur de sel and pepper.

PORK T-BONE WITH JALAPEÑO AND GARLIC DRESSING

It looks like a T-bone. It has a bone separating the loin and a nugget of tenderloin like a T-bone. But it's just called a center-cut loin chop. I'd rather call this great cut what it is. And treat it like what it is, too. As I do with its beefy counterpart, I look for the thickest one I can lay my hands on. That way the tenderloin stays juicy and you get a nice, dark, tasty crust.

Seasoning Blend

2 tablespoons garlic salt

2 tablespoons lemon pepper

2 tablespoons coarsely ground fresh black pepper

2 tablespoons mild chile powder, preferably Chimayo (see Sources page 378), Ancho, or Hatch

Finishing Dressing

2 tablespoons Apricot Compote (see below)

Zest of 1 lemon, grated on a Microplane grater

2 tablespoons freshly squeezed lemon juice

1 jalapeño chile, grated on a Microplane grater, stopping before the seeds

1 tablespoon honey

1 garlic clove, peeled, halved, germ removed, and grated on a Microplane grater

1 teaspoon kosher salt

1 teaspoon finely ground fresh black pepper

1 cup extra virgin olive oil

¼ cup finely chopped flat-leaf parsley

Eight 1¼-inch-thick center-cut pork chops, about 12 ounces each

About ½ cup canola or vegetable oil

16 tablespoons (8 ounces) unsalted butter, melted

1 bunch thyme sprigs, tied in an Herb Bundle (page 365)

2 lemons, halved and seeds removed

Fleur de sel

Finely ground fresh black pepper

1 recipe Apricot Compote (page 347)

1. Preheat all grates of a well-oiled charcoal or gas grill to medium-high.

2. Combine all of the seasoning blend ingredients.

   Place the apricot compote, zest, juice, jalapeño, honey, garlic, salt, and pepper in a jar with a tight-fitting lid and shake to combine. Add the oil and parsley, shake, and set aside.

   Sprinkle the seasoning blend evenly on all sides of the chops.

   Using your hands or a brush, evenly, but lightly, coat the chops with canola oil.

3. It is preferable that the chops be moved to a clean area of the grate when flipped during the initial charring. Depending on the grill size, they may need to be cooked in batches to ensure there is a clean portion of the grill to flip to.

   Place the chops on the grate, and, keeping the lid open, do not move the chops until they are well marked and lightly charred, about 2 minutes. Flip, brush with butter using the herb bundle, keep the lid open, and repeat on the second side for about 2 minutes.

   Brush the chops with butter using the herb bundle, and close the lid. Open the lid every few minutes, flipping, jockeying, and stacking throughout the remaining cooking time.

   Cook about 8 minutes for medium, about 10 minutes for medium well, and about 15 minutes for well-done.

4. Give the dressing a quick shake and drizzle about half on a cutting board. Top with the chops, and let rest for about 5 minutes.

   Separate the meat from the bone and then slice the meat on a diagonal into ¼-inch slices, drizzling with the remaining dressing, and making sure all slices are coated.

   Sprinkle with fleur de sel and pepper. Serve with apricot compote on the side.

PORK CHOPS POUNDED WITH SEASONING

SERVES 8

Usually, people pound chops to get them really tender and to make them cook really quickly. Only after they have Schnitzel-thin cutlets do they add seasoning. But as long as I'm pounding, I like to whack chile pepper, dried oregano, and dry mustard into the meat. You'll be shocked by the flavor lift you get.

Seasoning Blend

2 tablespoons mild chile powder, preferably Chimayo (see Sources page 378), Ancho, or Hatch

2 tablespoons dried oregano, preferably Mexican

2 tablespoons dry mustard

1 tablespoon garlic salt

1 teaspoon finely ground fresh black pepper

1 teaspoon cayenne pepper

Basting Butter

8 tablespoons (4 ounces) unsalted butter

4 garlic cloves, peeled, halved, germ removed, and thinly sliced

Finishing Dressing

2 lemons

2 tablespoons finely chopped flat-leaf parsley

2 tablespoons finely chopped chives

1 tablespoon fresh marjoram leaves

1 teaspoon granulated sugar

1 medium shallot, peeled and grated on a Microplane grater

1 small garlic clove, peeled, halved, germ removed, and grated on a Microplane grater

1 teaspoon thinly sliced serrano, or other hot chile of choice (optional)

½ cup extra virgin olive oil

Six 1½-inch-thick pork rib chops, 8 to 10 ounces each

About ¼ cup canola or vegetable oil

½ bunch thyme and ½ bunch rosemary, tied in an Herb Bundle (page 365)

Kosher salt

Coarsely ground fresh black pepper

Fleur de sel

1. Preheat all grates of a well-oiled charcoal or gas grill to high.
2. Combine all of the seasoning blend ingredients.

   Place the butter and garlic in a small saucepan over medium heat and stir to combine as the butter melts.

   Using a Microplane grater, zest and then juice the lemons over a jar with a tight-fitting lid. Add the parsley, chives, marjoram, sugar, shallot, garlic, and chile, and shake to combine. Add the oil, shake, and set the dressing aside.
3. Working with a couple chops at a time, season on both sides with the seasoning blend and place between two sheets of plastic wrap. Using a meat tenderizer/pounder (see Sources page 378), pound to ¼-inch thickness.

   Using your hands or a brush, evenly, but lightly, coat with canola oil.
4. It is preferable that the chops be moved to a clean area of the grate when flipped during the initial charring. Depending on the grill size, they may need to be cooked in batches to ensure there is a clean portion of the grill to flip to.

Place the pork chops on the grate, with the lid open, and grill without moving the chops until they are well marked and lightly charred, about 3 minutes. Flip, brush with the garlic butter using the herb bundle, and, keeping the lid open, repeat on the second side, grilling for about 3 minutes.

If you notice the chops curling slightly around the edges or want to intensify the char, use a grill press(es) or a firebrick(s) (see Sources page 378) wrapped in heavy-duty aluminum foil to weigh them down.

Season lightly with salt and pepper, then flip back to the first side, jockeying and stacking the chops as needed. Close the lid, and cook for 2 minutes. Flip, brush with butter using the herb bundle, and cook on the second side for 2 minutes. Brush with the butter again.

5. Remove the chops from the grill and brush both sides one more time with the butter. Place on a serving platter.

   Give the dressing a quick shake to incorporate any ingredients that may have settled, and drizzle over the chops. Sprinkle with fleur de sel and pepper.

CHARRED THIN ASIAN PORK CHOPS

I like to think of this dish as Vietnamese inspired, because it's my take on those slightly sweet, lovably chewy chops you get over noodles or rice in Vietnamese restaurants. I soak the thin chops in a mixture of soy, cilantro, hot red pepper flakes, and even more garlic than you think you need.

Make sure you serve these immediately, because they're best when they're right off the grill.

TIP: If you can't find ¼-inch-thick chops, ask a butcher to cut "through the bone" for you.

Marinade
1 tablespoon crushed hot red pepper flakes
2 tablespoons boiling water
½ cup Japanese soy sauce
¼ cup fish sauce
¼ cup rice wine or dry sherry
¼ cup toasted sesame oil
¼ cup canola or vegetable oil
¼ cup water
½ cup firmly packed dark brown sugar
2 tablespoons freshly squeezed lemon juice
2 tablespoons finely chopped or grated fresh ginger
1 tablespoon finely ground fresh black pepper
8 garlic cloves, peeled, halved, germ removed, and finely chopped
½ cup finely chopped scallions, white and green portions

Sixteen ¼-inch-thick pork chops, about 2 ounces each
About ¼ cup canola or vegetable oil
¼ cup black sesame seeds
½ cup finely chopped scallions, white and green portions

Edible Wraps
4 cups rehydrated bean threads or white rice
1 head Bibb or other lettuce
¼ cup cilantro leaves
2 red bell peppers, seeds and membranes removed, thinly sliced
¼ cup chile paste, preferably Sriracha or sambal

1. Place the pepper flakes in a small bowl and pour the boiling water over them. Let sit for 1 to 2 minutes to rehydrate the flakes.

    Combine all of the marinade ingredients except the pepper flakes and the scallions in a blender, or in a large bowl, using an immersion/stick blender. Blend until well combined. Stir in the scallions, the pepper flakes, and the soaking water.

    Place the chops in an extra-large resealable plastic bag (or divide between two large bags). Pour over the marinade, squeeze out any excess air from the bag, and close. Roll the bag to evenly coat all of the meat. Refrigerate for at least 12 hours, or up to 24.

2. Preheat all grates of a well-oiled charcoal or gas grill to medium-high.

3. Remove the chops from the marinade, letting any excess marinade remain in the bag. Lightly pat dry with paper towels.

    Reserve 1 cup of the marinade for glazing the chops. Place in a small saucepan over medium heat and bring to a boil.

    Using your hands or a brush, evenly, but lightly, coat the chops with canola oil.

4. It is preferable that the chops be moved to a clean area of the grate when flipped during the initial charring. Depending on the grill size, they may need to be cooked in batches to ensure there is a clean portion of the grill to flip to.

    Place the chops on the grate, keeping the lid open, turning frequently during the cooking time, and brushing with the reserved marinade. Cook until the chops are completely glazed and well marked with char, about 10 minutes. You want the chops to become nicely charred and caramelized. Flip, jockey, and stack throughout the cooking as needed.

    If you notice the chops curling slightly around the edges, or want to intensify the char, use a grill press(es) or a firebrick(s) (see Sources page 378) wrapped in heavy-duty aluminum foil to weigh them down.

5. Remove the chops from the grill and sprinkle with sesame seeds and scallions.

    Serve the chops immediately, family style, with bean threads, lettuce, cilantro, bell peppers, and chile paste, each in individual bowls.

HAM STEAK GLAZED WITH DARK BROWN SUGAR

Ham steaks are already so tasty. All you have to do to make them really shine is dress them up a bit. So I apply a glaze that has just the right amount of sweetness from brown sugar and pineapple juice. The glaze bubbles and caramelizes until I have the glossiest, most enticing slabs of ham imaginable.

Marinade

2 cups pineapple juice

1 cup firmly packed dark brown sugar

1/4 cup Dijon mustard

1 teaspoon kosher salt

1/2 teaspoon ground cloves

4 garlic cloves, peeled, halved, germ removed, and grated on a Microplane grater

4 thyme sprigs, bruised lightly by rubbing between your fingers

2 to 3 cured and cooked 1-inch-thick ham steaks, about 7 inches in diameter, cut into quarters

2 to 3 tablespoons canola or vegetable oil

Finely ground fresh black pepper

1/4 cup coarsely chopped flat-leaf parsley

1. Place all of the marinade ingredients in a jar with a tight-fitting lid and shake to combine.

   Place the ham in an extra-large resealable plastic bag (or divide between two large bags) and pour the marinade over the top. Squeeze out any excess air from the bag and close. Roll the bag to evenly coat the meat. Refrigerate for at least 3 hours, or up to 12.

2. Preheat all grates of a well-oiled charcoal or gas grill to high.

3. Remove the ham from the bag and lightly pat dry with paper towels. Reserve 1 cup of the marinade for glaze. Place in a small saucepan and bring to a boil.

   Using your hands or a brush, evenly, but lightly, coat the ham with canola oil.

4. Place the ham on the grate and do not move until they are well marked and lightly charred, about 1 1/2 minutes. Flip and repeat on the second side, grilling for about 1 1/2 minutes. If you notice the ham curling, or want to intensify the char, use a grill press(es) or firebrick(s) (see Sources page 378) wrapped in heavy-duty aluminum foil to weigh them down.

   Continue to cook for 3 minutes, flipping occasionally and brushing with glaze.

5. Remove from the heat, season with black pepper, and sprinkle with parsley.

PORK TENDERLOINS GLAZED WITH PEACH PRESERVES AND ROSEMARY

SERVES 8

Pork tenderloin is an impressive cut even if you just treat it to a dusting of salt and pepper. So just guess how tremendously delicious it becomes after a peach nectar brine, a chile seasoning blend, and a glaze packed with peach preserves. Plus, while it's cooking, I use a few sprigs of rosemary like a paintbrush to brush the meat with butter.

Brine

1 tablespoon crushed hot red pepper flakes
2 tablespoons boiling water
4 cups peach nectar
2 cups water
¼ cup kosher salt
¼ cup firmly packed dark brown sugar
4 garlic cloves, peeled, halved, germ removed, and grated on a Microplane grater
1 tablespoon finely ground fresh black pepper

3 pork tenderloins, about 1¼ pounds each, silverskin removed

Seasoning Blend

2 tablespoons mild chile powder, preferably Chimayo (see Sources page 378), Ancho, or Hatch
2 tablespoons dry mustard
1 tablespoon firmly packed dark brown sugar
1 tablespoon garlic salt
1 teaspoon finely ground fresh black pepper
1 teaspoon cayenne pepper

Glaze Finishing/Dressing

1 cup peach preserves
Juice of ½ lemon
4 garlic cloves, peeled, halved, germ removed, and thinly sliced
1 tablespoon apple cider vinegar
1 tablespoon fresh rosemary leaves
1 teaspoon coarsely ground fresh black pepper

About ¼ cup canola or vegetable oil

6 tablespoons (3 ounces) unsalted butter, melted
1 bunch rosemary, tied in an Herb Bundle (page 365)

Fleur de sel

1. Place the pepper flakes in a small bowl and pour the boiling water over them. Let sit for 1 to 2 minutes to rehydrate the flakes. In a large bowl, combine all of the brine ingredients, including the pepper flakes and the soaking water, stirring to dissolve the salt and sugar.

   Place the tenderloins in an extra-large resealable plastic bag (or divide between two to three large bags) and pour the brine over the top. Squeeze out any excess air from the bag and close. Refrigerate for at least 2 hours, but preferably up to 12.
2. Preheat all grates of a well-oiled charcoal or gas grill to medium-high.
3. Combine all of the seasoning blend ingredients.

   Combine all of the glaze ingredients in a jar with a tight-fitting lid and shake to combine. Pour half of the glaze into a baking dish or disposable aluminum pan, preferably a 13½ × 9⅝ × 2¾-inch lasagna pan. Set the remaining glaze aside to use as finishing/dressing.
4. Remove the tenderloins from the brine and lightly pat dry with paper towels.

   Sprinkle the seasoning blend evenly on all sides.

   Using your hands or a brush, evenly, but lightly, coat the tenderloins with canola oil.
5. Place the tenderloins on the grate. Do not move until the tenderloins are well marked and lightly charred on the first side, about 2 minutes. Continue to roll the tenderloins to the remaining sides, basting with butter using the herb bundle, until all sides are well marked and lightly charred, about 2 minutes per side. Flip, jockey, and stack throughout the cooking time as needed.

   Roll the tenderloins in the pan of glaze and place back on the grate.

   Continue to move the tenderloins between the pan and the grate, dredging in the glaze in the pan throughout the remaining cooking time, about 5 minutes for a tenderloin that is still slightly pink, and 8 to 10 for more well-done.
6. Give the dressing a quick shake and pour on a cutting board. Top with the tenderloins and let rest for 5 minutes.
7. Slice the tenderloins on the diagonal, dredging in the dressing to coat. Sprinkle with fleur de sel.

ASIAN PORK MEATBALL SKEWERS

SERVES 6 TO 8

I took everything I love about Asian street food and channeled it into these juicy little pork meatballs. You're going to love the way the fish sauce, shallots, and garlic become this deep, salty-sweet punch of flavor and create this beautiful color after spending just a few minutes on a hot grill. Don't be afraid of the addition of fish sauce: It may seem pungent when you sniff the bottle, but once it's cooked, it adds a totally different and completely essential salty tang that you just can't get from anything else. The skewers make the perfect pass-around snack for a party.

Glaze
¼ cup freshly squeezed lime juice
¼ cup firmly packed light brown sugar
2 teaspoons grated fresh ginger
4 garlic cloves, peeled, halved, germ removed, and grated on a Microplane grater
1 tablespoon finely chopped scallion, white and green portions

Meatballs
2 pounds ground pork
¼ cup fish sauce
¼ cup finely chopped shallots
¼ cup finely chopped scallions, white and green portions
¼ cup finely chopped cilantro
1½ tablespoons finely chopped garlic
1½ tablespoons finely chopped fresh ginger
2 tablespoons finely chopped lemongrass
2 tablespoons finely chopped flat-leaf parsley
1½ tablespoons finely ground fresh black pepper

1½ teaspoons kosher salt
1 small hot chile, preferably Thai bird

1 tablespoon toasted sesame oil
1 tablespoon (½ ounce) unsalted butter
1 lime, cut into quarters, seeds removed
¼ cup finely chopped scallions, white and green portions
2 tablespoons black sesame seeds

Edible Wraps
1½ cups Asian Dipping Sauce (page 372)
4 cups rehydrated bean threads
18 lettuce leaves, preferably green leaf or Bibb
About ½ cup cilantro leaves
4 small hot chiles, preferably Thai bird, thinly sliced

1. Cover 8 long wooden skewers with water and let soak for 1 hour (or plan on using metal skewers).
2. Place a cast-iron griddle on one area of a well-oiled charcoal or gas grill and pre-heat to medium-high.
3. Place all of the glaze ingredients in a jar with a tight-fitting lid and shake to combine. Set aside.
4. Place the pork and the fish sauce in the bowl of a food processor and combine. Add the remaining meatball ingredients and pulse to combine. Depending on the size of your food processor, this may need to be done in batches.

   Roll the meat into forty 1-inch meatballs.

   Place 5 meatballs on each skewer. The meatballs should be evenly spaced and not touching, with enough room at the ends of the skewers for moving them.

   Gently flatten the sides of the meatballs so that there are four sides, again making sure there is still room between each meatball and at the ends.
5. Add the sesame oil and butter to the top of the griddle. Based on the size of your griddle, working in batches, place the skewers on the griddle and brown on each of the four sides for 1 minute per side.

   Transfer to the grate, allowing any large exposed portion of the wooden skewers to hang off the edge of the grill or over another indirect area so they do not burn.

   Grill until nicely caramelized, brushing with the glaze to coat, about 2 minutes per side.
6. Remove from the heat. Squeeze the lime over the meatballs, and sprinkle with the scallions and sesame seeds.
7. Divide the dipping sauce among eight small bowls.

   Serve family style, wrapping the meatballs, bean threads, cilantro, and chiles in the lettuce.

BEER-AND-CARAWAY-BRAISED BRATWURST

SERVES 6 TO 12

It's game day. You're almost finished smoking six racks of ribs, but suddenly your small party has become a blowout. Instead of stressing, look to this perfectly porky sausage to fill out your meal. Stuffed in a soft bun, it's the ultimate hand-held, no-fuss food. Because I always end up hanging out and eating all day, I grill the brats, and then let them wallow in a bath of beer spiked with onions and garlic, so they stay moist and get all yeasty and delicious. Extras like mustard, sauerkraut, or caramelized onions certainly don't hurt.

Beer Bath
24 ounces beer (not light) or lager
1 large sweet white onion, thinly sliced
12 unpeeled garlic cloves, crushed
1/4 cup canola or vegetable oil
1 tablespoon caraway seeds, crushed with a
    rolling pin or heavy-bottomed pan
4 flat-leaf parsley sprigs
4 thyme sprigs
1 1/2 teaspoons crushed hot red pepper flakes
    (optional)

12 uncooked bratwurst
1/4 to 1/2 cup canola or vegetable oil
12 soft rolls
2 batches Grilled Sweet Onions (page 313)
About 5 cups sauerkraut
Mustard of choice

1. Position two heavy-duty aluminum foil–wrapped firebricks about 4 inches apart on one area of a well-oiled charcoal or gas grill, and preheat all areas to high.

2. Combine the beer bath ingredients in a baking dish or disposable aluminum pan, preferably a 13½ × 9⅝ × 2¾-inch lasagna pan. Place the uncovered dish on the bricks, close the lid, and preheat until hot, about 45 minutes.

3. Add the bratwurst to the bath. It's OK if the bratwurst touch and are not completely submerged in the bath. Close the lid and cook for 20 minutes, flipping the bratwurst once halfway through the cooking.

4. Meanwhile, pour a film of canola oil into a baking dish or disposable pan.

5. Remove the bratwurst from the bath, roll in the oil to lightly coat, and place evenly across the grate with about an inch between each. Turn to brown and caramelize deeply on all sides, about 2 minutes per side.

6. The brats can be served at this point, or held in the beer bath over very low heat with the lid closed for up to 1 hour. Occasionally test the heat of the bath. The bath should remain warm, 140°F, but should not boil.

Serve the brats on soft rolls, topped with onions and/or sauerkraut, and mustard.

GRIDDLED AND GRILLED ITALIAN SAUSAGES WITH PEPPERS AND ONIONS

SERVES 8

Ah, the smells and bustle of New York's Feast of San Gennaro, a street festival that the mention of Italian sausage brings me back to in an instant. Because it's a totally different sausage than bratwurst (page 58), my other favorite backyard-party link, you've got to treat it differently. Its grind means it has a fabulous coarse texture but also much less tolerance for overcooking. So instead of direct-heat grilling, I prefer griddling—using a cast-iron griddle or your shallowest cast-iron skillet (see Sources page 378)—which gets the casing really snappy and cooks the insides more gradually and evenly. Serve them right away, tucked into Italian rolls and piled with roasted peppers and grilled onions.

1 tablespoon extra virgin olive oil, plus additional as needed

1 tablespoon (½ ounce) unsalted butter, plus additional as needed

8 uncooked sweet or hot Italian sausages

1 recipe Grilled Sweet Onions (page 313)

1 recipe Roasted Marinated Peppers (page 331)

1½ teaspoons coarsely chopped fresh rosemary leaves

2 tablespoons roughly chopped flat-leaf parsley

Eight Italian rolls, or 6 inch-pieces of Italian bread split like rolls, lightly toasted on the grill

1 to 2 whole, large garlic cloves, peeled and lightly crushed

1. Place a cast-iron griddle on one area of a well-oiled charcoal or gas grill and pre-heat to medium. Preheat the exposed grate to low.
2. Add 1 tablespoon of the olive oil and 1 tablespoon of the butter to the top of the griddle.

   Once the butter has melted, keeping the natural bow of the sausage consistent, lay all of the sausages in a row on the griddle. Close the lid and cook for 5 minutes.

   Check to see if the sausages are nicely crisp on the first side. If they are, flip them over; if not, continue to cook with lid open until crisp.

   Flip and cook, with the lid closed, for an additional 5 minutes, or until the second side is crisp.

   Move the sausages to the low-heat grate.

   At this point, there should be residual fat on the griddle from the sausages. If there isn't, add an additional 1 tablespoon each of oil and butter.
3. Stir the onions, peppers, rosemary, and parsley together.

   Letting any excess oil run off and remain in the bowl, spread as many peppers and onions as will fit without crowding on the griddle. They may need to be done in batches. Cook for 5 minutes to reheat.

   Place the sausages (proportional to the number of peppers and onions that will fit on the griddle) on top of the mixture, close the lid, and cook for 5 minutes.

   Repeat with the remaining sausages peppers, and onions, as needed.
4. Rub the rolls with the garlic and fill each with the sausage, peppers, and onions.

BABY BACK PORK RIBS GLAZED WITH HONEY

SERVES 6 TO 8

Honey has long been a buddy to barbecuers. It caramelizes beautifully, plus it's a great flavor carrier—you can infuse it with anything from jalapeños to fruit juice—and thickener for sauces. Those who compete on the barbecue circuit often harness honey for a technique virtually unknown to recreational cooks: They drizzle onto their smoked ribs a mixture of honey, butter or margarine, and a splash of fruit juice just before giving the racks a final blast of smoke. Don't ask me how, but along with candying the meat a bit, the potion brings the ribs to a new degree of tenderness.

Mustard Moisturizer
¼ cup prepared yellow mustard
¼ cup water
1 tablespoon Worcestershire sauce
1 tablespoon apple cider vinegar

Seasoning Blend
6 tablespoons mild chile powder, preferably Chimayo (see Sources page 378), Ancho, or Hatch
3 tablespoons sweet paprika
3 tablespoons firmly packed dark brown sugar
1½ teaspoons dry mustard
2¼ teaspoons garlic salt
2¼ teaspoons kosher salt
2¼ teaspoons coarsely ground fresh black pepper
¾ teaspoon Old Bay Seasoning (see Sources page 378)
1 teaspoon ground cinnamon (optional)

4 racks baby back pork ribs, about 2¾ pounds each, membrane does not need to be removed (see Note)

Wrapping Mixture
1 cup firmly packed light brown sugar
1 cup honey
¼ cup apple juice

Honey BBQ Sauce
1 cup APL BBQ Sauce (page 362), or your favorite BBQ sauce
½ cup honey
2 tablespoons apple cider vinegar
½ Granny Smith apple, peeled, cored, and grated on a Microplane grater

About ½ cup Apple Juice Spray (page 364)

NOTE: I don't remove the membrane from the back of the ribs. It helps hold it all together.

1. Preheat an indirect barbecue with a drip pan and fruitwood (preferably apple), a ceramic cooker with deflector plate and fruitwood (preferably apple), or a charcoal or gas grill with a box or packet of fruitwood (preferably apple) to 275°F.

2. Combine all of the mustard moisturizer ingredients.

   Combine all of the seasoning blend ingredients.

   Rub a thin layer of the moisturizer on all sides of the racks and lightly sprinkle with the seasoning blend on all sides. The remaining seasoning blend will be used later in the cooking.

3. If using a ceramic cooker, the racks can be placed an inch apart on a rib rack (see Sources page 378). They might need to be trimmed to fit the cooking surface so that the lid can close. If using a larger indirect or direct barbecue, no additional trimming is necessary.

   Place the ribs in the cooker and cook for 2 hours.

4. Meanwhile, combine the wrapping mixture ingredients.

5. Tear off 8 sheets of heavy-duty aluminum foil. Working with 2 sheets of foil at a time, place a quarter of the wrapping mixture on the foil, top with a rack of ribs, and wrap in the foil, crimping to seal. Wrap with the second sheet of foil. Repeat for the remaining 3 racks of ribs.

   If using a ceramic cooker, stack the packets on top of each other. If using a smoker, place the ribs on sheet pans for easier movement.

   Place the packets back in the cooker, meat side down, and cook for 1 hour, flipping halfway through.

6. Remove the racks from the cooker and let rest in the foil packets for 20 minutes.

7. Remove the ribs from the foil and dust lightly on both sides with additional seasoning blend.

   Place the ribs back in the cooker, meat side up, for 30 minutes.

8. Meanwhile, combine the BBQ sauce ingredients.

9. Remove the racks from the cooker and brush with an even, but not too thick, layer of sauce. The layer should evenly coat the ribs, but should not clump.

   Place back in the cooker, meat side up, for 25 minutes to tighten up the sauce.

10. Paint a cutting board with some of the remaining sauce.

11. Remove the ribs from the cooker and place on the prepared cutting board, adding additional sauce as needed to cover, but not excessively coat. Spray twice with apple juice spray.

    Cut the ribs from the racks and dredge to coat the exposed sides with the remaining BBQ sauce.

ST. LOUIS–CUT SPARERIBS LAYERED WITH APRICOT FLAVORS

SERVES 6 TO 8

Before I knew real Southern barbecue, ribs, to me, meant either spareribs or baby backs. But when I started competing, I discovered the trim, tidy St. Louis cut. It's a little more expensive than spareribs, but because each rib is the same size, the racks cook more evenly, which means every bite of these ribs has an ultratender, delicate meatiness. They're slightly fattier than baby back or loin back ribs, so I add some extra acidity to my apricot BBQ sauce to cut the richness.

Mustard Moisturizer
¼ cup prepared yellow mustard
¼ cup water
1 tablespoon Worcestershire sauce
1 tablespoon apple cider vinegar

Seasoning Blend
6 tablespoons mild chile powder, preferably Chimayo (see Sources page 378), Ancho, or Hatch
3 tablespoons sweet paprika
3 tablespoons firmly packed dark brown sugar
1½ teaspoons dry mustard
2¼ teaspoons garlic salt
2¼ teaspoons kosher salt
2¼ teaspoons coarsely ground fresh black pepper
¾ teaspoon Old Bay Seasoning (see Sources page 378)
1 teaspoon ground cinnamon (optional)

4 racks St. Louis–cut pork spareribs, about 2½ pounds each, membrane does not need to be removed (see Note page 63)

Wrapping Mixture
1 cup firmly packed light brown sugar
1 cup honey
¼ cup apricot nectar

Apricot BBQ Sauce
1 cup APL BBQ Sauce (page 362) or your favorite BBQ sauce
½ cup apricot preserves
2 tablespoons apple cider vinegar
2 tablespoons water

About ½ cup Apple Juice Spray (page 364)

1. Preheat an indirect barbecue with a drip pan and fruitwood (preferably apple), a ceramic cooker with deflector plate and fruitwood (preferably apple), or a charcoal or gas grill with a box or packet of fruitwood (preferably apple) to 250°F.

2. Combine all of the mustard moisturizer ingredients.

   Combine all of the seasoning blend ingredients.

   Rub a thin layer of the moisturizer on all sides of the racks and lightly sprinkle with the seasoning blend on all sides. The remaining seasoning blend will be used later in the cooking.

3. If using a ceramic cooker, place an inch apart on a rib rack (see Sources page 378). They might need to be trimmed to fit the cooking surface so that the lid can close. If using a larger indirect or direct barbecue, no additional trimming is necessary.

   Place the ribs in the cooker and cook for 3 hours.

4. Meanwhile, combine the wrapping mixture ingredients.

5. Tear off 8 sheets of heavy-duty aluminum foil. Working with 2 sheets of foil at a time, place a quarter of the wrapping mixture on the foil, top with a rack of ribs, meat side down, and wrap in the foil, crimping to seal. Wrap with the second sheet of foil. Repeat for the remaining 3 racks of ribs.

   If using a ceramic cooker, stack the packets on top of each other. If using a smoker, place the ribs on sheet pans for easier movement.

   Place the packets back in the cooker, meat side down, and cook for 1½ hours, flipping halfway through.

6. Remove the ribs from the cooker and let them rest in the foil packets for 20 minutes.

7. Remove the ribs from the foil and dust lightly on both sides with additional seasoning blend.

   Place back in the cooker, meat side up, for 30 minutes.

8. Meanwhile, combine the BBQ sauce ingredients.

9. Remove the ribs from the cooker and brush with an even, but not too thick, layer of sauce. The layer should evenly coat the ribs, but should not clump.

   Place back in the cooker, meat side up, for 25 minutes to tighten up the sauce.

10. Paint a cutting board with some of the remaining sauce.

11. Remove the ribs from the cooker and place on the prepared cutting board, adding additional sauce as needed to cover, but not excessively coat. Spray twice with apple juice spray.

    Cut the ribs from the racks and dredge to coat the exposed sides with the remaining BBQ sauce.

RELIABLE PORK SPARERIBS

When I want to feed a big group of friends with ribs, I go straight for spareribs, which are inexpensive, really meaty, and long on porky flavor. And, man, do they get pretty after I add a tangy mustardy mix, my pork seasoning blend, and plenty of sauce—though not too much, because I really want the meat to shine. Keep in mind that while St. Louis-cut ribs cook relatively quickly and come out of the smoker uniformly tender, spareribs take a bit longer and are beautifully tender in some places and satisfyingly chewy in others.

Mustard Moisturizer
¼ cup prepared yellow mustard
¼ cup water
1 tablespoon Worcestershire sauce
1 tablespoon apple cider vinegar

Seasoning Blend
6 tablespoons mild chile powder, preferably Chimayo (see Sources page 378), Ancho, or Hatch
3 tablespoons sweet paprika
3 tablespoons firmly packed dark brown sugar
1½ teaspoons dry mustard
2¼ teaspoons garlic salt
2¼ teaspoons kosher salt
2¼ teaspoons coarsely ground fresh black pepper
¾ teaspoon Old Bay Seasoning (see Sources page 378)
1 teaspoon ground cinnamon (optional)

4 racks pork spareribs, about 3 pounds each, membrane does not need to be removed (see Note, page 63)

About 1 cup Apple Juice Spray (page 364)

Wrapping Mixture
1 cup firmly packed light brown sugar
1 cup honey
¼ cup apple juice

BBQ Sauce
1 cup APL BBQ Sauce (page 362), or your favorite BBQ sauce
¼ cup water

1. Preheat an indirect barbecue with a drip pan and fruitwood (preferably apple), a ceramic cooker with deflector plate and fruitwood (preferably apple), or a charcoal or gas grill with a box or packet of fruitwood (preferably apple) to 250°F.

2. Combine all of the mustard moisturizer ingredients.

    Combine all of the seasoning blend ingredients.

    Rub a thin layer of the moisturizer on all sides of the racks and lightly sprinkle with the seasoning blend on all sides. The remaining seasoning blend will be used later in the cooking.

3. If using a ceramic cooker, place the ribs an inch apart on a rib rack (see Sources page 378). They might need to be trimmed to fit the cooking surface so that the lid can close. If using a larger indirect or direct barbecue, no additional trimming is necessary.

    Place the ribs in the cooker, spraying with the apple juice spray every half hour after 2 hours of cooking. Cook for 4 hours.

4. Meanwhile, combine the wrapping mixture ingredients.

5. Tear off 8 sheets of heavy-duty aluminum foil. Working with 2 sheets of foil at a time, place a quarter of the wrapping mixture on the foil, top with a rack of ribs, meat side down, and wrap in the foil, crimping to seal. Wrap with the second sheet of foil. Repeat for the remaining 3 racks of ribs.

    If using a ceramic cooker, stack the packets on top of each other. If using a smoker, place the ribs on sheet pans for easier movement.

    Place the packets back in the cooker, meat side down, and cook for 1½ hours, flipping halfway through.

6. Remove the racks from the cooker and let the ribs rest in the foil packets for 20 minutes.

7. Remove the ribs from the foil and dust lightly on both sides with additional seasoning blend.

    Place back in the cooker, meat side up, for 30 minutes.

8. Meanwhile, combine the BBQ sauce and water.

9. Remove the ribs from the cooker and brush with an even, but not too thick, layer of sauce.

    Place back in the cooker, meat side up, for 25 minutes to tighten up the glaze.

10. Paint a cutting board with some of the remaining sauce.

11. Remove the ribs from the cooker and place on the prepared cutting board, adding additional sauce as needed to cover, but not excessively coat. Spray twice with apple juice spray.

    Cut the ribs from the racks and dredge to coat the exposed sides with the remaining BBQ sauce.

GLAZED PORK LOIN WITH CILANTRO AND GARLIC

When I was little, I would beg my mom to make pork chops, because she'd top them with this sweet, sticky condiment called Saucy Susan. It's a sort of jam made from apricots, and ever since she first combined the two ingredients, I've been obsessed with how well the fruit goes with pork. Nowadays, I pay homage to the sweet-tart flavor of the fruit by brining the loin in apricot nectar and later building upon the flavors with a glaze made from apricot preserves and lemon.

TIP: This dish is a crowd pleaser, so I'll double it and have two for a party.

Brine
1 teaspoon crushed hot red pepper flakes
1 tablespoon boiling water
2 cups apricot nectar
2 cups water
½ cup kosher salt
½ cup granulated sugar
10 garlic cloves, peeled, halved, germ removed, and grated on a Microplane grater

One 6½- to 7-pound pork loin

Seasoning Blend
2 tablespoons mild chile powder, preferably Chimayo (see Sources page 378), Ancho, or Hatch
1 tablespoon sweet paprika
1 tablespoon firmly packed dark brown sugar
¾ teaspoon dry mustard
½ teaspoon garlic salt
½ teaspoon lemon pepper
½ teaspoon coarsely ground fresh black pepper
½ teaspoon kosher salt
¼ teaspoon Old Bay Seasoning (see Sources page 378)
¼ teaspoon ground cumin

Glaze
½ cup apricot preserves
1½ tablespoons freshly squeezed lemon juice
3 tablespoons finely chopped cilantro or flat-leaf parsley
1 garlic clove, peeled, halved, germ removed, and grated on a Microplane grater

About 2 tablespoons canola or vegetable oil

Fleur de sel
Finely ground fresh black pepper

1. Place the pepper flakes in a small bowl and pour the boiling water over them. Let sit for 1 to 2 minutes to rehydrate the flakes. Combine all the brine ingredients in a blender, or in a large bowl using an immersion/stick blender. Stir in the pepper flakes and the soaking water.

   Place the loin in an extra-large resealable plastic bag, pour the brine over the top, squeeze out any excess air from the bag, and close. Roll the bag to evenly coat the meat. Refrigerate for at least 6 hours, or up to 12.

2. Preheat an indirect barbecue with a drip pan and fruitwood (preferably apple), a ceramic cooker with deflector plate and fruitwood (preferably apple), or a charcoal or gas grill with a box or packet of fruitwood (preferably apple) to 250°F.

3. Combine all of the seasoning blend ingredients.

   Place all of the glaze ingredients in a jar with a tight-fitting lid and shake to combine. Set aside.

4. Remove the loin from the brine and lightly pat dry with paper towels.

   Sprinkle the rub evenly on all sides.

   Using your hands or a brush, evenly, but lightly, coat the loin with canola oil.

   Insert a remote thermometer into the center of the meat.

5. Place the loin in the cooker and cook until the internal temperature reaches 135°F, about 1 hour and 15 minutes.

6. Give the glaze a quick shake to reincorporate any ingredients that may have settled. Brush the loin with the glaze and return to the cooker until the internal temperature reaches 145°F, about 15 minutes. At this point the meat will be slightly pink in the center; cook for an additional 5 to 10 minutes for more well-done.

7. Pour about half of the remaining glaze on a cutting board and top with the loin. Let rest for 10 minutes.

8. Slice the meat into ¼-inch slices. Dredge the slices in the glaze, adding additional as needed to coat the exposed sides. Sprinkle with fleur de sel and pepper.

BONE-IN PORK BUTT WITH GREEN APPLE AND CRUSHED HOT RED PEPPER

SERVES 8 TO 10

At the 2005 World Pork Expo (aka the Great Pork BarbeQLossal), my first-ever competition, a barbecue vet came up to me and whispered, "Just think apple." I never did get his name, but I did apply his advice. After all, apple is a very friendly flavor to pork. Yet I wasn't just going to dump some apple juice in my sauce. I wanted to hit the flavor from many different angles. So along with apple juice and jelly, I used apple cider vinegar for its lively acidity and grated green apple for its freshness and crunch. The effect borders on the subliminal: You're not going to taste it and think, "Aha, that must be apple jelly!" But the warm, familiar association the flavors conjure up makes this dish a winner. Plus, the crushed red pepper in there creates a rollercoaster of flavor: Some bites bring a rush of heat, which mellows during the next few bites only to come roaring back. Oh, and did I mention that I won Grand Champion?

Injection

3 cups apple juice

1½ cups water

6 tablespoons firmly packed light brown sugar

3 tablespoons kosher salt

1 teaspoon Worcestershire sauce

1 teaspoon Maggi Seasoning (see Sources page 378) or Japanese soy sauce

One 7- to 9-pound bone-in pork butt

Mustard Moisturizer

6 tablespoons prepared yellow mustard

6 tablespoons water

1½ tablespoons Worcestershire sauce

1½ tablespoons apple cider vinegar

Seasoning Blend

¼ cup mild chile powder, preferably Chimayo (see Sources page 378), Ancho, or Hatch

2 tablespoons sweet paprika

2 tablespoons firmly packed dark brown sugar

1½ teaspoons dry mustard

¾ teaspoon garlic salt

¾ teaspoon coarsely ground fresh black pepper

3/4 teaspoon kosher salt

1/2 teaspoon Old Bay Seasoning (see Sources
page 378)

About 1/4 cup canola or vegetable oil

1 cup Apple Juice Spray (page 364)

Wrapping Mixture

1 tablespoon (1/2 ounce) unsalted butter or
margarine, melted

1/4 cup honey

1/4 cup firmly packed light brown sugar

1/4 cup prepared yellow mustard

1/4 cup water

BBQ Sauce

1 cup APL BBQ Sauce (page 362), or your
favorite BBQ sauce

1 cup apple jelly

1 green apple, peeled, and grated on a
Microplane grater

2 tablespoons apple cider vinegar

1 tablespoon crushed hot red pepper flakes

Fleur de sel

1. Combine the injection ingredients, stirring to dissolve the sugar and salt.

   Place the pork in a baking dish or disposable aluminum pan. Working in a grid pattern, inject the pork butt with an injecting needle (see Sources page 378). Let stand for 2 hours at room temperature.

2. Preheat an indirect barbecue with a drip pan and fruitwood (preferably apple), a ceramic cooker with deflector plate and fruitwood (preferably apple), or a charcoal or gas grill with a box or packet of fruitwood (preferably apple) to 250°F.

3. Lightly pat the butt dry with paper towels.

   Combine all of the mustard moisturizer ingredients.

   Combine all of the seasoning blend ingredients.

   Lightly moisten the entire surface area of the pork with the moisturizer, sprinkle lightly with the seasoning blend, and using your hands or a brush, blot all sides to evenly, but lightly, coat with canola oil. (The remaining seasoning blend will be used later in the cooking.)

   Place a remote thermometer in the thickest part of the butt, avoiding contact with the bone.

4. Place the meat, fat side down, in the cooker, until the internal temperature reaches 130°F, about 3 hours.

5. Spray with the apple juice spray and continue to cook until the internal temperature reaches 160°F, about 3 hours.

6. Meanwhile, combine the wrapping mixture ingredients.

   Tear off 2 sheets of heavy-duty aluminum foil and place over a baking dish or disposable aluminum pan, preferably a $13\frac{1}{2} \times 9\frac{5}{8} \times 2\frac{3}{4}$-inch lasagna pan.

7. Remove the pork from the cooker, take out the thermometer, place the meat on the foil, pour over the wrapping mixture, and double wrap in the foil. Reinsert the thermometer, avoiding the bone, and transfer the wrapped pork in the pan back to the cooker.

   Cook until the internal temperature reaches 193°F, $2\frac{1}{2}$ to 3 hours.

8. Meanwhile, line a small cooler with a beach towel, or other large towels, to insulate the inside of the cooler.

9. Remove the pork from the cooker. Take out the thermometer, wrap the foiled pork completely in plastic wrap, place back in the baking dish or disposable pan (use a clean pan if there has been any leakage), and transfer the pork in the pan to the cooler. Fold over the towel to cover. Close the cooler, and let rest for 1 hour.

10. Place a cooling or other flat rack inside a baking dish or disposable pan that will hold the pork butt.

    Remove the butt from the cooler and carefully unwrap on a sheet pan. At this point the meat will be very tender. Carefully transfer to the rack in the pan and sprinkle moderately with the seasoning blend.

    Place the pan with the pork back in the cooker for 30 minutes.

11. Meanwhile, combine all of the BBQ sauce ingredients.

12. Remove the pan from the cooker and drizzle the meat on all sides with the barbecue sauce.

    Place back in the cooker for 20 minutes to tighten up the glaze.

13. Remove the pork butt from the cooker and spray with apple juice spray.

    Using bear paws (see Sources page 378) or heat-proof gloves (see Sources page 378), pull the pork, being sure to leave some in a semipulled, semichunk state. Mix with about half a cup of the remaining sauce and season with fleur de sel.

PICNIC SHOULDER MARINATED IN CITRUS, GARLIC, AND CUMIN

A bunch of my cooks at Daisy May's are Latino, and I'm consistently amazed by their ability to draw intense flavors from cuts neglected by fancy meat markets. Picnic shoulder is no glamour cut like the chop or tenderloin or even the butt, but tasting this dish—the juicy meat, the burst of acidity, the punchy heat—which one of them made for staff lunch, makes you wonder why this dish isn't on the menu of every restaurant in America.

Mojo Marinade
1½ cups freshly squeezed orange juice
½ cup freshly squeezed lime juice
8 garlic cloves, peeled, halved, germ removed, and grated on a Microplane grater
1 tablespoon ground cumin
1 tablespoon dried oregano, preferably Mexican
1 tablespoon kosher salt

Injection and Brine
4 cups water
¼ cup kosher salt
About 1 cup strained marinade (from above)

One 7- to 9-pound picnic shoulder
1 cup water, for the cooking bag
About ½ cup canola or vegetable oil

Glaze
½ cup firmly packed light brown sugar
¼ cup apple cider vinegar

½ cup coarsely chopped cilantro
Fleur de sel
Finely ground fresh black pepper

1. Combine all of the marinade ingredients in a blender, or in a large bowl using an immersion/stick blender. Strain through a fine-mesh strainer, preferably lined with cheesecloth (to remove any small pieces that could clog the injecting needle), into a clean bowl or storage container. Refrigerate for at least 12 hours, or up to 2 days to allow the flavors to mingle.

   Reserve and refrigerate 1 cup of the marinade to toss with the final cooked, pulled pork.

2. For the injection and brine mixture, combine the water and salt in a large bowl, stirring to dissolve the salt. Add the remaining marinade to the brine.

3. Place the picnic shoulder in a baking dish or disposable aluminum pan. Working in a grid pattern, inject with an injecting needle (see Sources page 378), using about 2 cups of the liquid. Place in an extra-large resealable plastic bag, or in a large container, with the remaining brine and refrigerate at least 8 hours or up to 12.

4. Preheat an indirect barbecue with a drip pan and fruitwood (preferably apple), a ceramic cooker with deflector plate and combination of fruitwood (preferably apple), or a charcoal or gas grill with a box or packet of fruitwood (preferably apple) to 275°F.

5. Set a cooling or other flat rack over a sheet pan.

   Remove the shoulder from the brine, place on the rack, and lightly pat dry with paper towels.

   Place the shoulder in an oven cooking bag (see Sources page 378) or wrap tightly in plastic wrap. If using the bag, pour in the water. If using plastic wrap, cut a 1-inch incision in the plastic wrap, pour in the water, and wrap tightly in a second layer of plastic wrap.

   If using the cooking bag or the plastic wrap, wrap the whole shoulder in heavy-duty aluminum foil. Place in a baking dish or disposable aluminum pan, preferably a 13½ × 9⅝ × 2¾-inch lasagna pan.

   To prevent leakage, attach a piece of foam-backed tape (see Sources page 378) to the outside of the wrapped shoulder near the thickest part, and insert the remote thermometer, avoiding contact with the bone.

6. Place the shoulder in the cooker and cook until the internal temperature reaches 195°F, about 7 hours.

7. Remove from the cooker and let rest, skin side down, still wrapped, for 2 hours.

8. Meanwhile, about 30 minutes before the end of the resting period, increase the temperature of the cooker for crisping the skin. If using a ceramic cooker, remove the deflector plate and increase the temperature to 375°F. If using a charcoal or gas grill increase the temperature of the grate to high.

   Remove the reserved marinade from the refrigerator and let come to room temperature.

   Pour a film of canola oil into a baking dish or disposable pan.

   Place the glaze ingredients in a jar with a tight-fitting lid and shake to combine.

9. Place a grilling basket (see Sources page 378) on the work surface.

   Carefully remove the shoulder from all of the wrappings. Some sticking may occur. Place, skin side down, in the oil.

   Transfer the shoulder, skin side down, to the grilling basket. The basket will not close completely.

Transfer in the basket, still skin side down, over the direct heat, and cook until the skin is very crisp, 15 to 20 minutes.

10. Give the glaze a quick shake to reincorporate any ingredients that may have settled.

Remove the shoulder from the cooker. Open the basket enough to brush with the glaze on all sides.

Place back over the direct heat, skin side up, for about 5 minutes to tighten the glaze.

11. Remove from the cooker.

Remove the skin and cut into 1-inch pieces for serving.

Using bear paws (see Sources page 378) or heat-proof gloves (see Sources page 378), pull the meat, being sure to leave some in a semipulled, semichunk state.

Toss the meat with the reserved marinade and the cilantro. Season to taste with fleur de sel and pepper. Garnish with the crisped skin.

PORK BLADE CHOPS, AKA SPEEDY PULLED PORK

SERVES 8

Smoking a giant shoulder to make pulled pork can be a major time commitment, but imagine if you could break that shoulder down into more manageable pieces that become superflavorful and succulent in three hours instead of eighteen. Well, your butcher has done it for you: Pork blade chops are cut from the shoulder, so you get the same fat-streaked, collagen-rich meat. Plus you get even more smokiness and flavor because you have so much surface area to work with. As for saving all that time, well, I won't tell anyone if you don't.

Brine

6 cups apple juice

3 cups water

3/4 cup firmly packed dark brown sugar

1/4 cup kosher salt

1 1/2 tablespoons Worcestershire sauce

1 1/2 tablespoons Maggi Seasoning (see Sources page 378) or Japanese soy sauce

Eight 3/4- to 1-inch-thick pork blade chops, about 1 pound each

Seasoning Blend

1/4 cup mild chile powder, preferably Chimayo (see Sources page 378), Ancho, or Hatch

2 tablespoons sweet paprika

2 tablespoons firmly packed dark brown sugar

1 1/2 teaspoons dry mustard

3/4 teaspoon garlic salt

3/4 teaspoon coarsely ground fresh black pepper

3/4 teaspoon kosher salt

1/2 teaspoon Old Bay Seasoning (see Sources page 378)

Wrapping Mixture

1 tablespoon (1/2 ounce) unsalted butter or margarine, melted

1/4 cup honey

1/4 cup firmly packed dark brown sugar

1/4 cup prepared yellow mustard

2 tablespoons apple juice

BBQ Sauce

1 1/2 cups APL BBQ Sauce (page 362), or your favorite BBQ sauce

1 1/2 cups apple jelly

3 tablespoons apple cider vinegar

1 1/2 tablespoons crushed hot red pepper flakes

Fleur de sel

1. In a large bowl, combine all of the brine ingredients, whisking to dissolve the salt and sugar.

   Place the blade chops into an extra-large resealable plastic bag (or divide between two large bags), pour the brine over, squeeze out any excess air from the bag, and close. Refrigerate for at least 3 hours, or up to 6.

2. Preheat an indirect barbecue with a drip pan and fruitwood or together with a combination of hardwoods (such as apple with oak and hickory), a ceramic cooker with deflector plate and fruitwood or together with a combination of hardwoods (such as apple with oak and hickory), or a charcoal or gas grill with a box or packet of fruitwood or together with a combination of hardwoods (such as apple with oak and hickory) to 275°F.

3. Combine the seasoning blend ingredients.

4. Remove the chops from the brine and lightly pat dry with paper towels.

   Sprinkle the seasoning blend evenly on all sides of the chops.

5. Place the chops in the cooker for 2 hours.

6. Meanwhile, combine all of the wrapping mixture ingredients.

   Tear off 8 sheets of heavy-duty aluminum foil, each large enough to wrap 2 chops.

7. Remove the chops from the cooker. Place 2 chops on top of a double-layered piece of foil and top with one-quarter of the wrapping mixture. Wrap tightly in the foil. Repeat with the remaining chops, foil, and mixture.

   Place back in the cooker for 1½ hours.

8. Remove the packets and let rest for 30 minutes.

9. Carefully unwrap and place the chops back in the cooker for 45 minutes.

10. Meanwhile, combine the BBQ sauce ingredients. Pour into a bowl, baking dish, or disposable aluminum pan, preferably a 13½ × 9⅝ × 2¾-inch lasagna pan.

11. Remove the chops from the cooker, coat in the BBQ sauce, and return to the cooker for 15 minutes.

12. Remove the chops from the cooker.

    Serve the chops whole, or shred and serve as pulled pork, adding the remaining sauce as needed while shredding. Season with fleur de sel.

"GET A BOOK" WHOLE PORK SHOULDER

SERVES 16 TO 18

A long time ago, just before I fell in love with the whole shoulder, I had the pleasure of watching one made by Chris Lilly, the many-times barbecue competition champ and the man who oversees the amazing, gigantic shoulders hand-pulled at Big Bob Gibson's in Decatur, Alabama. There's a reason old pros like Chris love the shoulder (it's made up of the picnic shoulder *and* the butt): It holds moisture so beautifully. My task as a chef, then, falls to giving it a flavor boost, since its size and shape means there's less smoke penetration and less space to add spice crust flavor. Fortunately, my apricot nectar–spiked injection and tangy apricot BBQ sauce are up to the task. I'm not going to beat around the bush—this is a major time commitment and you might have to sacrifice some sleep. But barbecuing a whole shoulder is something everyone should do *at least* once in his life, because, oh man, is it worth it!

TIP: Heat-proof gloves really come in handy for moving the whole shoulder in and out of the cooker.

Injection
6 cups apricot nectar
4 cups water
½ cup firmly packed dark brown sugar
½ cup kosher salt
1 tablespoon Worcestershire sauce
1 tablespoon Maggi Seasoning (see Sources page 378) or Japanese soy sauce

One 15- to 17-pound whole pork shoulder

Mustard Moisturizer
6 tablespoons prepared yellow mustard
6 tablespoons water
1½ tablespoons Worcestershire sauce
1½ tablespoons apple cider vinegar

Seasoning Blend
¼ cup mild chile powder, preferably Chimayo (see Sources page 378), Ancho, or Hatch
2 tablespoons sweet paprika
2 tablespoons firmly packed dark brown sugar
1½ teaspoons dry mustard
¾ teaspoon garlic salt
¾ teaspoon coarsely ground fresh black pepper

¾ teaspoon kosher salt
½ teaspoon Old Bay Seasoning (see Sources page 378)

¼ to ½ cup canola or vegetable oil
About 1 cup Apricot Juice Spray (page 364)

Wrapping Mixture
1 tablespoon (½ ounce) unsalted butter or
   margarine, melted
¼ cup honey
¼ cup firmly packed dark brown sugar
2 tablespoons apricot nectar

BBQ Sauce
2 cups APL BBQ Sauce (page 362), or your
   favorite BBQ sauce
1 cup apricot jelly
2 tablespoons apple cider vinegar
1 tablespoon crushed hot red pepper flakes

Fleur de sel

1. Combine all of the injection ingredients together in a large bowl, stirring to dissolve the sugar and salt.

   Place the shoulder in a large baking dish or disposable pan. Working in a grid pattern, inject the pork butt with an injecting needle (see Sources page 378), using all of the injecting liquid. A lot of the liquid will not remain inside the shoulder and will gather in the bottom of the pan. Let stand in the residual injection for 2 hours, at room temperature.

2. Preheat an indirect barbecue with a drip pan and a combination of fruitwood and hardwood (preferably apple and oak or hickory), a ceramic cooker with deflector plate and combination of fruitwood and hardwood (preferably apple and oak or hickory), or a charcoal or gas grill with a box or packet with a combination of fruitwood and hardwood (preferably apple and oak or hickory) to 250°F.

3. Combine the mustard moisturizer ingredients.

   Combine the seasoning blend ingredients.

4. Lift the shoulder, letting any excess liquid run off and remain in the pan. Remove the shoulder from the pan and lightly pat dry with paper towels.

   Lightly moisten the entire surface area of the shoulder with mustard moisturizer and sprinkle with the seasoning blend.

   Using your hands or a brush, evenly, but lightly, coat the shoulder with canola oil.

   Place a remote thermometer in the thickest part of the shoulder, avoiding contact with the bone.

5. Place the shoulder, fat side down, in the cooker, and cook until the internal temperature reaches 130°F, about 3 to 3½ hours.

6. Spray with apricot juice spray, and continue spraying every hour during the cooking until the internal temperature reaches 160°F, about 3 hours.

7. Meanwhile, combine all of the wrapping mixture ingredients.

   Tear off 2 sheets of heavy-duty aluminum foil that will be large enough to encase the shoulder and place over a baking dish or disposable aluminum pan.

8. Remove the shoulder from the cooker and place, skin side down, on the foil in the pan. Pour the wrapping ingredients on top. One sheet at a time, seal the foil, to keep all of the ingredients intact.

   Reinsert the thermometer, avoiding the bone, and transfer the wrapped pork in the pan back to the cooker. Cook until the internal temperature reaches 193°F, 3½ to 3¾ hours.

9. Meanwhile, line a small cooler with a beach towel or other large towels to insulate the inside of the cooler.

10. Remove the pork from the cooker and carefully unwrap, letting the juices remain in the pan.

    Line a work surface with heavy-duty aluminum foil. Wrap the shoulder completely, using additional foil as needed. Then wrap completely in plastic wrap. Place into a new baking dish or disposable pan and then into the cooler. Wrap with the towels to cover the top of the whole shoulder. Close the lid, and let rest for 1 hour.

11. At this point the meat will be very tender. Place a cooling or other flat rack over a baking sheet.

    Remove the meat from the cooler and carefully unwrap. Place the meat on the rack and place back in the cooker for 30 minutes.

12. Meanwhile, combine the BBQ sauce ingredients.
13. Remove the meat from the cooker and brush on all sides with the sauce.

    Place back in the cooker for 20 minutes.
14. Remove from the cooker and spray with apricot juice spray.

Using bear paws (see Sources page 378) or heat-proof gloves (see Sources page 378), pull the pork, being sure to leave some in a semipulled, semichunk state.

Mix with about 1½ cups of the remaining sauce, or additional to taste. Season with fleur de sel.

RACK OF PORK BRINED WITH CRAB BOIL SPICES

SERVES 6

I know what you're thinking: Using crab boil spices with pork sounds weird just for the sake of being weird. But one day I picked up a box, looked at the ingredients—bay leaves, peppercorn, cayenne, red pepper flakes—and thought, crab? These are some of my favorite spices to use with pork! Now instead of buying and mixing all these spices for a pork brine, I'll often grab a box of crab boil spices. In this case, I submerge the meat for an especially short amount of time, because I want some of the flavor penetration and succulence you get from brining, but also some of the traditional juiciness of unbrined meat.

Crab Boil Brine
2 cups apple cider
2 cups water
½ cup firmly packed dark brown sugar
¼ cup kosher salt
1 sachet of crab boil spices (see Note),
   preferably Zatarain's (see Sources page 378)
8 unpeeled garlic cloves, crushed

One 6-bone rack of pork, bones not frenched,
   about 4 pounds

Seasoning Blend
2 tablespoons mild chile powder, preferably
   Chimayo (see Sources page 368), Ancho, or
   Hatch
1 tablespoon sweet paprika
1 tablespoon firmly packed dark brown sugar
¾ teaspoon dry mustard

¾ teaspoon pimentón (see Sources page
   368), or other smoked paprika
½ teaspoon garlic salt
½ teaspoon coarsely ground fresh black
   pepper
½ teaspoon kosher salt
¼ teaspoon Old Bay Seasoning (see Sources
   page 368)

Red Pepper Glaze
½ cup red pepper jelly, preferably spicy
1 tablespoon apple cider vinegar

Finishing Dressing
½ cup extra virgin olive oil
½ lemon, seeds removed
¼ cup finely chopped chives
Fleur de sel
Finely ground fresh black pepper

NOTE: Sachets of crab boil spices are available in most supermarkets. If you can't find them or you prefer to use Old Bay Seasoning, make a sachet by placing ⅓ cup of Old Bay in a double layer of cheesecloth, bundle, and tie the top with kitchen twine.

1. Combine all of the brine ingredients in a medium saucepan. Bring to a boil, remove from the heat, cool, and refrigerate for at least 8 hours or up to 12.

2. Separate the bones of the rack by cutting between each of the bones, starting at the top between two bones, cutting through, and stopping about ¼ to ½ inch above the meat of the chop.

3. Place the rack in an extra-large resealable plastic bag. Pour the brine over the rack, squeeze out any excess air from the bag, and close. Refrigerate for at least 6 hours, or up to 12.

4. Preheat an indirect barbecue with a drip pan and fruitwood (preferably apple), a ceramic cooker with deflector plate and fruitwood (preferably apple), or a charcoal or gas grill with a box or packet of fruitwood (preferably apple) to 250°F.

5. Combine all of the seasoning blend ingredients.

6. Remove the pork from the brine and lightly pat dry with paper towels. Sprinkle with the seasoning blend ingredients on all sides.

   Place the pork in the cooker, and cook until the internal temperature reaches 135°F, about 1½ hours.

7. Meanwhile, put the glaze ingredients in a jar with a tight-fitting lid and shake to combine. If the jelly is especially thick, the mixture may need to be warmed in a small saucepan over medium heat, stirring to combine as the jelly melts.

8. Remove the meat from the cooker and brush on all sides with the glaze.

   Place back in the cooker and continue to cook until the internal temperature reaches 145°F, about 15 minutes. At this point the meat will be slightly pink in the center; cook for an additional 5 to 10 minutes for more well-done.

9. Drizzle the olive oil on a cutting board. Squeeze the lemon over the top, followed by the chives. Sprinkle fleur de sel and pepper on the board.

   Remove the meat from the cooker and transfer to the cutting board. Let rest for 10 minutes.

10. Slice into individual chops and dredge the exposed cut sides in the mixture. Season again with fleur de sel and pepper.

CROWN ROAST OF PORK

Just about two and a half hours in the barbecue brings just the right amount of smoke to this tremendously impressive cut of meat. I make it look especially regal, not by filling the top with the standard ground pork, but by serving it with a fresh, lively salad of peppery arugula and marinated tomatoes. It's dramatic, different, and perfect for warm weather.

TIP: For a larger group simply ask your butcher to create a crown roast with more bones.

Brine
1 tablespoon crushed hot red pepper flakes
2 tablespoons boiling water
4 cups water
2 cups apple cider
1¼ cups firmly packed dark brown sugar
¼ cup granulated sugar
¼ cup kosher salt
10 garlic cloves, peeled, halved, germ removed, and grated on a Microplane grater
1½ teaspoons Worcestershire sauce
Two 18-ounce packets Goya Sazón Azafrán (see Sources page 378) (see Note)

One 7½- to 8-pound crown roast of pork, with 8 to 10 bones (see Tip)

Seasoning Blend
2 tablespoons dry mustard
2 tablespoons sweet paprika
1 tablespoon granulated garlic or garlic powder
1 tablespoon kosher salt
1 tablespoon finely ground fresh black pepper
2 teaspoons Old Bay Seasoning (see Sources page 378)

Glaze
2 garlic cloves, peeled, halved, germ removed, grated on a Microplane grater
2 teaspoons crushed hot red pepper flakes
¼ cup apple cider vinegar
¼ cup honey
1 teaspoon kosher salt

¼ to ½ cup canola or vegetable oil

16 thyme sprigs

Finishing Dressing
½ cup extra virgin olive oil
½ lemon, seeds removed
¼ cup finely chopped chives
Fleur de sel
Finely ground fresh black pepper

1 recipe Dressed Arugula (page 348)
1 recipe Marinated Tomatoes (page 349)

NOTE: Goya Sazón Azafrán contains MSG. If you want to avoid it, substitute a combination of ¾ teaspoon chile powder, ¾ teaspoon ground cumin, ¾ teaspoon garlic salt, and ¾ teaspoon turmeric. The roast will not have quite the punch or color as it would with the Sazón.

1. Place the pepper flakes in a small bowl and pour the boiling water over them. Let sit for 1 to 2 minutes to rehydrate the flakes. Combine all of the remaining brine ingredients in a blender, or in a bowl using an immersion/stick blender. Stir in the pepper flakes and the soaking water.

    Place the roast in an extra-large resealable plastic bag. Pour over the brine, squeeze out any excess air from the bag, and close. Refrigerate for 2 to 3 hours.

2. Preheat an indirect barbecue with a drip pan and hardwood (preferably hickory, oak, or pecan), a ceramic cooker with deflector plate and hardwood (preferably hickory, oak, or pecan), or a charcoal or gas grill with a box or packet of hardwood (preferably hickory, oak, or pecan) to 300°F.

3. Combine all of the seasoning blend ingredients.

    Place all of the glaze ingredients in a jar with a tight-fitting lid and shake to combine. Set aside.

4. Remove the roast from the brine and lightly pat dry with paper towels.

    Sprinkle the seasoning blend over the entire roast, both outside and inside areas.

    Using your hands or a brush, evenly, but lightly, coat the roast with canola oil.

    Place 2 to 3 thyme sprigs into each of the cracks in the roast.

    Transfer the roast to a cooling or other flat rack.

    Insert a remote thermometer horizontally into a thick portion of the roast, running in the direction of a bone, but not touching one.

5. Place in the cooker and cook to desired doneness: about 2½ hours for medium (140°F), about 2¾ hours for medium-well (145°F), and about 3 hours and 15 minutes for well (155°F).

6. Remove the roast from the cooker, give the glaze a quick shake to reincorporate any ingredients that may have settled, and brush all exposed areas with the glaze.

    Return the roast to the cooker for 5 to 10 minutes to tighten the glaze.

7. Drizzle the olive oil on a cutting board. Squeeze the lemon over the top, followed by the chives. Sprinkle fleur de sel and pepper on the board.

    Remove the meat from the cooker and transfer to the cutting board. Let rest for 10 minutes.

8. If serving without the salad, slice into individual chops and dredge the exposed cut sides in the mixture on the board. Season again with salt and pepper.

    If serving with the salad, transfer the roast to a platter and surround with the arugula and tomatoes. Serve the roast and salad at the table, by first dishing out the salad and then cutting the roast into chops, dredging in the mixture on the board before serving.

CRISPY SUCKLING PIG WITH SPICY SWEET-SOUR GLAZE

SERVES 18 TO 20

Big hogs are fantastic—if you're feeding eighty people. But when your crowd is smaller, suckling pigs are the way to give your guests the dramatic effect that comes from serving an entire animal. And there's no easier or quicker way to make them than in a Caja China (see Sources page 378). Developed by Roberto Guerra, who gave me this recipe, this relatively inexpensive device gives you meat that's nearly dripping with juice and skin as crisp as a potato chip. To cut through the beautiful fattiness, a tangy, garlicky mojo performs like a pro. Traditionally, it's made with the juice from sour oranges, but I usually substitute a mixture of regular orange and lime juice if sour oranges are not available.

Cooking in the Caja China is a ton of fun, but you have to be prepared. And it is essential to have a friend to lend a hand.

Beyond the pig and the items on the ingredient list, you will need to order a #2 Caja China (this will come with two internal racks, "S" hooks, and an extra-large injecting needle). It requires assembly, and I strongly recommend you put it together well in advance of cooking the pig.

Other items to purchase:

Extra-large cooler with at least a 120-quart capacity
Ice, enough to fill the cooler twice
About 80 pounds brick charcoal
Lighting fluid or other starters (page 18)
Rake
Large ash can
Fireproof gloves
Fire extinguisher
One 6-foot-table you aren't afraid to get dirty, or one large, thick piece of plywood set on two sawhorses to create a work surface that can be hosed down.

Mojo Marinade

7½ cups freshly squeezed orange juice

2½ cups freshly squeezed lime juice

40 garlic cloves, peeled, halved, germ
removed, and grated on a Microplane
grater

5 tablespoons ground cumin

5 tablespoons dried oregano, preferably
Mexican

5 tablespoons kosher salt

Salt Water Brine

5 gallons (80 cups) water

4 cups kosher salt

7½ gallons (120 cups) ice

One 40- to 45-pound suckling pig, dressed,
skin on (see Note page 94)

4 cups kosher salt, for rubbing on the skin

Glaze

1 pound firmly packed dark brown sugar,
about 2¼ cups

½ cup apple cider vinegar

Juice of 8 limes

6 garlic cloves, peeled, halved, germ removed,
and grated on a Microplane grater

10 serrano, or other small, hot chiles of
choice, thinly sliced (optional)

Coarsely ground fresh black pepper

NOTE: If you have never cooked a whole pig before, you might be surprised to see that the kidneys might be attached to the animal when you receive it. The kidneys are often left on as a way to judge how fresh the animal is and whether or not it has been frozen. If the kidneys are still attached, they are easily cut out.

1. Combine all of the marinade ingredients in batches in a blender, or in a large bowl using an immersion/stick blender. Strain through a fine-mesh strainer into a clean bowl or storage container and refrigerate for at least 12 hours, or up to 1½ days before cooking the pig to allow the flavors to mingle.

2. In a 120-quart-capacity cooler, combine the water and salt for the brine, stirring and/or whisking to dissolve the salt. Add the ice.

3. Place the pig in the cooler, feet up, with the cavity exposed.

    Using the provided injecting needle, and the brine in the cooler, inject the shoulders and the hams going through the flesh side (as opposed to the skin side) in a grid-like pattern.

    Close the cooler and let brine for 12 hours.

4. Drain the liquid using the spout on the cooler. Any residual brine or ice can remain in the cooler with the pig.

    Pour the marinade into the cavity of the pig. Fill a large garbage bag with ice and place on top of the pig. Close the cooler, and let marinate for 12 hours.

5. Meanwhile, about 1 hour before removing the pig from the marinade, set up your work area and the Caja China.

    Place the provided drip pan in the bottom of the Caja China.

    If you don't have a work surface large enough to hold the pig, position a large

piece of thick plywood on two sawhorses. Place the bottom rack on the surface with the triangular pieces facing down.

6. Remove the bag of ice from the top of the pig.

    Keeping the marinade in the cooler, lift the pig, and place, belly side down with the legs extended, on the rack.

    Pour salt over all of the pig's skin and, using your hands, rub it into the skin, letting any excess remain on the surface. Let sit for 30 minutes.

    Rub the pig again with any residual salt and let sit for another 30 minutes.

7. Hose down the pig to remove any excess salt.

    Position the top rack on the skin side of the pig with the triangles facing up. Secure the two racks together by attaching the "S" hooks. Depending on the size of the pig, you may need to go through the skin and flesh on the sides of the belly.

8. Place the pig into the cooker, skin side down, and pour the marinade into the cavity.

    Place the cover (from here on out known as the ash pan) on the top of the box, and then top with the charcoal grid.

    Pour 18 pounds of charcoal onto the screen and light, using lighter fluid or other fire starters.

    Once the charcoal is lit, 20 to 25 minutes, using a rake, spread the charcoal evenly over the charcoal grid.

    Timed cooking begins now. The pig

will be cooked in about 5½ hours, or slightly longer as needed to crisp the skin. Do not move the ash pan (not even to peek) until instructed to do so (see below).

9. For 5 hours, every hour, spread 9 pounds of new charcoal over the hot coals.

    At the 5-hour mark (after the new charcoal has been added and spread), carefully lift only the grid, shaking any ash off of the existing coals. The coals will continue to be used. Move the grid with the coals temporarily to rest on the long handles of the cooker. Remove the ash pan from the top of the box and dispose of all of the ashes. If you place the ashes on the ground, be sure to hose them down before continuing.

10. Lift the pig and flip to be skin side up.

    Using a chef's knife cut large "X's" a quarter inch deep into the skin surface on all exposed areas of the pig.

    Replace the ash pan and top with the charcoal grid containing the coals. Add 9 more pounds of coals.

    Cook the pig for 30 minutes to crisp the skin.

11. Meanwhile, combine all of the glaze ingredients in a large jar (a juice jar is a good size) with a tight-fitting lid and shake to combine. If you don't have a juice jar, mix in a sauce pan.

12. Lift a corner of the ash pan and peek at the pig. The skin should be puffed up and crisped. If it isn't, continue to cook, peeking every 10 minutes.

    If the pig does not seem to be crisping evenly, check out the placement of the coals on the grid. They may need to be spread out more or moved over the areas that aren't crisping.

13. Once crisp, lift off the ash pan and char-

coal grid together and let rest on the handles of the Caja China.

    Brush the glaze over all of the skin.

    Replace the pan and the grid, and cook for an additional 5 to 10 minutes to tighten the glaze.

14. Lift off the ash pan and charcoal grid together and let rest on the handles.

    Lift the pig out of the cooker and transfer to the work area, skin side up.

    Undo the "S" hooks, remove the top rack, gently lifting to tease off any skin that may have stuck.

15. The pig can be served up by peeling back the skin, cutting it into large pieces, and serving alongside meat that has been pulled using bear paws (see Sources page 378) or heat-proof gloves (see Sources page 378). But, it is also great fun to peel back the skin, cut into manageable pieces, and let everyone come up and pick out what they like. Season the meat with pepper.

Glazing in action.

WHOLE PIG ON A SPIT

SERVES ABOUT 50 PEOPLE

Oh yeah, baby. I'm talking about a 100-plus-pound oinker, the showpiece of an old-fashioned pig pickin'. I use what I call the Adam Perry Lang Cocoon Technique, wrapping the slowly spinning hog in plastic wrap, which intensifies flavor and maximizes the moisture in the meat. This dig-a-hole-in-your-yard, half-a-day project takes some serious effort, but follow my lead and it'll be the unbelievably juicy, wickedly crisp-skinned stuff of backyard party legend.

Injection

2 gallons (32 cups) water

1 cup kosher salt

1 cup granulated sugar

30 unpeeled garlic cloves, crushed

1 teaspoon crushed hot red pepper flakes

1 gallon (16 cups) apple juice

One 120-pound pig, dressed, skin on (see Note page 94)

Basting Butter

4 pounds unsalted butter

1 sweet white onion, coarsely chopped

5 heads of garlic, cut in half horizontally

6 thyme sprigs

4 sage sprigs

2 rosemary sprigs

About 2 cups canola or vegetable oil

Seasoning Blend

1 cup garlic salt

1 cup lemon pepper

1 cup mild chile powder, preferably Chimayo (see Sources page 378), Ancho, or Hatch

1 cup coarsely ground fresh black pepper

Herb Bundle

1 bunch thyme

1 bunch sage

1 bunch marjoram

1 bunch rosemary

Glaze

1 cup honey

Juice of 1 lemon

1 tablespoon red wine vinegar

1/4 cup coarsely chopped flat-leaf parsley

4 garlic cloves, peeled, and grated on a Microplane grater

1 recipe Herb Sauce (page 371)

Coarsely ground fresh black pepper

1. Combine all of the injection ingredients, and ideally let sit for 24 hours, allowing the flavors to develop. Strain.
2. Remove the pig's trotters and reserve for another use, if desired. Place the pig, feet side up, in the cooler. Inject the shoulders, hams, loins, and belly, going through the flesh side (as opposed to the skin side) in a grid-like pattern. If using a cooler to store, pack with ice and close the top, or if you have the means, refrigerate. Let sit for 12 hours.
3. Set up your spit.
4. Position the pig on the spit according to the manufacturer's instructions.
5. Combine all of the basting butter ingredients in a baking dish or disposable pan and place in the center under the animal to catch the majority of drippings. Combine the seasoning blend ingredients. Tie together all of the herbs using kitchen twine and attach to a dowel, about 3 feet long and ½ inch in diameter (see Herb Bundle page 365). Place all of the glaze ingredients in a large jar (a juice jar is a good size) with a tight-fitting lid and shake to combine. Set aside.
6. Spread about 18 pounds of charcoal about 2½ feet away from, but parallel to, the pig. The coals should be in a mound next to the pig. Using anything but lighter fluid, light the coals.
7. To know that the coals are properly placed to cook the pig, watch the pig. The skin should begin to sweat very lightly and start to render fat. If the sweating or rendering is too aggressive, using a rake, move the coals about 6 inches away from the pig. Conversely if the pig is not sweating, use the rake to move the pile closer to the pig.
8. During the cooking time, you will be adding about 9 pounds of coals per hour, but the time frame will vary based on weather conditions. Coals should be added when the charcoal is almost completely ashed over and is not letting off as much heat. Do not wait too long to add new coals.
9. After 2 hours, using an industrial-size roll of food-safe plastic wrap, tie the wrap to one end of the spit. Guide the wrap and let the natural movement of the spit help with the wrapping. Continue to unroll and wrap until the pig is covered by and completely encased in plastic wrap. The pig will be injected with water between its skin and the wrap, so it will need to be watertight. If in doubt, add an extra layer. Using 1 to 2 gallons of water, inject water, using an injecting needle, between the wrap and the skin of the pig.
10. Continue cooking for 4 hours.
11. Carefully, because excess liquid will have built up, cut the plastic wrap. Slowly remove to avoid tearing the skin. Using your hands (protected with heat-proof gloves), smear the seasoning blend over the meat, covering all areas as best you can.
12. Cook for 1 hour and then brush with the butter every 30 minutes, using the herb bundle. Continue to cook until the internal temperature in the shoulder is 165°F, for slicing, about 4 hours. Or cook to 195°F, for pulling, about 7 hours.
13. Give the glaze a quick shake and brush the pig using the herb brush. Continue to cook for 30 minutes to tighten the glaze.
14. Cut the meat directly from the spit and serve. Or give knives to all of your guests. The meat can be served directly from the pig or transferred to serving platters, dressed with herb sauce, and sprinkled with pepper.

CRISP AND UNCTUOUS PORK BELLY

SERVES 8

Man, do the Brits know how to cook pork! I was strolling through London's Borough Market, on a tip from my friend and bottomless source of inspiration Jamie Oliver, when I stumbled across a stall that made the most amazing pork belly (which, for anyone who's skeptical, is just uncured bacon, and who doesn't love bacon?). So of course, I got the recipe. And of course, I cook my version on the barbecue. The belly cooks slowly inside a foil packet in its natural juices, so it develops a luscious texture. Then right before it's done, I unwrap it and crank up the heat to crisp the skin. If you like it sweet, homemade applesauce and a bit of hot English mustard make the flavor explode. It also goes great with a side of Kale with Bacon (page 344). But here's a warning: Your friends will want to stuff their faces with super-rich slices, so you'll have to play the parent and offer them just enough.

TIP: Here's a cool trick. After the belly is all jiggly and tender, I sandwich it in a grill basket. That way, it's easily moved around and keeps its shape as it crisps.

One 4-pound piece fresh, uncured, skin-on pork belly

Marinade
1 cup water
¼ cup extra virgin olive oil
¼ cup freshly squeezed lemon juice
¼ cup apple cider vinegar
10 garlic cloves, peeled, halved, germ removed, and thinly sliced
2 tablespoons fresh rosemary leaves
2 tablespoons fresh thyme leaves
2 tablespoons kosher salt

1 tablespoon coarsely ground fresh black pepper
2 tablespoons thinly sliced serrano or other small, hot chile of choice (optional)

2 cups water
2 tablespoons (1 ounce) unsalted butter, softened

Glaze
¼ cup bourbon
¼ cup firmly packed dark brown sugar
2 tablespoons finely chopped flat-leaf parsley
1 tablespoon apple cider vinegar
½ teaspoon crushed hot red pepper flakes (optional)

About ⅓ cup canola or vegetable oil

Finishing Dressing

¼ cup extra virgin olive oil

1 tablespoon lemon juice

2 tablespoons finely chopped chives

Kosher salt

Finely ground coarse black pepper

Hot English mustard

8 sliced Cuban-style rolls, or eight 6-inch pieces of soft, unseeded, Italian bread, split like rolls

1 recipe Applesauce (page 345)

1 recipe Dressed Arugula (page 348)

1. Combine all of the marinade ingredients in a blender, or in a large bowl using an immersion/stick blender, and blend to combine thoroughly.

   Place the pork belly in a large resealable plastic bag, pour the marinade over the top, squeeze out any excess air from the bag, and close. Roll the bag to evenly coat the pork belly. Refrigerate for at least 12 hours, or up to 1 day.

2. Preheat an indirect bbq with a drip pan and fruitwood (preferably apple), a ceramic cooker with deflector plate and fruitwood (preferably apple), or a charcoal or gas grill with a box or packet of fruitwood (preferably apple) to 275°F.

3. Place the belly in a baking dish or disposable aluminum pan, preferably a 13½ × 9⅝ × 2¾-inch lasagna pan. Pour over the marinade, add the water and the butter, cover the top with heavy-duty aluminum foil, and crimp the edges to tightly seal.

   Place in the cooker and cook for 5½ hours.

4. Remove from the cooker and let rest in the pan, still covered, for 2 hours.

5. Meanwhile, about 30 minutes before the end of the resting period, increase the temperature of the cooker for crisping the skin. If using a ceramic cooker, remove the deflector plate and increase the temperature to 375°F. If using a charcoal or gas grill, increase the temperature of the grate to high.

   For the glaze, pour the bourbon in a small saucepan and place over medium heat. Cook off the alcohol, being careful of a possible flare-up, 7 to 10 minutes. The strong alcohol smell will subside.

   Place the remaining glaze ingredients into a jar with a tight-fitting lid and pour over the warm bourbon. Close the lid and shake to combine. Set aside.

   Pour a film of canola oil into a baking dish or disposable pan.

   Place a grilling basket (see Sources page 378) on the work surface.

6. Carefully remove the belly from the pan and place, skin side down, in the oil. Turn over in the oil. Transfer the belly to the grilling basket and close.

   Place the basket over the direct heat, skin side down, and cook to crisp the skin, about 15 to 20 minutes.

7. Give the glaze a quick shake to reincorporate any ingredients that may have settled.

   Remove the belly from the cooker and brush on all sides with the glaze.

   Place the belly back over the direct heat, skin side up, for about 5 minutes to tighten the glaze. Flip and repeat on the second side, cooking for about 5 minutes.

8. Drizzle the olive oil over the cutting board, followed by the lemon juice. Sprinkle with the chives, salt, and pepper.

   Carefully, because it will be exceptionally tender, remove the belly from the basket, place on the cutting board, skin side up, and let rest for 10 minutes before cutting.

9. Sprinkle the belly with salt, pepper, chives, and parsley, and cut the belly into slices (if you have one, an electric knife works well here), dredging in the dressing as it is cut. Spread mustard on the rolls, place a slice on each roll, and top with applesauce and greens.

TENDER PIG TROTTERS

Braised by the French, pickled by Southerners, pigs' feet have some die-hard fans. I love them, too, but I do them a bit differently. I incorporate a bit of a braise, to help bring out that unctuous, gelatinous loveliness, and then hit them with smoke. Besides garlic and tons of herbs, I add lemon to provide some relief from the richness. The heat of chiles helps, too, and gives the trotters this stunning deep amber color. These are the perfect addition to a big spread, because they'll be a fun surprise to curious guests, and the lovers of trotters at the table will forever sing your praises.

4 pig trotters, split

Brine
6 quarts (24 cups) water
¾ cup kosher salt

Braising Ingredients
2 cups water
2 tablespoons freshly squeezed lemon juice
2 tablespoons canola or vegetable oil
1 cup thinly sliced sweet white onion
10 unpeeled garlic cloves, crushed
2 thyme sprigs
1 teaspoon dried oregano, preferably Mexican
1 teaspoon crushed hot red pepper flakes
1 teaspoon kosher salt
1 teaspoon coarsely ground fresh black
    pepper

Glaze
½ cup freshly squeezed lemon juice
½ cup granulated sugar
6 small hot chile peppers, preferably Thai
    bird, cut into very thin rings
4 garlic cloves, peeled and crushed

About 2 tablespoons canola or vegetable oil

Kosher salt

1. Place the trotters in an extra-large storage container or nonreactive stockpot that will allow for them to be covered completely by the water.

   Combine the water and the salt, stirring to dissolve the salt. Pour over the trotters.

   Refrigerate for at least 12 hours, or up to 24.

2. Preheat an indirect barbecue with a drip pan and fruitwood (preferably apple), a ceramic cooker with deflector plate and fruitwood (preferably apple), or a charcoal or gas grill with a box or packet of fruitwood (preferably apple) to 325°F.

3. Combine all of the braising ingredients in a large bowl.

4. Remove the trotters from the brine and rinse. Lightly pat dry with paper towels.

   The size of the trotters will dictate the pans used. The goal is to have the trotters in an even layer with as little excess room as possible. Depending on the size of the cooker, the pans will need to be stacked and rotated halfway through the cooking.

   Place the trotters in the pan(s), skin side down, and pour in enough of the braising liquid to come about ¼ inch up the sides of the trotters. Cover the top of the pan(s) with heavy-duty aluminum foil, crimping to seal the edges.

   Place the pan(s) in the cooker, stacking as needed. Cook for 5½ hours, rotating the pans once, halfway through cooking.

5. Remove the trotters from the cooker and let rest in the pan, still covered, for 2 hours.

6. Meanwhile, about 30 minutes before the end of the resting period, increase the temperature of the cooker for crisping the skin. If using a ceramic cooker, remove the deflector plate and increase the temperature to 375°F. If using a charcoal or gas grill, increase the temperature of the grate to high.

   Place the glaze ingredients in a jar with a tight-fitting lid and shake to combine.

   Pour a film of canola oil into a baking dish or disposable pan.

   Place a grilling basket(s) (see Sources page 378) on the work surface.

7. Remove the trotters from the pan. Place, skin side down, in the oil and dredge to lightly coat.

   Lay the trotters in an even layer in the basket. Depending on their size, you may need to do this in two baskets or in batches.

   Place the basket over the direct heat, skin side down, and cook to crisp the skin, 15 to 20 minutes.

8. Give the glaze a quick shake to reincorporate any ingredients that may have settled.

   Remove the trotters from the cooker and brush on all sides with the glaze.

   Place back over the direct heat, skin side up, for about 5 minutes to tighten the glaze. Flip and repeat on the second side.

   Remove from the cooker, sprinkle with salt, and serve immediately.

SMOKED "BAKED" HAM

Tricking out a ham for a stunning holiday (or any-day) centerpiece is a task I accept with relish. I love figuring out ways to add an element of smoky authenticity along with the traditional blast of slightly acidic, fruity reinforcements. My glaze handles this, mixing pineapple preserves and juice, plus it grabs onto the flavors of the barbecue, so you get plenty of beautiful smoke.

Wrapping Mixture/Glaze
½ cup pineapple juice
½ cup pineapple preserves
½ cup firmly packed dark brown sugar
½ cup honey
5 garlic cloves, peeled, halved, germ removed, and grated on a Microplane grater
2 tablespoons apple cider vinegar
1 tablespoon prepared yellow mustard
1 tablespoon mild chile powder, preferably Chimayo (see Sources page 378), Ancho, or Hatch
1 tablespoon finely chopped jalapeño chile
1 tablespoon fresh thyme leaves
Pinch ground cloves, plus additional to taste
5 medium to large sage leaves, cut into chiffonade (see Note)

One 6- to 8-pound, bone-in, spiral cut or cooked/cured ham, preferably from the shank end
½ bunch thyme and ½ bunch sage, tied in an Herb Bundle (page 365)

NOTE: To chiffonade the sage, stack the leaves and roll as tightly as possible into a cylinder. Cut across the roll so that when unrolled the sage will be in thin, ribbon-like strips.

1. Preheat an indirect barbecue with a drip pan and fruitwood (preferably apple), a ceramic cooker with deflector plate and fruitwood (preferably apple), or a charcoal or gas grill with a box or packet of fruitwood (preferably apple) to 275°F.

2. Combine all of the wrapping mixture/glaze ingredients. Add additional ground cloves to taste. Reserve 1 cup of the mixture to use later to glaze.

   Place the ham in an extra-large resealable plastic bag and pour the remaining wrapping mixture/glaze over the top. Squeeze out any excess air from the bag, close, and roll to coat the ham evenly in the mixture.

   Lay out 4 sheets of heavy-duty aluminum foil in a crisscross pattern that will be large enough to encase the ham.

   Turn the ham out in the center of the sheets, letting any excess marinade drip on the surface of the ham.

   Wrap the ham, using one sheet of foil at a time, to cover completely.

   Insert a remote thermometer into the thickest part of the ham, avoiding the bone.

3. Place the ham in the cooker and cook until the internal temperature reaches 140°F, about 3 hours and 45 minutes.

4. Remove from the cooker and let rest, still wrapped in the foil, for 15 minutes.

5. Carefully remove the ham from the foil and place in a baking dish or disposable aluminum pan, preferably a 13½×9⅝ × 2¾-inch lasagna pan. Brush with some of the reserved glaze using the herb bundle.

   Place the ham, still in the pan, back in the cooker to tighten the glaze. Cook for 15 minutes, basting with the glaze using the herb bundle, a few times during the cooking.

6. Remove the ham from the cooker and rest in the pan for 15 minutes.

7. Pour some of the glaze on a cutting board and top with the ham. Bring to the table whole, or slice before serving, dredging the slices in the glaze.

CARAMEL SMOKED BACON

Right after Marc Farris, the guy behind BBQ TV, finished interviewing me for a segment, we got down to some important business: swapping recipes. That's what happens whenever you put two barbecue lovers together. When he mentioned this one for bacon, I knew it would become part of my arsenal. I like to think of it as double-caramel bacon because the bacon caramelizes after about two hours in the barbecue, and then the sugar in my coriander-studded glaze melts into, well, caramel. This creates two delicious layers of flavor, and that's not even counting the blast of lip-tingling heat that comes from the crushed peppercorns mixed in with the sugar. Try these with my corn griddle cakes with fried eggs for an unforgettable brunch.

TIP: Since you're dealing with some sticky sugar, it helps greatly to have a Silpat (see Sources page 378), the silicone-coated mat that nothing can stick to. After you use it for bacon, you might not want to use it for baking cookies, but believe me, it's worth it.

½ cup firmly packed light brown sugar

¼ cup water

1 tablespoon whole coriander seeds, coarsely crushed

1 tablespoon coarsely ground fresh black pepper

1 tablespoon crushed hot red pepper flakes

One 4½- to 5-inch-thick piece of slab bacon, 1¼ to 1¾ pounds, cut into 16 slices, each about ¼ inch thick

¼ cup coarsely chopped flat-leaf parsley

1. Preheat an indirect barbecue with a drip pan and fruitwood (preferably apple), a ceramic cooker with deflector plate and fruitwood (preferably apple), or a charcoal or gas grill with a box or packet of fruitwood (preferably apple) to 275°F.
2. Line two half sheet pans (or other pans that will fit your cooker) with Silpats (see Sources page 378).
3. Combine the sugar, water, crushed coriander, black pepper, and pepper flakes in a medium saucepan. Bring to a boil over medium to medium-high heat.

   Remove from the heat and, either in the pan or in a large bowl, toss the bacon in the sugar mixture to evenly coat all the slices.

   Arrange the bacon on the sheet pans, leaving a half inch between the slices.
4. Place the tray(s) in the cooker. Depending on the size of your cooker and the pans used to fit the cooker, the pans will need to be stacked and rotated halfway through the cooking.

   Cook for 1½ hours to 2 hours, or until the bacon is caramelized and cooked to your liking. At 1½ hours the bacon will be caramelized, but at 2 hours it will be crispier.
5. Remove the bacon from the cooker and sprinkle with the parsley.

   Let cool for a few minutes before serving.

NEW MEXICAN CHILE PORK STEW

SERVES 8

After training in some of the best kitchens out there, I don't do much back-of-the-box cooking. But when I came across an intriguing mix of Mexican oregano, dehydrated garlic, and chiles in a New Mexico grocery store, I decided to buy it and try the recipe printed on the bag. And what do you know? The marinated pork shoulder stewed with these Southwestern spices quickly became one of my favorite recipes. Over the years, I tweaked this freak success and started making it on the barbecue, letting the smoke flavor seep in before covering the pot so the pork could break down into a luscious mass. This chile-based stew cooked on the barbecue makes serving a crowd simple whether you eat it with warm tortillas for dinner or eggs for breakfast. It also makes great leftovers.

One 4-pound piece of pork shoulder, cut into 1-inch cubes

1 pound of whole pod dried chiles, preferably New Mexican (see Sources page 378), stems and seeds removed (see Note)

4 cups boiling water

2 tablespoons dried oregano, preferably Mexican

2 tablespoons granulated garlic or garlic powder

2 tablespoons granulated onion or onion powder

1 tablespoon ground cumin

½ cup plus 2 to 4 tablespoons firmly packed dark brown sugar

2 tablespoons kosher salt, plus additional for seasoning

2 cups thinly sliced sweet white onion

10 garlic cloves, peeled, halved, germ removed, and grated on a Microplane grater

4 cups low-sodium chicken stock

1½ to 3 tablespoons apple cider vinegar

8 cups cooked white rice

16 flour tortillas, warmed

½ cup thinly sliced raw chiles, preferably serrano or jalapeño

½ cup cilantro leaves

NOTE: When working with dried or fresh chiles it is important to avoid any contact with your eyes. Some stronger chiles can also leave a burning sensation on the skin, so wearing gloves is recommended.

1. Place the chiles in a large glass bowl, pressing lightly with your hands so that the chiles fit. Pour the water over the top. The water will only come about one-third of the way up the chiles, but the steam will help to soften them all. Cover the top of the bowl with plastic wrap to form a tight seal, and let sit, covered, to steam for 30 minutes.

2. Using a slotted spoon, place all of the chiles in a food processor. Reserve 1 cup of the soaking liquid. Pour the remaining liquid in the processor. Add the oregano, granulated garlic, granulated onion, cumin, ½ cup of the dark brown sugar, and 2 tablespoons of the salt. Blend until smooth, adding additional liquid only as necessary to make a smooth paste.

   Strain the pepper mixture through a medium strainer to remove any small pieces of pepper and/or skin. Let cool.

3. Place the onions, garlic, and meat in an extra-large resealable plastic bag, and roll to combine. Add the chile paste, squeeze out any excess air from the bag, close, and roll again to thoroughly combine.

   Refrigerate for at least 12 hours, or up to 1 day.

4. If using an indirect cooker, preheat to 275°F. If using a charcoal or gas grill, preheat the grates in one area to high and leave another off for indirect cooking.

5. Place the meat and the bag's contents in a small roasting pan or deep baking dish or pan that can take a direct flame. The pan should have about a 15-cup capacity. Add the chicken stock and stir to combine.

   Place the roasting pan over medium-high to high heat over two burners on the stovetop, or directly on the grill and bring to a simmer.

   Carefully remove from the direct heat and place into the preheated cooker or, if using the grill, move to the indirect heat and keep the internal grill temperature at 275°F.

   Cook for 3 to 3½ hours, or until the pork is fork tender.

6. Remove from the cooker and season with the remaining 2 to 4 tablespoons of the brown sugar and the vinegar and salt.

   Serve with white rice, flour tortillas, chiles, and cilantro.

BEEF

AND

VEAL

WHAT IS BEEF?

Remember the first time you had a good steak? I mean a *really* good steak. After years of tolerating decent beef, someone put a steak in front of you that blew your mind, something with a deep char on the outside and a rosy center, something that tasted so beautifully beefy that you knew you'd never forget it. Re-creating that experience yourself is much easier than you think. But it requires an understanding that starts with a fundamental but often overlooked question, one that you and I must consider even before talking about cooking: What is beef?

The simple answer, of course, is meat from cattle. But let's go a bit deeper. What you and I casually call beef is essentially muscle (the red stuff), connective tissue (the translucent stuff), and fat (the whitish stuff). So what does that mean for you, the cook? Well, different cuts of meat are composed of different muscles and have different amounts of connective tissue and fat so they respond differently to heat and cooking. Generally, the more an animal uses a particular muscle (think the shoulder), the tougher the meat. The muscle located at the cow's saddle (basically, the lower back), on the other hand, gets much less use and is very tender. More connective tissue means tougher meat, though properly applied heat can transform even the toughest meat into something soft and luscious. Then there's fat, beautiful fat. It's not the only thing that makes beef juicy, tender, and tasty, but a steak that's evenly riddled with fat has even more potential to be succulent and tender and to explode with flavor.

The goal of this chapter is not to make you an expert on the science of beef. Leave that to me. Rather, it's about sharing a few simple principles that will guide you to the best beef for your particular budget and culinary purpose, and teach you how to cook it so that you get the best from what you have.

THE IMPORTANCE OF FAT (THE GRADES)

You don't hear this nearly enough nowadays, but fat is your friend—at least when it comes to delicious beef. There are basically two types of fat in beef: the fat outside the meat, which I call external fat, and the fat interspersed throughout the meat, known as marbling. This second type—you'll recognize it as the whitish flecks of fat that dot the reddish meat—is so important that the USDA grading system is basically devoted to classifying it. Because when it comes to beef, more of this fat, particularly if it's evenly dispersed throughout the meat, is a good thing. It means more flavor (mainly because melted fat tastes really, really good) and meat that seems more juicy and tender.

You've probably heard the terms before: prime, choice, select. These are the USDA grades determined, more or less, by the degree of marbling in what's called the eye of the animal's rib section. Prime has the greatest degree, choice the second, and select the third. And whatever grade the eye of the rib gets is the grade applied to the rest of the meat from that particular animal.

Generally, the higher the grade, the more you'll pay per pound for your beef. But I have good news: You don't always have to splurge on prime to get a great beef experience. First of all, USDA grading isn't the last word on quality. For reasons I'll explain in a minute, I've found that choice beef that has been raised without growth hormones and antibiotics can sometimes out-perform certain prime beef. Especially if it's in that top range of choice, which I'll show you how to spot.

And second, for certain kinds of cooking, I consider choice a better value than prime. I've noticed that any cut of beef that you cook at low temperature for more than three hours will lose a lot of its fat during the process. If you've paid a premium for prime's higher degree of marbling, the fat that you skim off the surface of your stew, for instance, is almost literally money down the drain.

On the other hand, when you cook meat quickly with high heat, this fat melts, lubricating the meat, and mostly stays put. And you get to enjoy the benefits of this fat, to experience steak the way it should be. So when I'm making, say, Porterhouse, strip, or hanger steaks, which are best served by this cooking method, I always splurge on the highest grade I can afford.

BLACK ANGUS AND THE REST

Genetics matter. I've ogled and eaten beef from every breed of cattle out there and discovered that different breeds can offer different flavor and levels of fat. And my pick for the breed that, pound for pound, produces the beefiest meat with the best marbling is Black Angus. Let's get one thing straight: I'm not talking about the beef that makes up the so-called "Angus Steak Burger" ballyhooed by some fast food chains. I mean Black Angus sold under the Certified Angus Beef (CAB) label. CAB is essentially a brand that sets particularly strict parameters for its beef, including fat distribution, size, and the genealogy of the cattle from which it comes. Champagne does something very similar within the world of sparkling wine. Neither is foolproof, but they do offer a reliable assurance that you're getting what you're paying for.

GRAIN VERSUS GRASS

This is how I think about it: If the breed sets the bar for how good an animal's meat can be,

then what that animal eats and how it's raised determines whether it reaches its potential. There are two basic feeding programs—grain finished and grass finished—but within those I've seen a lot of variation. I say grass and grain "finished," because during the first part of their lives, just about all cattle eat grass on pasture. The two distinct diets begin when the animals that will be grain-fed are moved to feedlots. As you can imagine, each diet has a very different effect on the meat. Here's my take:

Grain

I'll just come right out and say it: Most of the time, I prefer meat from grain-finished cattle. Other variables aside, cattle that eat this calorie-dense food in a feedlot environment typically develop fat more quickly (and therefore reach a high level of fattiness at a younger age) than those that eat food that's not as calorie-dense (like grass). In the same way, a guy who eats only rice porridge will probably get fatter than a guy who eats only salad. And, as you know, fat plays a major role in flavor and in how juicy and tender beef seems when you take a bite. And, as Americans, you and I have grown up on meat from grain-finished cows. I can't overstate the appeal, whether conscious or subconscious, of this familiar flavor.

Grass

There are some great things about grass-finished beef. In some important ways, it can be great for the environment and for our health. But I've seen and sampled my fair share of beef from grass-fed cattle and have found that its marbling rarely matches that of grain-finished beef. It also tends to have a strong flavor that doesn't jibe with what many people consider the quintessential beef experience. To top it all off, I've noticed that the flavor is less consistent. There's a reason: While the corn and grain that make up the country's grain feed tend to be pretty homogenous, the grass grown in, say, Idaho, can differ significantly from that grown in Illinois. Yet there is good news. I recently sampled some truly great grass-finished beef. It didn't have that buttery finish of grain-finished, but it did deliver a similar richness and depth of flavor. A few farmers are taking the lead and doing grass-finished beef right. I'm sure more will soon follow.

HORMONES AND ANTIBIOTICS

"Natural beef" has a nice ring to it. But I see a crucial distinction between the government's definition of natural and the standards maintained by those farmers whom I consider true-blue advocates of top-notch beef. The USDA's official designation refers to beef that is "minimally processed and contains no

artificial flavors, added colors, or preservatives." By those standards, just about every whole cut of beef is natural. When I refer to all-natural beef, I mean meat from cattle that have never (ever!) been given antibiotics or growth hormones.

To increase the amount of meat that they get from each animal, some ranchers give cattle growth hormones. Bones and muscles grow like mad—think weight lifters on steroids—but collagen and marbling will never develop as they would have, no matter the breed or the way the animal's fed. Antibiotics are slightly different. Like growth hormones, they have an incidental effect of causing animals to grow quickly, but mainly, they're used to keep animals from getting sick. It's not that great beef never comes from these cows—I've seen some stunning marbling on meat from cows that weren't naturally raised, but were, for instance, of a superior breed. But if you let your eyes be your guide when selecting meat at the market, you'll be drawn again and again to hormone- and antibiotic-free meat.

My main "beef" with hormones and antibiotics goes beyond how they affect meat directly, because again I've seen beautifully marbled beef that doesn't meet my definition of all natural. Their use indicates a way of raising cattle that substitutes science for a genuine understanding of the animal. It's easy to give an animal an implant to bulk it up and a shot to prevent it from getting sick. It's more difficult to rely only on thoughtful feeding and raising. That care pays off in ways that just avoiding growth hormones and antibiotics can't account for. In other words, I believe in what natural meat delivers and what it represents.

Aging

I love aged beef, because, done right, aging can transform a good steak into a phenomenal one.

That fact demolishes the persistent notion that, in matters of meat, fresh is always best. Here's my jab at the fetish for freshness (stick around for the uppercut): No matter how good beef is, believe me, you wouldn't want to eat it right off the animal. Happily for us, by the time it travels from slaughterhouse to supermarket, as long as it hasn't been frozen before it comes out of rigor mortis, its taste and texture have improved. With further, careful aging, it can improve exponentially.

There are two types of aging: wet and dry. The former, by far the most common type of aging, essentially entails vacuum-packing meat and refrigerating it. The meat becomes more tender as its enzymes break down the muscle fibers. The flavor stays pretty much the same. Dry aging is my knockout punch. Not only does it produce more tender meat, but since the meat isn't wrapped, it also has a chance to lose moisture, which intensifies a steak's beefy flavor, sort of like when a grape dehydrates and evolves into a raisin. It changes the flavor profile, giving the steaks this amazing, almost mushroom-y flavor. In the process, I find dry-aged steaks sacrifice some traditional juiciness, though as long as the beef is nicely marbled, the melted fat will compensate. So will the huge payoff in flavor.

Dry aging, of course, takes more than just time. A dedicated room with rigorously controlled temperature, humidity, and airflow makes sure the meat matures properly. You can probably tell that dry-aged beef particularly excites me.

Yet it's not as simple as dry-aged is better. Not all the time. First, its intense beefiness and different sort of juiciness isn't for everyone. Second, there are plenty of situations for which I wouldn't recommend it. If you were following a recipe whose goal is to infuse meat with a boldly flavored marinade or stew it with spices and flavorful liquid, using more expensive dry-aged meat isn't necessary. But if you're after pure, intense beefiness, especially for high-heat cooking methods like direct grilling, nothing beats dry-aged beef, and your culinary goal should be treating it simply to highlight the amazingly complex flavor.

By the way, some restaurants and markets make a big deal of how long a certain cut of beef has been aged, proudly touting the exact amount of time on their menus or labels. Sorry, but I don't buy it. The effect of dry aging on a particular cut of meat is not entirely predictable. Sometimes the maximum benefit is achieved after six weeks, sometimes after eight weeks, and sometimes even longer. It depends on many factors, including the temperature at which the meat is aged. So find a source for dry-aged meat that you trust, and pay little mind to numbers.

VEAL

OK, I know this is a sensitive subject. So before I dive in, I'll just say that whether I'm buying veal, chicken, lamb, or pork, I try to seek out meat from animals raised with animal welfare in mind when I can.

So what is veal? Well, while beef typically comes from cattle that are around 20 months old, veal comes from calves that are typically just 13 to 20 weeks old. There's also what's called bob veal, which comes from calves that are less than a week old. This is the inexpensive meat favored by chain restaurants when they serve cutlets and most of the time it's been frozen. I don't like it. I don't cook it.

Then there's what's called nature veal, which comes from calves that have been raised on milk or formula. If you've ever had succulent ultratender veal in a really good Italian restaurant, this is what they use. It gives you what I think is the iconic veal chop—big, thick, tender, and luscious.

In the last several years, there has been a movement (a small one, to be sure) toward veal raised on grass, grain, or a combination of the two. Some farmers even raise the calves on pasture instead of keeping them in pens or in crates. As you might expect, the different diet and husbandry (calves in a pasture move around a lot more than those in a pen) make for different meat—it's darker (but will turn that familiar lighter color after it's cooked), it's sometimes not as tender, and it has a greater depth of flavor. Different, but often quite delicious.

When I'm direct grilling, I tend to cook my beef rare or medium rare, depending on my mood, the people I'm cooking for, and the particular cut. But with veal, I usually go for medium, which I think maximizes its characteristic tenderness and juiciness.

SELECTING BEEF

TRUST YOUR SENSES. Look for meat that has an even, bright color. Traces of ice or frost mean meat was incorrectly stored and improperly wrapped.

Pick meat that looks moist but not wet. Beware of liquid pooling on the surface of the meat or in its container. For vacuum-packed meat, liquid in the bag is OK. A broken inner seal, however, is not.

Poke the meat with your finger. Pick meat that gives a little but springs back. Avoid meat that feels squishy or stiff.

KNOW YOUR FAT. Choosing beef is not just about choosing between prime and choice. There's variation within each grade, so when you spring for prime, buy the meat that gives you the most bang for your buck—that is, meat in the glorious upper range of prime. The same goes for buying choice and select. It's easy to do if you know what to look for: You want meat with the most visible, evenly distributed mar-

bling. The distribution is particularly important and often overlooked. Clumpy fat means some bites may taste juicy and delicious, while others may seem dry and bland.

You want meat with some external fat, because it'll keep the edges from drying out. Mostly, though, it renders out during cooking. You can always trim this fat before you cook, but I'd rather not pay for something I'm not going to use.

DON'T BE FOOLED BY LABELS. Some labels mean something, like those that give the USDA grade or say "Certified Angus Beef." But most of the information blaring is marketing nonsense. I've seen it all: "Certified and pure!" one exclaims. Oh yeah, certified by whom? Pure how?

BE A DOGGEDLY DEMANDING CUSTOMER. Scrutinize meat before you by it. Relentlessly compare individual packages. Ask the butcher if you can inspect the meat in his case. Ask him about how his meat was aged. If you're not happy with what you see, ask if he has any more in the back. And if you still can't find the bright color or degree of marbling you're after, shop somewhere else. Your persistence could mean the difference between a pretty good steak and one your friends will be talking about for weeks.

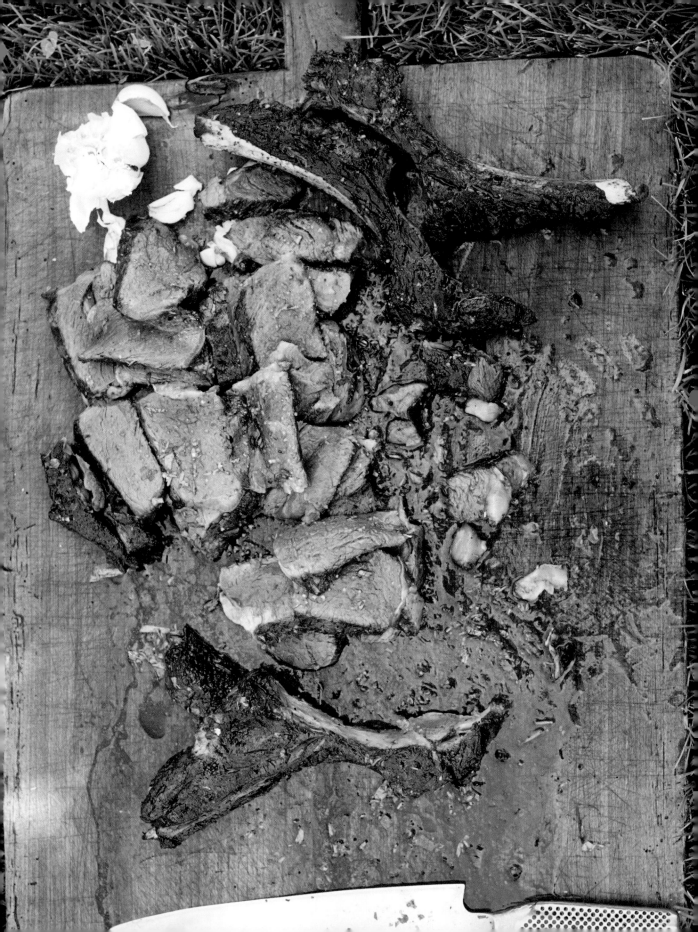

SALT AND PEPPER DRY-AGED "COWBOY-CUT" RIB EYE

SERVES 8

The rib eye has long been my hands-down favorite steak, because it's always juicy and contains the ultrarich, hypermarbled deckle, which I'd call the ultimate nugget of beef. Dry aging makes it even better, contributing an intense, minerally, almost mushroom-y essence. The perfect rib-eye is what I was going for when I built the dry-aging room at Mario Batali and Joe Bastianich's Carnevino, in Las Vegas, where I'm the meat-meister. But just as important as using properly aged steaks is treating them right, creating an irresistible char and not detracting from the flavor-packed meat by adding more than a dusting of salt and pepper. You'll notice that I recommend letting the steak rest for only 10 minutes. That's because dry-aged steaks have already lost a lot of their moisture during the aging process, so it doesn't take as long for the juices to redistribute throughout the meat.

TIP: This method also works exceptionally well for dry-aged Porterhouse and dry-aged shell steaks.

Eight 1½- to 1¾-inch-thick dry-aged rib eye, cowboy-cut steaks, about 20 ounces each
Kosher salt
Whole black peppercorns, crushed with the bottom of a heavy pan
About ¼ cup canola or vegetable oil
2 sticks (16 tablespoons, 8 ounces) unsalted butter, cold and unwrapped (see Note)
½ bunch of thyme, and ½ bunch of Rosemary, tied in an Herb Bundle (page 365)
2 large garlic cloves, peeled

Finishing Dressing
½ cup extra virgin olive oil
2 tablespoons coarsely chopped flat-leaf parsley
Fleur de sel
Coarsely ground fresh black pepper

NOTE: Melting the butter directly from the stick can be time-consuming if doing a large amount of steaks. If it is preferable, start with softened butter, and use the herb bundle to apply.

1. Preheat all grates of a well-oiled charcoal or gas grill to high.
2. Season the steaks with salt and pepper on both sides and work it in with your hands.

   Using your hands or a brush, evenly, but lightly, coat the steaks with canola oil.
3. It is preferable that the steaks be moved to a clean area of the grate every time they are flipped. Depending on the grill size, they may need to be cooked in batches to ensure there is a clean portion of the grill to flip to.

   Place the steaks on the grate, decrease the heat to medium, close the lid, and do not move the steaks until they are well marked and have a light char, about 3 minutes. Flip, close the lid, and repeat on the second side, grilling for 3 minutes.

   Press 1 stick of the butter on the top of one of the steaks, running it across the surface as it melts. Repeat with the remaining steaks, using the second stick of butter as needed. Brush with the herb bundle, flip the steaks, and repeat with the butter and herb brush on the second side. If the butter gets too soft, or the pieces too small, place in a small bowl and use the herb brush to apply.

   Continue to cook with the lid down as much as possible; flip, jockey, and stack as needed, and open to brush with butter using the herb bundle toward the end of cooking.

   Cook to desired doneness: about 4 minutes per side for rare, about 5 minutes per side for medium rare, about 7 minutes per side for medium, and 9 to 10 minutes per side for medium well to well-done.
4. Remove the steaks from the grill and place in a baking dish or disposable pan. Aggressively starting with the bone, rub both sides of the steaks with the garlic cloves. Brush again with the butter using the herb bundle, and let rest for 3 to 5 minutes.
5. Drizzle the olive oil on a cutting board. Sprinkle with the parsley, fleur de sel, and pepper. Cut the end of the herb brush off and finely chop with the mixture on the board. Finely chop the remaining portions of the garlic cloves as well.

   Place the steaks on top and pour some of the juices from the pan over the meat.

   Cut to separate the meat from the bone and slice the meat on a diagonal into 1/4-inch slices. Dredge in the dressing, top with additional pan juices, and sprinkle with fleur de sel and pepper.

Seasoning, pressing in seasoning, preparing board dressing

WORCESTERSHIRE MARINATED AND GLAZED BONELESS RIB EYE STEAKS

SERVES 8

If you don't feel like splurging for a dry-aged rib eye, you can still turn this cut into an intensely beefy steak. Here's my secret: Worcestershire sauce. I love it because its flavor recedes into the background while enhancing the taste of whatever it touches. I give the steak a double dose—in the marinade and in the brown sugar glaze. Not only does this pump up the flavor, it gives the meat a killer mahogany gloss.

Marinade
1 tablespoon crushed hot red pepper flakes
1 tablespoon boiling water
1 cup extra virgin olive oil
20 garlic cloves, peeled, halved, germ
    removed, and thinly sliced
1/4 cup Worcestershire sauce
2 tablespoons firmly packed dark brown
    sugar
2 rosemary sprigs
2 thyme sprigs

8 boneless rib eye steaks, about 14 ounces
    each

Seasoning Blend
2 tablespoons garlic salt
2 tablespoons lemon pepper
2 tablespoons coarsely ground black pepper
2 tablespoons mild chile powder, preferably
    Chimayo (see Sources page 378), Ancho, or
    Hatch

Glaze
1/2 cup Worcestershire sauce
1/2 cup of dark brown sugar
4 tablespoons (2 ounces) unsalted butter,
    melted

About 1/4 cup canola or vegetable oil
1/2 recipe Compound Butter (page 366),
    softened at room temperature
1/2 bunch rosemary and 1/2 bunch thyme, tied
    in an Herb Bundle (page 365)

Finishing Dressing
1/2 cup extra virgin olive oil
2 tablespoons coarsely chopped flat-leaf
    parsley
2 tablespoons thyme leaves
Fleur de sel
Coarsely ground fresh black pepper

1. Place the pepper flakes in a small bowl and pour the boiling water over them. Let sit for 1 to 2 minutes to rehydrate the flakes. Combine all of the remaining marinade ingredients including the pepper flakes and the soaking water.

   Place the steaks in an extra-large resealable plastic bag (or divide between two large bags). Pour over the marinade, squeeze out any excess air from the bag, and close. Roll the bag to evenly coat all of the meat. Refrigerate for at least 2 hours, but preferably up to 24.

2. Preheat all grates of a well-oiled charcoal or gas grill to high.

3. Combine all of the seasoning blend ingredients.

   Combine all the glaze ingredients in a jar with a tight-fitting lid and shake to combine. Pour into a baking dish or disposable aluminum pan, preferably a $13^{1}/2 \times 9^{5}/8 \times 2^{3}/4$-inch lasaga pan.

4. Remove the steaks from the bag, letting any excess marinade run off into the bag. Lightly pat dry with paper towels.

   Generously season both sides of the steaks with the seasoning blend.

   Using your hands or a brush, evenly, but lightly, coat with canola oil.

5. It is preferable that the steaks be moved to a clean area of the grate every time they are flipped. Also, the steaks will need to be moved to a raised rack or a section covered with heavy-duty aluminum foil once glazed. Depending on the grill size, they may need to be cooked in batches to ensure there is a clean portion of the grill to flip to and an area for glazing. If you will not be using a rack area, place a large piece of heavy-duty aluminum foil over one area of the grill.

   Place the steaks on the grate, decrease the heat to medium, close the lid, and do not move the steaks until they are well marked and have a light char, about 2 minutes. Flip, close the lid, and repeat on the second side, grilling for 2 minutes.

6. Brush the steaks generously on both sides with the compound butter using the herb bundle. Continue to cook with the lid down as much as possible; flip, jockey, and stack as needed. During the last 2 to 3 minutes of the cooking time, dip each steak into the glaze, turning to coat lightly and letting any excess run off and remain in the pan. Move to the raised-rack area or foiled section and turn off the heat under that section. Close the lid and cook to desired doneness.

   Cook about 2 minutes per side for rare, about 3 minutes per side for medium rare, about 4 minutes per side for medium, about 5 minutes per side for medium well, and about 8 minutes per side for well-done.

7. Remove the steaks from the grill and place in a baking dish or disposable pan. Brush with the butter using the herb bundle, and let rest for 3 to 5 minutes.

8. Drizzle the olive oil on a cutting board. Sprinkle with the parsley, thyme, fleur de sel, and pepper. Cut the end of the herb brush off and finely chop with the mixture on the board.

   Place the steaks on top, and pour some of the juices from the pan over the meat.

   Cut to separate the meat from the bone and slice on a diagonal into 1/4-inch slices. Dredge in the dressing, top with additional pan juices, and sprinkle with fleur de sel and pepper.

BUTTER-BOMBED PORTERHOUSE

The Porterhouse gives you the best of both worlds: Separated by a T-shaped bone, the tender filet and the full-figured, fat-riddled strip steak lounge side by side, a pair as simpatico as Butch Cassidy and the Sundance Kid. It's wet-aged, so it needs an injection of flavor, which I take care of with a marinade with good old Montreal Steak Seasoning, a mix of pungent granulated garlic and onion, paprika, and dried herbs. Halfway through the cooking, I take a whole clove of garlic and rub it on the bone. The heady smell you get is like aromatherapy for meat lovers.

TIP: When you're choosing a Porterhouse, keep in mind that the ones flaunting a bigger portion of the filet will have a chewier strip.

Marinade
1 tablespoon crushed hot red pepper flakes
2 tablespoons boiling water
1/2 cup Worcestershire sauce
1/4 cup Dijon mustard
2 tablespoons honey
1 tablespoon Japanese soy sauce
1/2 cup coarsely chopped sweet white onion
10 garlic cloves, peeled, halved, germ removed, and grated on a Microplane grater
1 tablespoon Montreal Steak Seasoning (see Sources page 378)
1 teaspoon dried oregano, preferably Mexican

Four 1½-inch-thick Porterhouse steaks, about 1½ pounds each

Resting Butter
8 tablespoons (4 ounces) unsalted butter
1/4 cup finely chopped flat-leaf parsley
1 tablespoon freshly squeezed lemon juice
1 tablespoon Worcestershire sauce
4 garlic cloves, peeled, halved, germ removed, and grated on a Microplane grater
1 teaspoon crushed hot red pepper flakes

Kosher salt
Finely ground fresh black pepper
About 1/4 cup canola or vegetable oil
2 large, whole garlic cloves, peeled
1 bunch of rosemary, tied in an Herb Bundle (page 365)

Fleur de sel

1. Place the pepper flakes in a small bowl and pour the boiling water over them. Let sit for 1 to 2 minutes to rehydrate the flakes. Combine all of the remining marinade ingredients in a blender, or in a bowl using an immersion/stick blender. Stir in the pepper flakes and the soaking water.

   Place the steaks in an extra-large re-sealable plastic bag (or divide between two large bags). Pour over the marinade, squeeze out any excess air from the bag, and close. Roll the bag to evenly coat all of the meat in the marinade, and refrigerate for at least 1 hour or up to 3.

2. Place a lightly oiled cast-iron griddle on one area of a well-oiled charcoal or gas grill. Preheat all areas to high.

3. In a small saucepan, combine all of the resting butter ingredients, stirring to combine as the butter melts. Pour about ½ cup of the butter into a small bowl and set aside. Pour the remainder into a baking dish or disposable aluminum pan, preferably a 13½ × 9⅝ × 2¾-inch lasagna pan.

4. Remove the steaks from the bag, letting any excess marinade drip into the bag. Lightly pat dry with paper towels.

   Season lightly with salt and pepper and, using your hands or a brush, evenly, but lightly, coat with canola oil.

5. It is preferable that the steaks be moved to a clean area of the griddle and grate every time they are flipped. Depending on the griddle and grill size, they may need to be cooked in batches to ensure there is a clean portion of the grill to flip to.

   Place the steaks on the griddle, close the lid, and do not move them for 3 minutes. Flip the steaks over on the griddle, close the lid, and do not move them for 3 minutes.

   Aggressively rub the bone and both sides of the steaks with the whole garlic (you may want to move each steak off of the heat temporarily), then brush with the ½ cup of butter using the herb bundle.

   Transfer the steaks to the grate.

   Continue to grill with the lid open, flipping, jockeying, and stacking throughout the cooking until you reach the desired doneness; about 3 minutes per side for rare, about 4 minutes per side for medium rare, about 5 minutes per side for medium, about 6 minutes per side for medium well, and about 8 minutes per side for well-done.

6. Remove the steaks from the grill, place in the resting butter, turn to coat, and let rest for 5 minutes.

7. Meanwhile, clean and re-oil the grill grates.

8. Place the steaks back on the grate and do not move them for 1 minute. Flip them over and repeat for 1 minute.

   Remove from the grill, place in the pan with the butter, and let rest for 5 minutes.

9. Drizzle some of the resting butter on the board and top with the steaks.

   Cut to separate the meat from the bone and slice the meat on a diagonal into ¼-inch slices. Dredge in the butter and top with and sprinkle with fleur de sel and pepper.

TERIYAKI MARINATED SHELL STEAK

SERVES 6 TO 8

Teriyaki has become such a familiar flavor—just mention the word and you immediately think of that easy-to-love combination of soy-sauce-saltiness and sticky sweetness. The bottled stuff works fine in this dish, but making the marinade at home takes almost no effort and pays off big time: Not only does chopped ginger and garlic add a bit of texture, but it tastes so much fresher and brighter.

TIP: A shell steak is also called a New York or Kansas City Strip Steak.

Marinade
1 tablespoon dry mustard
2 tablespoons water
½ cup sake
½ cup mirin
¼ cup Japanese soy sauce
2 tablespoons sesame oil
4 garlic cloves, peeled, halved, germ removed, and finely chopped
1 tablespoon finely chopped ginger
3 tablespoons finely chopped scallions, white and green portions
1 tablespoon granulated sugar
½ teaspoon finely ground fresh black pepper

6 shell steaks, 1 to 1¼ pounds each (see Tip)

Glaze
Generous pinch of crushed hot red pepper flakes (optional)
3 tablespoons rice wine vinegar
6 tablespoons firmly packed dark brown sugar
3 tablespoons water

About ¼ cup canola or vegetable oil

½ recipe Compound Butter (page 366), softened at room temperature
1 bunch thyme, tied in an Herb Bundle (page 365)

1. In a small bowl, stir together the dry mustard and the water to prevent the mustard from clumping when added to the other ingredients. Combine the mustard mixture with the remaining marinade ingredients.

   Place the steaks in an extra-large resealable plastic bag (or divide between two large bags). Pour over the marinade, squeeze out any excess air from the bag, and close. Roll the bag to evenly coat all of the meat in the marinade. Refrigerate for at least 3 hours, or up to 6.

2. Preheat all grates of a well-oiled charcoal or gas grill to high.

3. If using the pepper flakes, combine with the vinegar in a jar with a tight-fitting lid and let sit for 1 to 2 minutes for the flavors to develop. Add all of the remaining glaze ingredients to the jar and shake to combine. Pour into a baking dish or disposable aluminum pan, preferably a 13½ × 9⅝ × 2¾-inch lasagna pan.

4. Remove the steaks from the bag, letting any excess marinade remain in the bag. Lightly pat dry with paper towels.

   Using your hands or a brush, evenly, but lightly, coat with canola oil.

5. It is preferable that the steaks be moved to a clean area of the grate every time they are flipped. Also, the steaks will need to be moved to a raised rack or a section covered with heavy-duty aluminum foil once glazed. Depending on the grill size, they may need to be cooked in batches to ensure there is a clean portion of the grill to flip to and an area for glazing.

   If you will not be using a rack area, place a large piece of heavy-duty aluminum foil over one area of the grill.

   Place the steaks on the grate, decrease the heat to medium, close the lid, and do not move the steaks until they are well marked and lightly charred, about 2 minutes. Flip the steaks, close the lid, and repeat on the second side, grilling for 2 minutes.

   Flip the steaks again and continue to cook, with the lid open (flipping, jockeying, and stacking as needed), brushing with butter using the herb bundle about every minute, until you reach the desired doneness.

   Cook about 1 minute per side for rare, about 2 minutes per side for medium rare, about 4 minutes per side for medium, about 5 minutes per side for medium well, and about 6 minutes per side for well-done.

6. Turn off the heat under the section of the grate covered with foil, if using.

   Dip each steak into the glaze, turning to coat lightly and letting any excess run off and remain in the pan. Move to the raised-rack area or foiled section.

   Close the lid and and let sit with the glaze for 3 minutes.

7. Pour the remaining glaze on the cutting board, top with the steaks, and let rest for 5 minutes.

   Cut to separate the meat from the bone, and slice the meat on a diagonal into 3/8-inch slices.

MARINATED TENDERLOIN FILETS WITH SMOKED PAPRIKA

SERVES 8

When I'm craving the lushness of a perfect rosy-rare center, I grill the whole tenderloin and carve it up. But when I'm after deep, dark char and gleaming grill marks, I head straight for individual filets mignons. As if they don't get enough flavor from my herb infused oil, I hit them with compound butter to boost caramelization. And, as I love to do, toward the end of cooking I take a bundle of rosemary and thyme and use it to brush butter on each filet. It's a way to add an extra blast of herby perfume without the risk of burning the greenery.

TIP: Unlike the whole tenderloin, the tenderloin filets can be easily cooked to various degrees of doneness, which is a blessing when you're cooking for a group with different preferences.

Flavoring Oil
1 tablespoon crushed hot red pepper flakes
1 tablespoon boiling water
1 cup extra virgin olive oil
20 garlic cloves, peeled, halved, germ removed, and thinly sliced
2 rosemary sprigs
2 thyme sprigs

8 tenderloin filets mignons, 7 to 8 ounces each

½ recipe Compound Butter (page 366), softened at room temperature
1 tablespoon pimentón (see Sources page 378), or other smoked paprika
Kosher salt
Finely ground fresh black pepper
½ bunch rosemary and ½ bunch thyme, tied in an Herb Bundle (page 365)

1. Place the pepper flakes in a small bowl and pour the boiling water over them. Let sit for 1 to 2 minutes to rehydrate the flakes. Combine all of the flavoring oil ingredients including the pepper flakes and the soaking water in a blender, or in a bowl using an immersion/stick blender.

   Place the filets in an extra-large resealable plastic bag (or divide between two), pour over the flavoring oil, squeeze out the excess air from the bag, and close. Refrigerate for at least 2 hours, but preferably up to 24.

2. Preheat all grates of a well-oiled charcoal or gas grill to high.

3. Combine the compound butter with the paprika.

4. Remove the steaks from the bag, letting any excess marinade run off into the bag. Lightly pat dry with paper towels.

   Generously season all steaks on both sides with salt and pepper.

5. It is preferable that the steaks be moved to a clean area of the grate every time they are flipped. Depending on the grill size, they may need to be cooked in batches to ensure there is a clean portion of the grill to flip to.

   Place the steaks on the grate and decrease the heat to medium. Keep the lid open, and do not move the steaks until they are well marked and have a light char, about 2 minutes. Flip, keep the lid open, and repeat on the second side, grilling for 2 minutes.

   Flip the steaks again and continue to cook, with the lid open (flipping, jockeying, and stacking as needed), brushing with butter, using the herb bundle about every minute, until you reach the desired doneness.

Cook about 2 minutes per side for rare, about 3 minutes per side for medium rare, about 4 minutes per side for medium, about 5 minutes per side for medium well, and about 6 minutes per side for well-done.

6. Using the herb bundle, brush butter onto a cutting board, remove the steaks from the heat, and place on top. Brush each steak with additional butter and season with salt and pepper. Let rest for 5 minutes before serving.

BURGERS WITH GRIDDLED ONIONS

SERVES 8

Making patties from lean ground beef and hoping for perfectly juicy burgers is like building a ship out of bricks and hoping it floats. You have to start with the right meat. For me, the ultimate is a blend of 70 percent lean and 30 percent fatty. That generous touch of fat brings just the right amount of richness and lubricates the meat while it's cooking. I recommend making your own seasoning salt, because it's just as easy and much cheaper than buying a bottle of the premade kind. Remember to season only the outsides of your patties right before you cook them rather than mix the salt into the entire mass of meat, which will make your burgers rubbery. And also remember that the secret to an amazing salty, slightly crunchy crust is not high heat but a super-hot surface—an important distinction.

¼ cup water
1 teaspoon Worcestershire sauce
4 to 4¼ pounds 70/30 (70 percent lean, 30 percent fatty) ground beef, preferably a combination of chuck, sirloin and brisket (see Note)

Seasoning Salt
1 tablespoon garlic salt
1 tablespoon lemon pepper

Basting Butter
8 tablespoons (4 ounces) unsalted butter
4 garlic cloves, peeled, halved, germ removed, and grated on a Microplane grater
¼ cup finely chopped flat-leaf parsley
2 teaspoons freshly squeezed lemon juice
2 teaspoons Worcestershire sauce

2 teaspoons coarsely ground fresh black pepper
2 teaspoons kosher salt

2 tablespoons canola or vegetable oil
2 sweet white onions, cut into ½-inch slices
2 tablespoons (1 ounce) unsalted butter, plus additional for the buns
1½ teaspoons crushed hot red pepper flakes
1 bunch thyme tied in an Herb Bundle (page 365)
8 sesame seed buns
16 small slices mild cheddar cheese, or other sliced or crumbled cheese of choice (optional)

NOTE: Buying a 70–30 blend from the meat case will give you some great burgers, but you can go a step further by using a mix of different cuts. For the ultimate blend, ask your butcher to grind together about 2½ pounds of chuck, 1¼ pounds of sirloin, and ½ pound of brisket.

1. Combine the water and Worcestershire sauce and, using your hands, blend into the beef until evenly distributed.

    Divide the meat into eight equal parts, roll into balls (but do not overwork the meat because it will toughen your burgers), and flatten into discs about ½ inch thick and 4½ to 5 inches in diameter. Chill for at least 1 hour or up to 1 day.

2. Place a cast-iron griddle on one area of a well-oiled charcoal or gas grill. Preheat all areas to high.

3. Combine the seasoning salt ingredients.

    Combine all of the basting butter ingredients over medium heat and pour into a baking dish or disposable aluminum pan.

4. Swab the oil on the griddle, top with the onions, close the lid, and cook until golden, about 3 minutes. Flip, close the lid, and cook for another 3 minutes.

    If you have a grill press(es) or a firebrick(s) (see Sources page 378) wrapped in heavy-duty aluminum foil, it is ideal to keep on hand to maximize the caramelization.

    Brush the onions with the 2 tablespoons of butter, sprinkle with the pepper flakes, and continue to cook until caramelized and tender.

    Transfer the onions to a bowl and cover to keep warm while the burgers cook. Do not clean the griddle.

5. It is preferable that the burgers be moved to a clean area of the griddle and grill every time they are flipped. Depending on the griddle and grill size, they will need to be cooked in batches to ensure there is a clean portion of the griddle and grill to flip to. (It is best to read the full step below first before continuing.)

    Season both sides of the burgers, using about half of the seasoning salt.

    Place 4 burgers on the exposed grate, keeping the other half clean to flip to. Close the lid, and cook the burgers until the meat easily separates from the grate and is well marked, about 2 minutes. Flip the burgers to the clean section, close the lid, and cook without moving them for 2 minutes more.

    Season the burgers with the remaining seasoning salt.

    Transfer the burgers to the griddle, brush with the basting butter using the herb bundle, and continue to cook, flipping once (at this point the second 4 burgers can be started on the grate, see below) until you reach the desired doneness. Cook 2 to 3 minutes for rare, about 4 minutes for medium, and about 5 to 6 for well-done.

    Once the first 4 burgers are on the griddle, scrape the grates, re-oil, and repeat the grilling process. As the burgers reach the desired doneness on the griddle, transfer them to a sheet pan and cover with foil while the other burgers cook.

6. When all the burgers have been cooked, turn off the heat on all areas of the grill. Brush the buns with butter and top the burgers with the cheese, if using. Close the lid for 1 to 2 minutes to melt the cheese and toast the buns.

    Serve the burgers on the toasted buns.

BONELESS GRILLED SHORT RIBS WITH ASIAN FLAVORS

SERVES 6

Short ribs have become synonymous with long cooking. But go to any Korean restaurant, and you'll see thin slices of short ribs grilling over high heat, getting charred and smelling sensational. My interpretation of the Korean classic starts with a sweet-salty marinade of soy sauce and sugar with ginger, scallions, garlic, and sesame oil thrown in to really perk up the flavor. Then it's on to the super-hot grill, where the slices get glazed with brown sugar and rice vinegar and become all caramelized just before you tuck them into lettuce leaves or heap them over rice.

Marinade

4 garlic cloves, peeled, halved, germ removed, grated on a Microplane grater

¼ cup Japanese soy sauce

2 tablespoons fish sauce

2 tablespoons rice wine or dry sherry

2 tablespoons water

2 tablespoons toasted sesame oil

2 tablespoons canola or vegetable oil

1 tablespoon granulated sugar

3 tablespoons finely chopped scallions, white and green portions

1 tablespoon finely chopped or grated fresh ginger

½ teaspoon finely ground fresh black pepper

One 3-bone rack of plate short ribs, bones removed, and thinly sliced (see Note, page 138)

Glaze

Pinch of crushed hot red pepper flakes (optional)

1 tablespoon rice wine vinegar

2 tablespoons firmly packed dark brown sugar

1 tablespoon water

4 cups rehydrated bean threads or white rice

1 head Bibb or other lettuce

¼ cup cilantro leaves

2 red bell peppers, thinly sliced

¼ cup chile paste, preferably Sriracha or sambal

1. Combine all of the marinade ingredients.

   Place the beef in an extra-large resealable plastic bag (or divide between two large bags). Pour over the marinade, squeeze out any excess air from the bag, and close. Roll the bag to evenly coat all of the meat in the marinade. Refrigerate for at least 3 hours, or up to 6.

2. Preheat all grates of a well-oiled charcoal or gas grill to medium.

3. If using the pepper flakes in the glaze, combine the vinegar and flakes in a jar with a tight-fitting lid and let sit for 1 to 2 minutes to allow the flavors to develop. Add the sugar and water to the jar and shake to combine the glaze ingredients. Set aside.

4. Remove the meat from the marinade, letting any excess run off into the bag. Lightly pat the meat dry with paper towels.

5. If you have a grill press(es) or a firebrick(s) (see Sources page 378) wrapped in heavy-duty aluminum foil, it is ideal to keep on hand to keep the meat from lifting up and also to maximize the caramelization.

   Place the beef on the grate. Close the lid and cook, without moving the meat, until it is well marked and lightly caramelized, 5 to 7 minutes, flipping, jockeying, and stacking as necessary. Flip the pieces of meat, close the lid, and cook, without moving it, on the second side for 5 to 7 minutes. (If there are any slices that are slightly thicker, they may need an additional 1 to 2 minutes.)

   Give the glaze a quick shake to reincorporate any ingredients that may have settled. Brush each piece of the beef on both sides with the glaze and flip, jockey, and stack as needed. Cook for 1 to 2 minutes to tighten the glaze.

6. Remove the meat from the grill and slice on the diagonal into slices about 3/8 inch thick.

   Serve family style alongside the bean threads, lettuce, cilantro, peppers, and paste. Let each person assemble their own rolls.

NOTE ON BUYING AND CUTTING SHORT RIBS:

For Short Ribs with Fleur de Sel (page 186), I always ask the butcher for a 3-bone plate of short ribs cut from the center of the rack. The bones should all be the same size, approximately 9 inches long. Each plate should weigh about 5 pounds.

For a boneless version of this cut (Boneless Grilled Short Ribs with Asian Flavors, page 136), you can ask the butcher to remove the bones, but you can also easily do it yourself.

Position the plate so that the bones are running from top to bottom on the work surface. Your goal is to remove the bones, keeping the meat as intact as possible. Start with the bone farthest to the right. Run a boning knife along the entire length of the right side of the bone from top to bottom, making an incision down the full bone. Continue running the knife along the bone to loosen all of the meat and eventually lift out the full bone. Repeat with the remaining two bones.

Once the bones are removed, you will be left with a relatively flat piece of meat, except for the strips of meat remaining where the bones were. Cut these off and reserve to cook (keeping in mind that they will cook much more quickly), or reserve for another use. The remaining large piece of boneless meat will weigh $2^1/2$ to 3 pounds, and will be square-shaped.

Lay the square of meat on the work surface and cut it into three even square pieces. To ensure evenness of the slices, look at the thickness of the meat and make two small incisions to visualize and guide where you will be cutting. The goal is to finish with three squares of meat, each about $1/4$ inch thick.

The meat is now ready for Boneless Grilled Short Ribs with Asian Flavors (page 136).

For Flanken-Style Riblets (page 188), the meat is cut through the bone, so ask your butcher to cut them for you if they are not readily available. It is still best to start with a 3-bone center-cut plate of short ribs. When the butcher cuts across the bones, the resulting pieces of flanken alternate between rib and bone, perfect for riblets.

MARINATED SKIRT STEAK WITH GARLIC AND CILANTRO

SERVES 6 TO 8

Skirt steak has a deep, beefy flavor that can stand up to bold spices. So I take this inexpensive, easy-to-find cut and hit it with lots of garlic and a little honey to rev up the caramelization. The result is so outrageously good that it'll tempt you to take skirt steak outside of its standard role as fajita-filler. It's a really thin cut, so it should be served right after it's cooked. Have everything else ready before you throw it on the grill.

Marinade
1 tablespoon crushed hot red pepper flakes
2 tablespoons boiling water
1 cup freshly squeezed orange juice
½ cup freshly squeezed lime juice
2 tablespoons honey
1 tablespoon Japanese soy sauce
½ cup coarsely chopped sweet white onion
10 garlic cloves, peeled, halved, germ removed, and grated on a Microplane grater
1 tablespoon kosher salt
1 teaspoon ground cumin
1 teaspoon dried oregano, preferably Mexican

4 skirt steaks, about 1½ pounds each

Seasoning Blend
2 tablespoons mild chile powder, preferably Chimayo (see Sources page 378), Ancho, or Hatch
1 tablespoon garlic salt
1 tablespoon lemon pepper
1 tablespoon coarsely ground fresh black pepper

Resting Butter
8 tablespoons (4 ounces) unsalted butter
¼ cup finely chopped flat-leaf parsley or cilantro
1 tablespoon freshly squeezed lemon juice
1 tablespoon Worcestershire sauce
4 garlic cloves, peeled, halved, germ removed, and grated on a Microplane grater
1 teaspoon crushed hot red pepper flakes

About ¼ cup canola or vegetable oil

½ cup cilantro leaves

1. Place the pepper flakes in a small bowl and pour the boiling water over them. Let sit for 1 to 2 minutes to rehydrate the flakes. Combine all of the remining marinade ingredients in a blender, or in a bowl, using an immersion/stick blender. Stir in the pepper flakes and the soaking water.

   Place the skirt steaks in one extra-large resealable plastic bag (or divide between two large bags). Pour over the marinade, squeeze out any excess air from the bag, and close. Roll the bag to evenly coat all of the meat in the marinade. Refrigerate for at least 1 hour and up to 3.

2. Preheat all grates of a well-oiled charcoal or gas grill to high.

3. Combine all of the seasoning blend ingredients.

   In a small saucepan, combine all of the resting butter ingredients, stirring to combine as the butter melts. Pour into a baking dish or disposable aluminum pan, preferably a 13½ × 9⅝ × 2¾-inch lasagna pan.

4. Remove the steaks from the bag and lightly pat dry with paper towels.

   Season the steaks with the seasoning blend.

   Using your hands or a brush, evenly, but lightly, coat the steaks with canola oil.

5. If you have a grill press(es) or a firebrick(s) (see Sources page 378) wrapped in heavy-duty aluminum foil, it is ideal to keep on hand to keep the meat from lifting up and also to maximize the caramelization.

   Place the steaks on the grill, keep the lid open, and do not move the steaks until they are well marked and lightly charred, about 2 minutes. Flip the steaks, keep the lid open, and repeat on the second side, grilling for 2 minutes.

   Place the steaks into the pan of resting butter, dredging to thoroughly coat both sides in the butter.

6. Clean and re-oil the grill grates.

7. Letting any excess butter run off into the pan, place the steaks back on the grill, close the lid, and do not move them until you reach the desired doneness. Cook about 2 minutes for rare, about 3 minutes for medium, and about 4 minutes for well-done.

8. Remove from the grill and place in the butter, turning to coat, and let rest for at least 5 minutes, or up to 15.

9. Drizzle some of the butter on a cutting board, top with the steaks, and cut against the grain, on the diagonal, into ¼-inch slices. Sprinkle the cilantro leaves over the top.

FAJITA-STYLE MARINATED FLANK STEAK

SERVES 6 TO 8

I've done the research. I've cooked hundreds of steaks. And I've come to an important conclusion: Nothing makes better fajitas than flank steak. It's juicy, beefy, and has a high surface-area-to-interior ratio that lets you add lots of Mexican-inflected flavors like chiles, garlic, and cilantro. Tuck a few slices along with a few strips of bell pepper, blistered from the grill, into a warm flour tortilla, and you'll see what I mean.

Marinade
1 tablespoon crushed hot red pepper flakes
2 tablespoons boiling water
1 cup water
½ cup apple cider vinegar
¼ cup freshly squeezed lemon juice
2 tablespoons Worcestershire sauce
2 tablespoons Tabasco sauce, or your favorite hot sauce
1 tablespoon Japanese soy sauce
½ cup grated sweet white onion
10 garlic cloves, peeled and crushed
½ cup firmly packed dark brown sugar
¼ cup prepared yellow mustard
1 tablespoon kosher salt
2 teaspoons fresh thyme leaves

2 flank steaks, 1½ to 1¾ pounds each

Seasoning Blend
¼ cup mild chile powder, preferably Chimayo (see Sources page 378), Ancho, or Hatch
1½ teaspoons coarsely ground fresh black pepper

1½ teaspoons kosher salt

Resting Butter
8 tablespoons (4 ounces) unsalted butter
¼ cup finely chopped cilantro or flat-leaf parsley
1 tablespoon freshly squeezed lemon juice
4 garlic cloves, peeled, halved, germ removed, and grated on a Microplane grater
1 tablespoon dried oregano, preferably Mexican
1 tablespoon crushed hot red pepper flakes

About ¼ cup canola or vegetable oil

1 recipe Grilled Sweet Onions (page 313)
8 blistered peppers (See Roasted Marinated Peppers, page 331), peeled
8 to 16 flour tortillas (depending on size), warmed

1. Place the pepper flakes in a small bowl and pour the boiling water over them. Let sit for 1 to 2 minutes to rehydrate the flakes. Combine all of the remaining marinade ingredients in a blender, or in a bowl, using an immersion/stick blender. Stir in the pepper flakes and the soaking water.

   Place the flank steaks in one extra-large resealable plastic bag (or divide between two large bags). Pour over the marinade, squeeze out any excess air from the bag, and close. Roll the bag to evenly coat all of the meat in the marinade. Refrigerate for at least 1 hour and up to 3.

2. Preheat all grates of a well-oiled charcoal or gas grill to high.

3. Combine all of the seasoning blend ingredients together.

   In a small saucepan, combine all of the resting butter ingredients, stirring to combine as the butter melts. Pour into a baking dish or disposable aluminum pan, preferably a 13½ × 95/8 × 2¾-inch lasagna pan.

4. Remove the steaks from the bag and lightly pat dry with paper towels.

   Season the steaks with the seasoning blend.

   Using your hands or a brush, evenly, but lightly, coat the steaks with canola oil.

5. If you have a grill press(es) or a firebrick(s) (see Sources page 378) wrapped in heavy-duty aluminum foil, it is ideal to keep on hand to keep the meat from lifting up and also to maximize the caramelization.

   Place the steaks on the grill, keep the lid open, and do not move the steaks until they are well marked and lightly charred, about 2 minutes. Flip the steaks, keep the lid open, and repeat on the second side, grilling for 2 minutes.

   Place the steaks into the pan with the resting butter, dredging to thoroughly coat both sides in the butter.

6. Clean and re-oil the grill grates.

7. Letting any excess butter run off into the pan, place the steaks back on the grill, close the lid, and do not move them until you reach the desired doneness. Cook about 2 minutes for rare, about 3 minutes for medium, and about 4 minutes for well-done.

8. Remove from the grill and place in the butter, turning to coat, and let rest for at least 5 minutes, or up to 15.

9. Drizzle some of the butter on a cutting board, top with the steaks, and cut against the grain, on the diagonal, into ¼-inch slices. Serve with grilled onions, peppers, and flour tortillas.

TRI-TIP WITH HONEY-GARLIC GLAZE

SERVES 6 TO 8

Meat is a funny thing. Some cuts get popular and other equally awesome cuts remain under the radar. The tri-tip's status is especially strange. You'll never see more of this triangular piece of the sirloin than you do in southern California. But on the East Coast, though it's certainly accessible, no one seems to be trumpeting it. So I'll do the trumpeting: This über-underrated cut packs a ton of juice and flavor, despite its leanness. My honey-garlic glaze could make a block of tofu taste great, so just imagine what it does for juicy beef.

Flavor Paste
1/4 cup mild chile powder, preferably Chimayo (see Sources page 378), Ancho, or Hatch
1 tablespoon Worcestershire sauce
1 tablespoon Japanese soy sauce
1 tablespoon beef base in paste form, such as Better Than Bouillon (see Sources page 378)

2 tri-tip steaks, 2 to 3 pounds each

Seasoning Blend
1 tablespoon garlic salt
1 tablespoon lemon pepper
1 tablespoon coarsely ground fresh black pepper
1 teaspoon cayenne pepper

Honey-Garlic Glaze
2 tablespoons apple cider vinegar
1 teaspoon crushed hot red pepper flakes
1/4 cup apple juice
1/2 cup honey
1 tablespoon Worcestershire sauce
5 garlic cloves, peeled, halved, germ removed, and grated on a Microplane grater
4 tablespoons (2 ounces) unsalted butter

About 1/4 cup canola or vegetable oil

Finishing Dressing
1/2 cup extra virgin olive oil
1 tablespoon finely chopped lemon zest
1 tablespoon freshly squeezed lemon juice
1/4 cup finely chopped chives
Fleur de sel

1. Preheat one grate of a well-oiled charcoal or gas grill to high and another to low.
2. Stir the flavor paste ingredients together and spread on all sides of the tri-tips.

   Combine all of the seasoning blend ingredients.

   Combine the vinegar and pepper flakes for the glaze in a jar with a tight-fitting lid and let sit for 1 to 2 minutes for the flavors to develop. Add the apple juice, honey, Worcestershire sauce, and garlic to the jar. Melt the butter and pour over the top. Shake to combine the glaze ingredients. Set aside.

   Sprinkle the seasoning blend evenly on all sides of the tri-tips.

   Using your hands or a brush, evenly, but lightly, coat the tri-tips with canola oil.
3. Place the steaks on the high grate, keep the lid open, and do not move them until they are well marked and have a light char, 2 to 3 minutes. Flip, keep the lid open, and repeat on the second side, grilling for 2 to 3 minutes.

   Move to the low grate, close the lid, and cook for 10 minutes.

   Give the glaze a quick shake to reincorporate any ingredients that may have settled. Brush with the glaze and keep the tri-tips moving. Continue to brush with the glaze until desired doneness. Cook about 6 minutes for rare, about 7 minutes for medium, and about 9 minutes for well-done.
4. Drizzle the olive oil on a cutting board. Add the zest, juice, chives, and fleur de sel. Top with the meat and let rest for 5 minutes.
5. Slice the meat, against the grain, into ¼-inch slices, dredging them in the dressing. Sprinkle with fleur de sel.

HANGER STEAK WITH THYME, CRUSHED RED PEPPER, AND GARLIC

SERVES 8

The hanger is also known as the butcher's steak, because butchers used to save the boldly flavored, super-succulent cut for themselves. Now, however, the secret is out, and everyone seems to want the hanger, which means it's more readily available today than it's ever been. As long as you crank up the heat and make sure never to cook the meat past medium rare, you'll get a tremendously beefy steak with an exquisite chew. But I won't let you settle for anything less than the ultimate version, so I set that flavor off with some thyme, crushed hot red pepper, and garlic.

Marinade

2 teaspoons crushed hot red pepper flakes
2 teaspoons boiling water
¾ cup extra virgin olive oil
8 garlic cloves, peeled, halved, germ removed, and thinly sliced
1½ tablespoons firmly packed dark brown sugar
1½ tablespoons Japanese soy sauce
1½ tablespoons red wine vinegar
2 thyme sprigs

Four hanger steaks, about 14 ounces each

Seasoning Blend

1 tablespoon garlic salt
1 tablespoon coarsely ground fresh black pepper
1½ teaspoons mild chile powder, preferably Chimayo (see Sources page 378), Ancho, or Hatch

About ¼ cup canola or vegetable oil

½ recipe Compound Butter (page 366), softened at room temperature
½ bunch rosemary and ½ bunch thyme, tied in an Herb Bundle (page 365)

Fleur de sel
Finely ground fresh black pepper

1. Place the pepper flakes in a small bowl and pour the boiling water over them. Let sit for 1 to 2 minutes to rehydrate the flakes. Combine all of the marinade ingredients including the flakes and soaking water.

   Place the steaks in an extra-large resealable plastic bag (or divide between two large bags bags). Pour over the marinade, squeeze out any excess air from the bag, and close. Roll the bag to evenly coat all of the meat in the marinade. Refrigerate for at least 2 hours, but preferably up to 24.

2. Preheat all grates of a well-oiled charcoal or gas grill to high.

3. Combine the seasoning blend ingredients.

4. Remove the steaks from the bag, letting any excess marinade run off into the bag.

   Season the steaks on both sides with the seasoning blend.

   Using your hands or a brush, evenly, but lightly, coat the steaks with canola oil.

5. Place the steaks on the grate, decrease the heat to medium, keep the lid open, and do not move the steaks until they are well marked and lightly charred, about 2 minutes. Flip, keep the lid open, and repeat on the remaining side, grilling for 2 minutes.

   Flip again and continue to cook with the lid down, opening to brush with the compound butter, using the herb bundle, flipping, jockeying, and stacking as needed, until you reach the desired doneness. Cook about 2 minutes per side for rare, about 3 minutes per side for medium rare, about 4 minutes per side for medium, about 5 minutes per side for medium well, and about 6 minutes per side for well-done.

6. Spread some of the remaining butter on a cutting board using the herb brush. Cut the end of the herb brush off and finely chop. Combine with the butter on the board. Place the steaks on the board and let rest for at least 5 minutes.

7. Cut the steaks against the grain, on the diagonal, into ¼-inch slices. Season with fleur de sel and black pepper.

FLATIRON STEAKS MARINATED IN RED WINE

SERVES 8

Nothing beats tenderloin for silky tenderness, but if you're searching for a steak that delivers similarly supple slices without the sky-high asking price, look no further than the flatiron. And because it comes from the chuck blade, the flatiron also packs more flavor than its luxurious counterpart. I build on the beefiness with a red wine marinade, a simple-but-incredible seasoning blend with garlic salt and chile powder, and finally, some compound butter. Lay it on a hot grill and slice it thin.

Marinade

1 tablespoon crushed hot red pepper flakes
1 tablespoon boiling water
1 cup extra virgin olive oil
1/2 cup dry red wine, preferably Cabernet Sauvignon
1/4 cup red wine vinegar
2 tablespoons granulated sugar
1 tablespoon Worcestershire sauce
20 garlic cloves, peeled, halved, germ removed, and thinly sliced

Four 1 1/2-inch-thick flatiron steaks

Seasoning Blend

1/4 cup mild chile powder, preferably Chimayo (see Sources page 378), Ancho, or Hatch
2 tablespoons garlic salt
2 tablespoons coarsely ground fresh black pepper

About 1/4 cup canola or vegetable oil

Compound Butter (page 366)
1/2 bunch rosemary and 1/2 bunch thyme, tied in an Herb Bundle (page 365)

Fleur de sel
Finely ground fresh black pepper

1. Place the pepper flakes in a small bowl and pour the boiling water over them. Let sit for 1 to 2 minutes to rehydrate the flakes. Combine all of the marinade ingredients including the flakes and the soaking water.

   Place the steaks in an extra-large resealable plastic bag (or divide between two large bags). Pour over the marinade, squeeze out any excess air from the bag, and close. Roll the bag to evenly coat all of the meat in the marinade. Refrigerate for at least 2 hours, but preferably up to 24.

2. Preheat all grates of a well-oiled charcoal or gas grill to high

3. Combine all of the seasoning blend ingredients.

4. Remove the steaks from the bag, letting any excess marinade run off into the bag. Lightly pat dry with paper towels.

   Generously season all steaks on both sides with the seasoning blend.

   Using your hands or a brush, evenly, but lightly, coat with canola oil.

5. Place the steaks on the grate, decrease the heat to medium, keep the lid open, and do not move the steaks until they are well marked and lightly charred, about 2 minutes. Flip, keep the lid open, and repeat on the second side, grilling for 2 minutes.

   Flip again, and continue to cook with the lid down, opening to brush each steak with the butter, using the herb bundle, toward the end of the cooking time, flipping, jockeying, and stacking until you reach the desired doneness. Cook about 2 minutes per side for rare, about 3 minutes per side for medium rare, about 4 minutes per side for medium, about 5 minutes per side for medium well, and about 8 minutes per side for well-done.

6. Spread some of the remaining butter on a cutting board using the herb brush. Cut the end of the herb brush off and finely chop. Combine with the butter on the board. Place the steaks on the board and let rest for at least 5 minutes.

7. Cut against the grain, on the diagonal, into 1/4-inch slices. Season with fleur de sel and pepper.

VEAL RIB CHOPS WITH GARLIC, THYME, AND SAGE

SERVES 8

From the first bite through the silky meat of these thick chops to the fabulous slightly chewy bits that cling to the bone, veal chops are a thrill. They also make a brilliant base for flavor. After I get through with them, they're dripping with it and have a perfect glaze with a hint of sweetness and lemony tartness.

Marinade
1 cup extra virgin olive oil
3 tablespoons garlic salt
3 tablespoons fresh thyme leaves
1 tablespoon dried oregano, preferably
    Mexican
1 tablespoon finely ground fresh black pepper
2 teaspoons cayenne pepper

Eight 1½-inch-thick veal rib chops, about 7¾
    ounces each

Basting/Resting Butter
12 tablespoons (6 ounces) unsalted butter
¼ cup finely chopped flat-leaf parsley
4 garlic cloves, peeled, halved, germ removed,
    and grated on a Microplane grater
1 tablespoon freshly squeezed lemon juice
1 tablespoon Worcestershire sauce

1 bunch thyme, tied in an Herb Bundle (page
    365)

Glaze
6 tablespoons freshly squeezed lemon juice
3 tablespoons granulated sugar
3 tablespoons water
1 tablespoon fresh thyme leaves
1 tablespoon sage, cut in chiffonade (see
    Note)
1½ teaspoons serrano, Thai bird, or other
    small, hot chile of choice, thinly sliced

¼ cup finely chopped flat-leaf parsley
Fleur de sel
Finely ground fresh black pepper

NOTE: To chiffonade the sage, stack the leaves and roll as tightly as possible into a cylinder. Cut across the roll so that when unrolled, the sage will be in thin, ribbon-like strips.

1. Combine all of the marinade ingredients.

   Place the chops in an extra-large re-sealable plastic bag (or divide between two large bags). Pour the marinade over the chops, squeeze out any excess air from the bag, and close. Roll the bag to evenly coat all of the meat with the marinade. Refrigerate for at least 3 hours and up to 24.

2. Place a cast-iron griddle on one area of a well-oiled charcoal or gas grill and pre-heat to high. Preheat the other area to medium.

3. Combine all of the ingredients for the basting butter in a medium saucepan, stirring to combine as the butter melts. Pour into a baking dish or disposable aluminum pan, preferably a $13\frac{1}{2} \times 9\frac{5}{8} \times 2\frac{3}{4}$-inch lasagna pan.

   Place all of the glaze ingredients in a jar with a tight-fitting lid and shake to combine, being sure that the sugar has completely dissolved.

4. Remove the chops from the marinade. The oil may have solidified slightly on the meat. If it has, remove any excess by rubbing lightly with a paper towel. Some herbs and garlic will remain on the meat.

5. Place the chops on the griddle, close the lid, and do not move the chops for 3 minutes. Flip to the second side, still on the griddle; brush with the butter, using the herb bundle, close the lid, and do not move them for 3 minutes.

   Brush the chops again with butter, using the herb bundle, and move to the grate.

   Continue to cook, basting with the butter and using the herb bundle during the last few minutes of cooking. Flip, jockey, and stack as needed, until you reach the desired doneness: 4 to 5 minutes for medium, 6 to 7 minutes for medium well, and 8 to 9 minutes for well-done.

6. Remove from the grill, dredge in the butter, and let rest in the butter for 5 minutes.

   Lift from the butter and place back on the grate for 1 minute on each side.

7. Drizzle some of the butter on a cutting board, followed by the parsley, fleur de sel, and pepper. Top with the chops. If slicing, dredge each slice in the butter.

POUNDED VEAL ROUND WITH SLIVERED GARLIC AND OREGANO

SERVES 8

These super-thin veal cutlets have the lovable texture of scallopini but without the heaviness contributed by a wine sauce and a dredging in flour. I infuse them with herbs before grilling them quickly, so they stay nice and juicy. A drizzle of olive oil and a few squeezes of lemon make them sing.

One 4- to 4½-inch piece of veal round, about 2 pounds

Herb Blend
1 cup extra virgin olive oil
1 cup thinly sliced garlic
½ cup sage, cut in chiffonade (see Note)
1 tablespoon fresh rosemary leaves
1 tablespoon fresh thyme leaves
1 tablespoon fresh oregano leaves
1 tablespoon finely ground fresh black pepper

Kosher salt
3 lemons, each cut into quarters, seeds removed
¼ to ½ cup extra virgin olive oil
¼ cup coarsely chopped flat-leaf parsley
Fleur de sel
Finely ground fresh black pepper

NOTE: To chiffonade the sage, stack the leaves and roll as tightly as possible into a cylinder. Cut across the roll so that when unrolled, the sage will be in thin, ribbons-like strips.

1. Line a sheet with plastic wrap. Cut the veal round against the grain into 8 round pieces, each about ½ inch thick.

   Combine the oil with the garlic, sage, rosemary, thyme, oregano, and pepper. Pour into a baking dish or disposable aluminum pan, preferably a 13½ × 9⅝ × 2¾-inch lasagna pan.

   Working with a couple chops at a time, dredge in the herb dressing and place between two sheets of plastic wrap. Using a meat tenderizer/pounder (see Sources page 378), pound to ⅛-inch thickness, about 4 to 5 inches across.

   Place on the prepared sheet pan. Repeat with remaining pieces of veal. Refrigerate for at least 3 hours or up to 24.

2. Preheat all grates of a well-oiled charcoal or gas grill to high.

3. It is preferable that the pieces of veal be moved to a clean area of the grate every time they are flipped. Depending on the grill size, they may need to be cooked in batches to ensure there is a clean portion of the grill to flip to.

   If you have a grill press(es) or a firebrick(s) (see Sources page 378) wrapped in heavy-duty aluminum foil, it is ideal to keep on hand, to keep the meat from lifting up and also to maximize the caramelization.

   Peel off the top pieces of plastic wrap from each piece of veal, season with the kosher salt and, as quickly as possible, slap directly on the grate.

   Grill on the first side, with the lid open, without moving, until well marked and lightly charred, about 3 minutes. Flip to the second side, squeeze lemon juice over the top, keep the lid open, and grill it without moving for 3 minutes.

5. Transfer the veal to a serving platter.

   Drizzle the top of the veal with olive oil and additional lemon juice, sprinkle with parsley, and season with fleur de sel and pepper.

VEAL T-BONES WITH MARSALA SHALLOTS

When I was growing up, I was nuts for veal Marsala. The Marsala (an easy-to-find fortified wine from Italy) is ridiculously aromatic and felt like such a special treat. This recipe captures the spirit of that classic dish, but instead of drenching a glorious cut like the T-bone in sauce, I've turned caramelized shallots into these torpedoes of winy flavor.

Marinade
1 cup extra virgin olive oil
3 tablespoons garlic salt
3 tablespoons thyme leaves
1 tablespoon dried oregano, preferably
   Mexican
1 tablespoon coarsely ground fresh black
   pepper
2 teaspoons cayenne pepper

Eight 1½-inch-thick veal loin chops
   (T-bones), about 14 ounces each

Basting/Resting Butter
8 tablespoons (4 ounces) unsalted butter
¼ cup finely chopped flat-leaf parsley
4 cloves garlic, peeled, halved, germ removed,
   and grated on a Microplane grater
1 tablespoon freshly squeezed lemon juice
1 tablespoon Worcestershire sauce

Marsala Shallots
2 tablespoons (1 ounce) unsalted butter
3 cups thinly sliced shallots
2 tablespoons granulated sugar
6 garlic cloves, peeled, halved, germ removed,
   and grated on a Microplane grater
1 cup Marsala wine
1 tablespoon fresh thyme leaves
Juice from 1 lemon

1 bunch thyme, tied in an Herb Bundle (page
   365)

Kosher salt
Finely ground fresh black pepper
¼ cup extra virgin olive oil
¼ cup finely chopped flat-leaf parsley
4 lemons, each cut into quarters, seeds
   removed

1. Combine all of the marinade ingredients.

    Place the chops in an extra-large re-sealable plastic bag (or divide between two large bags). Pour the marinade over the chops, squeeze out any excess air from the bag, and close. Roll the bag to evenly coat all of the meat in the marinade. Refrigerate for at least 3 hours and up to 24.

2. Place a cast-iron griddle on one area of a well-oiled charcoal or gas grill and preheat to high. Preheat the other area to medium.

3. Combine all of the ingredients for the basting butter in a medium saucepan, stirring to combine as the butter melts. Pour into a baking dish or disposable aluminum pan, preferably a 13½ × 9⅝ × 2¾-inch lasagna pan.

4. Melt the 2 tablespoons of butter for the shallots in a medium-size sauté pan or skillet over medium-high heat. Toss the shallots with the sugar and add to the pan. Stir continuously until the shallots are richly caramelized, 6 to 8 minutes, being careful not to burn them. Add the garlic and cook for 1 minute more.

    Pour in the wine and deglaze the pan, scraping up any bits that may have stuck to the bottom of the pan. Stir in the thyme. Continue to simmer until the wine has almost completely evaporated and the shallots are glazed. Stir in the lemon juice, remove from the heat, and cover with foil to keep warm.

5. Remove the chops from the marinade and pat lightly with paper towels to remove any excess oil that may be clinging to the chops. Some herbs and garlic will remain on the meat.

6. Place the chops on the griddle, close the lid, and do not move them for 3 minutes.

    Flip to the second side, still on the griddle, brush with the butter, using the herb bundle, close the lid, and do not move them for 3 minutes.

    Brush again with the butter, using the herb bundle, and move the chops to the grate.

    Continue to cook, brushing with the butter during the last few minutes. Flip, jockey, and stack as needed, until you reach desired doneness: 4 to 5 minutes for medium, 6 to 7 minutes for medium well, and 8 to 9 minutes for well-done.

7. Remove the chops from the grill, dredge in the butter, and let rest in the butter for 5 minutes.

8. Lift the chops from the butter and place back on the grate for 1 minute on each side.

9. Transfer to a serving platter, season lightly with salt and pepper, top with the glazed shallots, drizzle with olive oil, and sprinkle the parsley over the top. Serve with lemon wedges on the side.

VERY FRENCH RACK OF VEAL

SERVES 8

Introduce one of the most impressive holiday cuts to the barbecue, and sparks will fly. The rosy meat absorbs just the right amount of smoke, and the paste that I slather on becomes a crust that'll have your guests gasping as you haul it to the table. Right before I let people dig in, I finish it with a scattering of herbs and a squeeze of lemon juice.

Two 5-bone racks of veal, bones frenched and the racks tied, each about 4½ pounds

Seasoning Paste
1 tablespoon crushed hot red pepper flakes
2 tablespoons boiling water
½ cup extra virgin olive oil
½ cup Dijon mustard
¼ cup thinly sliced garlic
2 tablespoons firmly packed light brown sugar
2 tablespoons sweet paprika
2 tablespoons thyme leaves
2 tablespoons sage, cut in chiffonade (see Note)
1 tablespoon coarsely ground fresh black pepper
1 tablespoon garlic salt

Glaze
½ cup honey
¼ cup freshly squeezed lemon juice

Finishing Dressing
¼ cup extra virgin olive oil
1 lemon, halved, and seeds removed
¼ cup finely chopped chives
¼ cup coarsely chopped flat-leaf parsley
Fleur de sel
Finely ground fresh black pepper

NOTE: To chiffonade the sage, stack the leaves and roll as tightly as possible into a cylinder. Cut across the roll so that when unrolled, the sage will be in thin, ribbons-like strips.

1. Place the pepper flakes in a small bowl and pour the boiling water over them. Let sit for 1 to 2 minutes to rehydrate the flakes. Combine all of the seasoning paste ingredients, including the pepper flakes and the soaking water.

   Lay out a triple layer of plastic wrap that will be large enough to completely wrap one of the racks.

   Place the first rack on the plastic and rub half of the seasoning blend on all sides of the meat. Wrap completely in the plastic wrap. Lay out a triple layer of plastic wrap and repeat with the second rack and the remaining seasoning paste. Refrigerate for at least 6 hours, or up to 8.

2. Preheat an indirect barbecue with a drip pan and hardwood (preferably hickory or oak), a ceramic cooker with deflector plate and hardwood (preferably hickory or oak), or a charcoal or gas grill with a box or packet of hardwood (preferably hickory or oak) to 250°F.

3. Place the glaze ingredients in a jar with a tight-fitting lid and shake to combine. Set aside.

4. Remove the meat from the plastic wrap.

   Insert a remote thermometer into the center of one of the racks.

5. Place the racks in the cooker. (They will be pulled out before desired doneness, glazed, and returned to the cooker.)

   Cook until the internal temperature registers 120°F, about 2 hours and 15 minutes.

6. Remove the racks from the cooker.

   Increase the temperature to 350°F.

   Give the glaze a quick shake to reincorporate any ingredients that may have settled and glaze all sides of the meat.

7. Place back in the cooker and cook until the racks reach desired doneness: about 15 to 20 minutes for medium (135°F), about 25 to 35 minutes for medium well (145°F), and about 30 to 45 minutes for well-done (150°F).

8. Drizzle the olive oil on a cutting board and squeeze the lemon juice on top. Sprinkle the chives, parsley, fleur de sel, and pepper over the mixture. Top with the rack and let rest for 15 minutes.

9. Slice the rack into individual chops, dredging to coat the chops in the dressing.

   Season the top with fleur de sel and pepper.

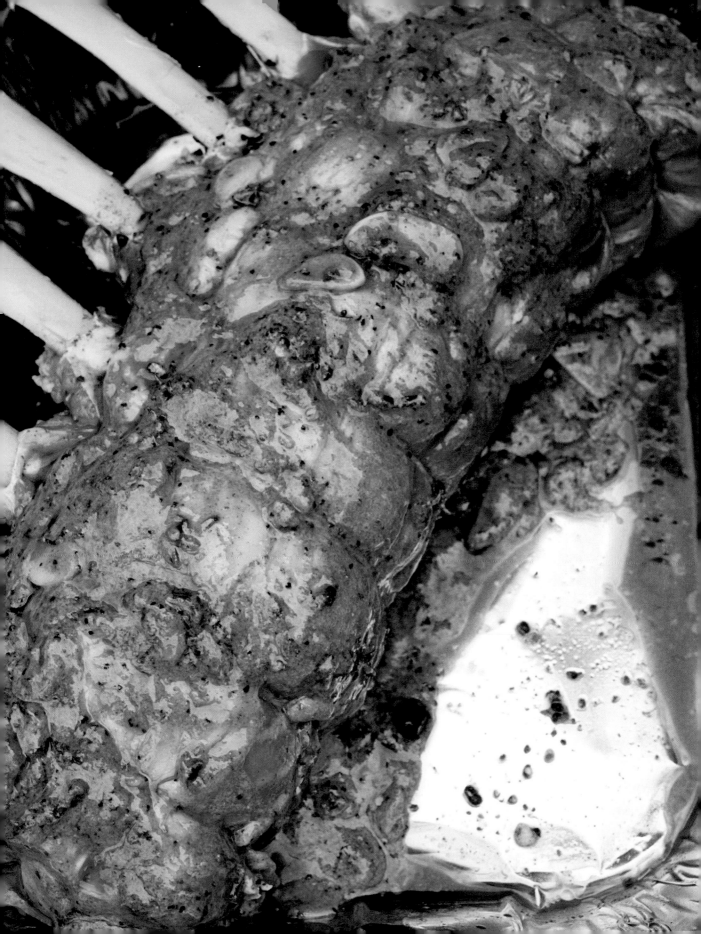

GRILLED AND BRAISED OSSO BUCO

SERVES 8

Fans of braising go crazy for *osso buco,* the Italian name for pieces of slow-cooked shank made by slicing across the bone. You get melting, luscious meat, plus you get to scoop out the jiggly, ultrarich marrow. What could be better, right? For the answer, just try it after you lay on some wood smoke, a flavorful accent that I promise you won't come across in Milan.

TIP: When making a braising baste, it is best to add cold wine and stock in the warm pan mixture. You'll get fewer lumps.

Marinade

½ cup extra virgin olive oil
¼ cup thinly sliced garlic
2 tablespoons fresh thyme leaves
2 tablespoons fresh rosemary leaves
2 tablespoons fresh marjoram leaves
1 tablespoon dried oregano, preferably Mexican
1 tablespoon finely ground fresh black pepper

8 pieces veal shank, cut for Osso Buco (see Note)

Braising Base

4 tablespoons (2 ounces) unsalted butter
2 cups finely chopped sweet white onion
10 garlic cloves, peeled, halved, germ removed, and grated on a Microplane grater
2 teaspoons kosher salt
2 tablespoons all-purpose flour
1 cup dry white wine, such as Sauvignon Blanc, cold
4 cups low-sodium chicken stock, cold
2 cups canned crushed tomatoes, drained

About 2 tablespoons kosher salt

¼ to ½ cup extra virgin olive oil
2 tablespoons freshly squeezed lemon juice
½ cup finely chopped flat-leaf parsley
2 tablespoons fresh marjoram leaves
Fleur de sel

NOTE: The pieces of veal should be 1½ to 2 inches thick and 1½ to 2 inches in diameter, with at least 1 inch of meat surrounding the bone.

1. Combine the marinade ingredients.

    Place the pieces of veal shank in an extra-large resealable plastic bag (or divide between two large bags). Pour over the marinade, squeeze out any excess air from the bag, and close. Roll the bag to evenly coat all of the meat in the marinade. Refrigerate for at least 12 hours and up to 24.

2. The meat will be initially charred over direct heat and then moved to indirect.

    Preheat all grates of a charcoal or gas grill to high.

    If using an indirect barbecue for the indirect portion of the cooking, preheat the cooker with hardwood (preferably hickory or oak) to 275°F.

3. In a roasting pan, baking dish, or saucepan that will hold the osso buco in a single layer, prepare the braising base. (Depending on your cooker, the osso buco may need to be divided between two pans for braising. The base can be prepared in one pan and then split as needed.)

    Place the butter in the pan over medium heat to melt it. Add the onions, garlic, and salt, and sauté until the onions are translucent, adjusting the temperature as needed to keep them from browning. Sprinkle the flour over the top and, stirring constantly, cook until there is no longer a raw flour smell, about 3 minutes.

    Pour in the wine and deglaze the pan, scraping any bits from the bottom. Cook until the wine has reduced by about half, about 5 minutes. Add the chicken stock and tomatoes, bring the mixture to a boil, and cook for 5 minutes. Remove from the heat and set by the cooker.

4. Remove the osso buco from the marinade and pat lightly with paper towels to remove any excess oil that may be clinging to the meat. Some herbs and garlic will remain on the meat. Season generously with salt.

    Place the meat on the grate, and keeping the lid open, grill for about 6 minutes until well marked and lightly charred, flipping, jockeying, and stacking as necessary. Flip and repeat on the second side, grilling for about 6 minutes.

    As the pieces are charred, place in the pan(s), presentation side up (the side that has the neatest appearance), along with the braising base. At this point do not cover the pans.

5. If using a ceramic cooker after the initial char, replace the deflector plate and use hardwood (preferably hickory or oak), adjusting the temperature to 275°F. If using a charcoal or gas grill, add a box or packet with hardwood (preferably hickory or oak) after the initial char, and adjust the temperature to 275°F.

    Place in the cooker, stacking the pans if needed. Because the pans are not covered, you may need to place a cooling rack over the bottom pan to secure the top pan. Cook for 1 hour, rotating them from top to bottom halfway through the cooking.

6. Remove the pans from the cooker. Cover the pan(s) tightly with heavy-duty aluminum foil. Return the pans to the cooker and cook, rotating the pans from top to bottom halfway through the cooking, until the meat is fork-tender, 2 to 2½ hours.

7. Remove from the cooker and let rest, covered, for 30 minutes.

8. Carefully remove the osso buco from the pans and arrange on a serving platter.

   With a large spoon or ladle, remove the fat from the top of the braising liquid and discard. Spoon the sauce over the meat.

   Combine the olive oil, lemon juice, parsley, and marjoram and drizzle over the meat. Finish with a sprinkling of fleur de sel.

WHOLE BEEF TENDERLOIN WITH WORCESTERSHIRE GLAZE

SERVES 6 TO 8

This luxurious larger cut provides succulent texture and unparalleled tenderness—perfect for serving a large group. But it's the cook's job to bring flavor to the very lean meat. And that's exactly what I do by rubbing it with soy and mustard, then a seasoning blend with granulated garlic and cayenne. By the time you're ready to grill, the meat has grabbed on to just enough of those tasty ingredients, but not so much that it overwhelms the flavor of the meat. A Worcestershire-honey glaze near the end of cooking is icing on the cake.

One 5-pound whole beef tenderloin, trimmed

Paste
1 tablespoon prepared yellow mustard
1 tablespoon Worcestershire sauce
1 tablespoon Japanese soy sauce
1 tablespoon beef base in paste form, such as Better Than Bouillon (see Sources page 378)

Seasoning Blend
2 tablespoons mild chile powder, preferably Chimayo (see Sources page 378), Ancho, or Hatch
2 tablespoons coarsely ground black pepper
1½ teaspoons cayenne pepper
1½ teaspoons granulated garlic or garlic powder
1½ teaspoons kosher salt

Glaze
½ cup Worcestershire sauce
½ cup honey
4 tablespoons unsalted butter

¼ to ½ cup canola or vegetable oil

1 bunch thyme, tied in an Herb Bundle (page 365)
½ cup Apple Juice Spray (page 364)

Finishing Dressing
½ cup extra virgin olive oil
½ cup finely chopped chives
Fleur de sel
Finely ground fresh black pepper

1. Preheat one grate of a well-oiled charcoal or gas grill to high and another to low.

2. Combine all of the paste ingredients.

   Combine all of the seasoning blend ingredients.

   Combine the Worcestershire sauce and the honey for the glaze in a jar with a tight-fitting lid. Melt the butter, pour into the jar, and shake to combine.

3. Rub the tenderloin with the mustard beef paste on all sides.

   Sprinkle the seasoning blend on all sides.

   Using your hands or a brush, evenly, but lightly, coat the tenderloin with canola oil.

   Insert a remote thermometer into the thickest part of the tenderloin.

4. Place the tenderloin on the grate set to high and, keeping the lid open, grill on the first side until well marked and lightly charred, 2 to 3 minutes. Turn the roast a quarter-turn, still over high and keeping the lid open, grill until well marked and lightly charred, 2 to 3 minutes. Turn two more times, to grill the third and fourth sides, each time keeping the lid open, and grilling until well marked and lightly charred, 2 to 3 minutes per side.

   Move the tenderloin to the low grate, close the lid, and cook, turning at least once, about halfway through the cooking (at 8 to 10 minutes), until the internal temperature reaches 115°F, 15 to 20 minutes.

Give the glaze a quick shake to reincorporate any ingredients that may have settled.

   Continue to cook over low, brushing with the glaze using the herb bundle every couple of minutes and spraying with apple juice spray. Flip and jockey as needed, cooking until you reach the desired doneness; about 5 minutes for rare (120°F), about 10 minutes for medium rare (125°F), about 15 minutes for medium (130°F), about 25 minutes for medium well (140°F), and about 35 minutes for well-done (150°F).

5. Drizzle the olive oil on a cutting board. Cut the end of the herb brush off and finely chop with the oil on the board. Sprinkle the chives, fleur de sel, and pepper over the oil. Top with the tenderloin and let rest for 5 minutes.

   Slice the tenderloin against the grain into ¼-inch slices, dredging the slices in the dressing.

QUICK-COOK BRISKET FLAT

I love the over-the-top richness of the point of the brisket, but sometimes (like when your finicky aunt is coming over) you need to look to a less fatty cut that looks neat on the plate. That's why the first cut flat, often called "lean brisket," shows up so often on the holiday table. But that doesn't mean you can't transform it into something any fan of brisket would love. The trick—aside from layering flavors like mustard, chile powder, and honey—is an especially short cooking time and a slightly higher temp, which helps keep the lean meat stay really juicy.

One 3½-pound beef brisket flat, fat trimmed to ¼ inch

5 garlic cloves, peeled, halved, germ removed, and grated on a Microplane grater

Paste

¼ cup mild chile powder, preferably Chimayo (see Sources page 378), Ancho, or Hatch

2 tablespoons prepared yellow mustard

2 tablespoons beef base in paste form, such as Better Than Bouillon (see Sources page 378)

Seasoning Blend

1 tablespoon garlic salt

1 tablespoon chili powder

1½ teaspoons lemon pepper

¾ teaspoon coarsely ground fresh black pepper

¾ teaspoon kosher salt

¼ teaspoon cayenne pepper

About ¼ cup canola or vegetable oil

Wrapping Mixture

¼ cup honey

¼ cup firmly packed dark brown sugar

1 tablespoon water

Finishing Sauce

1 cup APL BBQ Sauce (page 362), or your favorite BBQ sauce

1½ teaspoons apple cider vinegar

Fleur de sel

1. Preheat an indirect barbecue with a drip pan and hardwood (preferably hickory, oak, or pecan), a ceramic cooker with deflector plate and hardwood (preferably hickory, oak, or pecan), or a charcoal or gas grill with a box or packet of hardwood (preferably hickory, oak, or pecan) to 325°F.

2. Using the point of a paring knife, make 20 small incisions, each about ½ inch deep, no wider than a paring knife, and 2 inches apart from each other on the surface of the brisket. Press in the garlic.

   Combine the paste ingredients and spread on the brisket.

   Combine all of the seasoning blend ingredients and sprinkle evenly on the brisket.

   Using your hands or a brush, evenly, but lightly, coat the brisket with canola oil.

3. Place in the cooker, fat side down, and cook for 2½ hours.

4. Meanwhile, combine the wrapping mixture ingredients.

   Lay out a double sheet of aluminum foil, top with the brisket, and cover with the wrapping mixture. Securely wrap in the foil.

   Place back in the cooker and cook for 2 hours.

5. Meanwhile, line a small cooler with a beach towel or other large towels to insulate the inside of the cooler.

6. Remove the brisket from the cooker and carefully unwrap over a baking dish or disposable pan, reserving the liquid.

   Lay out a double sheet of aluminum foil, and top with the brisket.

   Strain all of the juices from the pan through a fine-mesh strainer set over a liquid measuring cup. Discard any solids. Allow the fat to come to the top, pour off, and discard. For the enhanced sauce, reserve ½ cup of the beef liquid.

   Pour the remaining defatted liquid over the brisket. Securely wrap in the foil, place in a baking dish or disposable pan, and transfer to the cooler. Cover the top with the towels, close the lid, and let rest for 1 hour.

7. Meanwhile, combine the reserved beef liquid, BBQ sauce, and vinegar.

8. Remove the brisket from the cooler, unwrap carefully, coat with the sauce, and place back in the cooker, fat side up. Cook for 30 minutes.

9. Paint the remaining sauce on a cutting board, top with the brisket, and let rest for 10 minutes.

10. Slice the brisket against the grain into ⅛-inch slices, dredging them in the sauce. Sprinkle with fleur de sel.

"GET A BOOK" WHOLE BEEF BRISKET

SERVES 8 TO 12

My Texas barbecue revelation happened in New Mexico. The displaced Texans tending the ranch where I worked blew me away with the most elemental food. It was just brisket cooked for what seemed like forever with post oak and coals. It emerged with that dark, nearly black, bark encasing juicy meat, some of it meltingly tender and unctuous and some with an appealing chew. Each slice was bordered by a pinkish hue—the mark of a steady flame. Over years of meditatively cooking (and eating) brisket, I tweaked Texas tradition until I found this recipe, which I consider the ultimate version—I call it "get a book" brisket, because it'll have you cooking for a *long* time. But whether you pass the time by reading, chatting with good friends, or dozing off, I promise you: The wait will be well worth it.

TIP: Whole briskets often come encased in a thick layer of fat. Trim this until you have a layer that's only about ¼ to ⅛ inch thick, depending on how thick a rim of fat you prefer on your sliced brisket.

Paste
6 tablespoons mild chile powder, preferably Chimayo (see Sources page 378), Ancho, or Hatch
3 tablespoons prepared yellow mustard
3 tablespoons beef base in paste form, such as Better Than Bouillon (see Sources page 378)

Seasoning Blend
¼ cup garlic salt
3 tablespoons coarsely ground fresh black pepper
2 tablespoons chili powder
1 tablespoon lemon pepper

2 teaspoons kosher salt
¾ teaspoon cayenne pepper

One 8- to 12-pound whole beef brisket, trimmed to fit your cooker (see Note)
About ¾ cup canola or vegetable oil

½ cup Apple Juice Spray (page 364)

Wrapping Mixture
½ cup honey
½ cup firmly packed dark brown sugar
4 tablespoons (2 ounces) unsalted butter or margarine, melted

Finishing Sauce
1 cup APL BBQ Sauce (page 362), or your favorite BBQ sauce
1½ teaspoons apple cider vinegar

Fleur de sel

1. Combine the paste ingredients and spread on all sides of the brisket.

   Combine all of the seasoning blend ingredients and sprinkle evenly on all sides of the brisket. You may not use all of the blend.

   Let sit at room temperature for 1 hour.

2. Preheat an indirect barbecue with a drip pan and hardwood (preferably hickory, oak, or pecan), a ceramic cooker with deflector plate and hardwood (preferably hickory, oak, or pecan), or a charcoal or gas grill with a box or packet of hardwood (preferably hickory, oak, or pecan) to 275°F.

3. Using your hands or a brush, evenly, but lightly, coat the brisket with canola oil.

   Insert a remote thermometer in the thickest part of the brisket.

4. Place in the cooker, fat side down. After 2 hours spray every hour with apple juice spray. Cook until the internal temperature reaches 165°F, about 6 to 7½ hours (the colder the meat is going into the cooker the longer it will take).

5. Meanwhile, combine the wrapping mixture ingredients.

6. Lay out a double sheet of aluminum foil, top with the brisket, and cover with the wrapping mixture. Securely wrap in the foil. Reinsert the thermometer.

   Place back in the cooker and cook until the internal temperature reaches 195°F, 2 to 2½ hours.

7. Meanwhile, line a small cooler with a beach towel or other large towels to insulate the inside of the cooler.

8. Remove the brisket from the cooker and carefully unwrap over a baking dish or disposable pan, reserving the liquid.

   Lay out a double sheet of aluminum foil and top with the brisket.

   Strain all of the juices from the pan through a fine-mesh strainer set over a liquid measuring cup. Discard any solids. Allow the fat to come to the top, pour off, and discard. For the enhanced sauce, reserve ½ cup of the beef liquid.

   Pour the remaining defatted liquid over the brisket. Securely wrap in the foil, place in a disposable pan, and transfer to the cooler. Cover the top with the towels, close the lid, and let rest for 1 hour.

   After the brisket has rested for about 30 minutes, increase the temperature of the cooker to 300°F.

9. Meanwhile, combine the reserved beef liquid, BBQ sauce, and vinegar.

10. Remove the brisket from the cooler, carefully unwrap, coat with the sauce, place back in the cooker, fat side up, and cook for 30 minutes.

11. Paint the remaining sauce on a cutting board, top with the brisket, and let rest for 10 minutes.

12. Slice the brisket against the grain into ⅛-inch slices, dredging in the sauce. When you're carving, you'll notice that the grain changes direction when you move from the flat to the point. Don't let it throw you—just make sure you're cutting against the grain at all times. Sprinkle with fleur de sel.

BURNT ENDS WITH MELTING GARLIC

SERVES 6 TO 8

Kansas City has made many great contributions to the world of barbecue, including this riff on barbecued brisket, which is one of my favorite things in the world. It's essentially twice-cooked brisket: the fatty point reduced to quivering tenderness by the smoker, cubed, tossed with tangy sauce, and then cooked again with jacked-up heat. Stirred into baked beans, burnt ends rev up the classic barbecue side. Piled between two pieces of white bread, they make an unforgettable sandwich.

2 brisket points, with the thin layer of fat still intact, 3 to 4 pounds each

Paste
½ cup prepared yellow mustard
¼ cup water
1 tablespoon Worcestershire sauce
¼ cup garlic salt
¼ cup chili powder
3 tablespoons coarsely ground fresh black pepper
1 tablespoon kosher salt
1 teaspoon cayenne pepper

Seasoning Blend
2 tablespoons garlic salt
1½ tablespoons coarsely ground fresh black pepper
1 tablespoon chili powder
½ tablespoon lemon pepper
½ tablespoon kosher salt
½ teaspoon cayenne pepper

About ¼ cup canola oil

Wrapping Mixture
½ cup honey
½ cup firmly packed dark brown sugar
4 tablespoons (2 ounces) unsalted butter or margarine, melted

Finishing Sauce
1 cup APL BBQ Sauce (page 362), or your favorite BBQ sauce
1½ teaspoons apple cider vinegar

1 recipe Melting Garlic (page 335) (optional)
Fleur de sel

1. Preheat an indirect barbecue with a drip pan and hardwood (preferably hickory, oak, or pecan), a ceramic cooker with deflector plate and hardwood (preferably hickory, oak, or pecan), or a charcoal or gas grill with a box or packet of hardwood (preferably hickory, oak, or pecan) to 325°F.
2. Combine the paste ingredients and spread on the brisket.

   Combine all of the seasoning blend ingredients and sprinkle evenly on the brisket.

   Using your hands or a brush, evenly, but lightly, coat the brisket with canola oil.
3. Place in the cooker, fat side down, and cook for 2½ hours.
4. Meanwhile, combine the wrapping mixture ingredients.
5. Lay out a double sheet of aluminum foil.

   Remove the brisket from the cooker, place on the foil, and cover with the wrapping mixture. Securely wrap in the foil.

   Place back in the cooker and cook for 3 hours.
6. Meanwhile, line a small cooler with a beach towel or other large towels to insulate the inside of the cooler.
7. Remove the brisket from the cooker and carefully unwrap the brisket over a baking dish or disposable pan, reserving the liquid.

   Lay out a double sheet of aluminum foil and top with the brisket.

   Strain all of the juices from the pan through a fine-mesh strainer set over a liquid measuring cup. Discard any solids. Allow the fat to come to the top, pour off, and discard. For the enhanced sauce, reserve ½ cup of the beef liquid.

Pour the remaining defatted liquid over the brisket. Securely wrap in the foil, place in a baking dish or disposable pan, and transfer to the cooler. Cover the top with the towels, close the lid, and let rest for 1 hour.
8. Meanwhile, combine the reserved beef liquid, BBQ sauce, and vinegar.
9. Remove the brisket from the cooler, carefully unwrap, and cut into 1½-inch cubes. Coat with some of the sauce, and toss with the Melting Garlic, if using. To keep the garlic from falling through the grates, transfer to a baking dish or disposable pan (if cooking cubes only, they can be cooked directly on the grate). Place back in the cooker for 30 minutes.
10. Toss with the remaining sauce and sprinkle with fleur de sel.

ANY TIME OF YEAR PRIME RIB

SERVES 6 TO 8

This holiday-worthy roast is easy on the eyes, expensive, and unbelievably good. Yet whether it becomes a once-a-year treat or a monthly indulgence, you'll relish every thick, smoky slab—each one a cross section of the pink-centered, tender eye, and the charred, magnificently marbled deckle (aka the rib-eye cap). The "prime" in its name once referred to the grade, but now it's just part of the name people use to refer to the cut. Still, while you can buy choice, I go for prime almost every time.

TIP: This method will also work well with a 7-bone section of prime rib, which can weigh as much as 18 pounds.

One 7- to 8-pound, 3-bone section of a standing rib roast

Flavor Paste
½ cup prepared yellow mustard
¼ cup water
1 tablespoon Worcestershire sauce
½ cup chili powder
2 tablespoons coarsely ground fresh black pepper
2 tablespoons kosher salt

Water, in a spray bottle

Glaze
½ cup water
4 garlic cloves, peeled and crushed
¼ cup mild chile powder, preferably Chimayo (see Sources page 378), Ancho, or Hatch
3 tablespoons beef base in paste form, such as Better Than Bouillon, (see Sources page 378)
1 tablespoon lemon pepper
1 tablespoon coarsely ground fresh black pepper
2 teaspoons cayenne pepper
1 tablespoon canola or vegetable oil

Finishing Dressing
½ cup extra virgin olive oil
3 tablespoons coarsely chopped flat-leaf parsley
Fleur de sel
Coarsely ground fresh black pepper

1. Place all the flavor paste ingredients in an extra-large resealable plastic bag and roll until well combined. (For a larger rack, cover with the base and wrap in plastic wrap.)

   Place the roast in the bag and roll to cover with the base. Squeeze out any excess air from the bag, close, and roll to evenly coat all of the meat in the marinade. Refrigerate for at least 2 hours and up to 1 day.

2. Preheat an indirect barbecue with a drip pan and hardwood (preferably hickory, oak, or pecan), a ceramic cooker with deflector plate and hardwood (preferably hickory, oak, or pecan), or a charcoal or gas grill with a box or packet of hardwood (preferably hickory, oak, or pecan) to 275°F.

3. Remove the prime rib from the bag and gently wipe off the base with paper towels. It does not have to be completely clean.

   Spray the prime rib lightly with water to moisten.

   Insert a remote thermometer, in the thickest part of the meat.

4. Place the prime rib in the cooker and cook until the internal temperature reaches 115°F, about 2 hours; a larger prime rib will take closer to 3 hours.

5. Meanwhile, place all of the glaze ingredients into a blender, or in a bowl using an immersion/stick blender, and blend until smooth.

6. Remove the prime rib from the cooker and, using a brush or your hands, spread the finishing glaze in an even layer on all sides. You will not use all of the glaze.

   Return the prime rib to the cooker.

   Continue to cook until the internal temperature reaches 125°F for medium rare, about 30 minutes. (A larger rack will take 30 to 45 minutes to reach medium rare, for a total cooking time of 3½ to 3¾ hours.) Although it is my preference not to cook prime rib past this temperature, continue to cook, if desired, monitoring the internal temperature until the prime rib reaches desired doneness.

7. Drizzle the olive oil on a cutting board. Add some of the remaining glaze, followed by the parsley, fleur de sel, and pepper. Place the prime rib on the board and let rest for 20 minutes.

8. Slice the prime rib, dredging the slices in the dressing to coat. Finish with additional fleur de sel to taste.

BONELESS RIB ROAST WITH MUSTARD AND PEPPER

SERVES 8

Sometimes my smoker seems more like a magic box than a cooking tool. When I was cooking in France, I noticed that people ate their steaks with lots of pepper and mustard, so I decided to apply those ingredients to a rib roast and throw it in the smoker. What came out was not at all what I'd expected—it was something even more exciting. Instead of bringing a sharp flavor, the pepper and the mustard teamed up with the beef juices to become a sauce that even mustard's most bitter enemy would slurp by the spoonful. Make more than you think you need, because this dish is great the next day.

One 6- to 7-pound boneless rib roast
12 garlic cloves, peeled, halved, and germ removed
1 tablespoon kosher salt
1½ teaspoons fresh thyme leaves

Flavor Paste
½ cup Dijon mustard
¼ cup water
1 tablespoon Worcestershire sauce
½ cup chili powder
¼ cup coarsely ground fresh black pepper
2 tablespoons kosher salt

4 tablespoons (2 ounces) unsalted butter, melted
1 bunch thyme, tied in an Herb Bundle (page 378)
½ cup Apple Juice Spray (page 364)
Fleur de sel
Finely ground fresh black pepper
Extra virgin olive oil

1. Using the point of a paring knife, make 20 incisions, each about ½ inch deep, no wider than a paring knife, and 1 inch apart from each other, on the surface of the roast.

   Finely chop the garlic and mound in a small pile on the work surface. Sprinkle with the salt. Using a chef's knife, chop the garlic with the salt and then rub the mixture against the board with the broad side of the knife. Continue chopping and rubbing until you have a smooth paste. Combine the garlic paste and the thyme leaves and press into the incisions.

   Combine the flavor paste ingredients in an extra-large resealable plastic bag.

   Place the roast in the bag, squeeze out any excess air from the bag, and close. Roll the bag to evenly coat all sides of the roast. Refrigerate for at least 2 hours, and preferably up to 24.

2. Preheat an indirect barbecue with a drip pan and hardwood (preferably oak, hickory, or pecan), a ceramic cooker with deflector plate and hardwood (preferably oak, hickory, or pecan), or a charcoal or gas grill with a box or packet of hardwood (preferably oak, hickory, or pecan) to 275°F.

3. Remove the meat from the bag, removing any excess paste, but some is OK.

   Insert a remote thermometer in the thickest part of the meat.

4. Place the roast in the cooker and cook until about 15 degrees below desired doneness, then pull from the cooker, glaze, and return to cook to desired doneness.

   For rare, remove from the cooker when the internal temperature reaches 105°F, about 2 hours and 20 minutes.

For medium rare, remove from the cooker when the internal temperature reaches 110°F, about 2½ hours.

For medium, remove from the cooker when the internal temperature reaches 115°F, about 2 hours and 40 minutes.

For medium well, remove from the cooker when the internal temperature reaches 125°F, about 3 hours.

For well-done, remove from the cooker when the internal temperature reaches 135°F, 3 hours and 15 minutes.

5. Remove the roast from the cooker, and increase the temperature to 350°F.

   Let the roast rest while the cooker comes to temperature, 20 to 30 minutes.

6. Brush the roast lightly with butter using the herb bundle, and return to the cooker.

   Cook, spraying with apple juice spray halfway through the remaining cooking time. Cook for about 20 additional minutes to reach the desired doneness: 120°F for rare, 125°F for medium rare, 130°F for medium, 140°F for medium well, and 150°F for well-done.

7. Remove the roast from the cooker and let rest for at least 20 minutes, or up to 2 hours before serving.

8. Slice into ¼-inch slices and season with fleur de sel, pepper, and a light drizzle of olive oil.

GERMAN DELI-STYLE TOP ROUND OF BEEF

SERVES 8 TO 10

I love roast beef, but this recipe takes the deli-case standard to a whole new level. I cook it slowly, so it picks up a lot of smoky flavor but not so long that it sacrifices a rosy, velvety center. You'll love it however you eat it, but I'd be neglecting my responsibilities as a chef if I didn't urge you to try my favorite version: sliced thin and piled on rye bread with Russian dressing and slivers of raw onion. Make this one a day in advance for easy entertaining.

2 tablespoons red wine vinegar
1 tablespoon Worcestershire sauce
2 tablespoons Dijon mustard

2 top round roasts, about 2¾ pounds each

Seasoning Blend
2 tablespoons coarsely ground fresh black pepper
2 tablespoons granulated garlic or garlic powder
2 tablespoons granulated onion or onion powder
2 tablespoons sweet paprika
2 tablespoons firmly packed dark brown sugar
2 tablespoons kosher salt

2 tablespoons canola or vegetable oil
2 tablespoons (1 ounce) unsalted butter, melted

Wrapping Mixture
10 garlic cloves, peeled, halved, germ removed, and thinly sliced
10 thyme sprigs

1. Combine the vinegar, Worcestershire sauce, and mustard, and rub on all sides of the meat to moisten.

   Place the seasoning blend ingredients in an extra-large resealable plastic bag, then roll the bag to combine.

   Add the beef to the bag, squeeze out any excess air from the bag, and close. Roll the bag to evenly coat all sides of the meat with the mixture. Refrigerate for at least 2 hours, or up to 1 day.

2. Preheat an indirect barbecue with a drip pan and hardwood (preferably hickory), a ceramic cooker with deflector plate and hardwood (preferably hickory), or a charcoal or gas grill with a box or packet of hardwood (preferably hickory) to 250°F.

3. Remove the roasts from the bag and wipe off the excess seasoning blend from the meat with paper towels. It does not have to be completely clean.

   Combine the oil and the butter and, using your hands or a brush, evenly, but lightly, coat the roasts with canola oil.

   Insert a remote thermometer in the thickest part of the meat.

4. Place the roasts in the cooker until the internal temperature reaches 115°F, 50 to 60 minutes.

5. Remove the roasts from the cooker, and increase the temperature to 375°F.

   Let the roasts rest while the cooker comes to temperature, 20 to 30 minutes.

6. Wrap each of the roasts in a double layer of heavy-duty aluminum foil.

   Return the roasts to the cooker and cook for 15 minutes. At this point the meat will be a rosy, medium rare, around 125°F. Although it is my preference not to cook roast beef past this temperature, continue to cook, if desired, monitoring the internal temperature until the roast beef reaches the desired doneness.

7. Meanwhile lay out sheets of plastic wrap large enough to wrap the roasts. Spread the garlic slivers and thyme leaves on the plastic, so when wrapped they will be evenly distributed on all sides of the roasts.

8. Remove the roasts from the cooker and wrap tightly in the plastic wrap. Let rest at room temperature until cool, then refrigerate.

9. To serve, slice the meat as thinly as possible.

CHUCK ROAST CRUSTED WITH GARLIC SALT AND INSTANT COFFEE

SERVES 6 TO 8

During a photo shoot for *Food & Wine* magazine, I decided to improvise a recipe for chuck roast. I thought, "Aha, I'll use coffee." There was only one problem—we didn't have good coffee on hand. So I used instant grounds, and you know what? They worked better than the more expensive stuff ever had. While freshly ground beans often linger in gritty bits on top of the meat, the granules of the instant stuff melt and become a beautiful glaze. Even those who don't love coffee go crazy for this dish, because the coffee transforms through cooking into a subtle accent, not something overpowering—a deep flavor that goes so well with the super-beefy chuck roast.

One chuck roast, about 4 pounds
8 garlic cloves, peeled, halved, and germ removed

Flavor Paste
2 tablespoons prepared yellow mustard
1 tablespoon beef base in paste form, such as Better Than Bouillon (see Sources page 378)

Seasoning Blend
1 tablespoon garlic salt
1 tablespoon chili powder
1 tablespoon lemon pepper
1 tablespoon regular (not decaffeinated) instant coffee
1 tablespoon mild chile powder, preferably Chimayo (see Sources page 378), Ancho, or Hatch

¾ teaspoon ground cumin
½ teaspoon dried oregano, preferably Mexican
½ teaspoon kosher salt
⅛ teaspoon cayenne pepper

Wrapping Mixture
¼ cup honey
2 tablespoons (1 ounce) unsalted butter or margarine, melted

½ cup Apple Juice Spray (page 364)
1½ teaspoons apple cider vinegar

Finishing Dressing
½ cup extra virgin olive oil
¼ cup coarsely chopped flat-leaf parsley
Fleur de sel
Finely ground fresh black pepper

1. Preheat an indirect barbecue with a drip pan and hardwood (preferably hickory, pecan, or oak), a ceramic cooker with deflector plate and hardwood (preferably hickory, pecan, or oak), or a charcoal or gas grill with a box or packet of hardwood (preferably hickory, pecan, or oak) to 275°F.

2. Using the point of a paring knife make 16 incisions, each about 1½ inches deep, no wider than a paring knife, and 2 inches apart from each other on the surface of the roast. Press in the halved garlic.

   Combine the paste ingredients and spread on all sides of the roast.

   Combine all of the seasoning blend ingredients and sprinkle evenly on all sides of the meat.

   Place a remote thermometer in the thickest part of the roast.

3. Place the roast in the cooker and cook until the internal temperature reaches 105°F, about 1½ hours.

4. Meanwhile combine the wrapping mixture ingredients.

   Combine the apple juice spray and the vinegar.

5. Lay out a double sheet of heavy-duty aluminum foil large enough to encase the roast. Remove the roast from the cooker, place on the foil, and pour over the wrapping mixture. Wrap tightly in the foil, and reinsert the thermometer.

   Cook until the internal temperature reaches 115°F, about 15 minutes.

6. Remove the roast from the cooker, and increase the temperature to 350°F.

   Let the roast rest while the cooker comes to temperature, 20 to 30 minutes.

7. Unwrap the roast, place back in the cooker, spraying generously with apple juice spray halfway through.

   Cook until the internal temperature reaches the desired doneness: about 5 minutes for rare (120°F); about 10 minutes for medium rare (125°F); about 15 minutes for medium (130°F); about 30 minutes for medium well (140°F); and about 50 minutes for well-done (150°F).

8. Drizzle the olive oil on the board and sprinkle the parsley, fleur de sel, and pepper over the top. Place the roast on the board and let rest for 10 minutes.

9. Slice against the grain into ¼-inch slices, dredging in the dressing to coat. Sprinkle with additional fleur de sel and pepper.

SHORT RIBS WITH FLEUR DE SEL

Taste a skillfully braised short rib—its ultratender, richly beefy meat giving way to even a plastic fork—and it's hard to believe that it can get any better. Yet the barbecue makes them even more compelling, creating something with the deep, intense beefiness of smoked brisket but also the satisfying chew of a steak. Anyone tempted to pour sauce on this one must first try a slice with just a sprinkling of good salt and tell me that doesn't make it explode with flavor.

Two 3-bone plates of short ribs (see Note on Buying and Cutting Short Ribs, page 138)

Mustard Moisturizer
¼ cup prepared yellow mustard
¼ cup water
1 tablespoon Worcestershire sauce
1 tablespoon apple cider vinegar

Seasoning Blend
¼ cup garlic salt
3 tablespoons coarsely ground fresh black pepper
2 tablespoons chili powder
1 tablespoon lemon pepper
1 tablespoon kosher salt
1 teaspoon cayenne pepper

¼ to ½ cup canola or vegetable oil

Wrapping Mixture
½ cup firmly packed light brown sugar
½ cup honey
3 tablespoons beef base in paste form, such as Better Than Bouillon (see Sources page 378)
2 tablespoons water
1 tablespoon (½ ounce) unsalted butter or margarine, melted

Finishing Dressing
½ cup extra virgin olive oil
3 tablespoons coarsely chopped flat-leaf parsley
Fleur de sel
Finely ground fresh black pepper

1. Preheat an indirect barbecue with a drip pan and hardwood (preferably hickory, oak, or pecan), a ceramic cooker with deflector plate and hardwood (preferably hickory, oak, or pecan), or a charcoal or gas grill with a box or packet of hardwood (preferably hickory, oak, or pecan) to 250°F.
2. Combine all of the ingredients for the mustard moisturizer and moisten all sides of the roasts.

   Combine all of the seasoning blend ingredients.

   Sprinkle the roasts with about half of the seasoning blend, covering all sides evenly.

   Using your hands or a brush, evenly, but lightly, coat the roasts with canola oil.
3. Place the roasts in the cooker, bone side down, and cook for 5 hours.
4. Meanwhile, combine all of the wrapping mixture ingredients.
5. Remove the racks from the cooker.

   Lay two sets of double sheets of heavy-duty aluminum foil large enough to wrap the roasts on the work surface, and pour half of the wrapping mixture on each.

   Top one set of foil with a rack, meat side down, close, and crimp to seal. Wrap with a second sheet of foil. Repeat with the remaining rack and foil.

   Place the racks back in the cooker, meat side down, and cook for 1 hour.
6. Remove the racks from the cooker, and increase the temperature to 275°F.

   Let the racks rest in the foil for 45 minutes.
7. Remove the racks from the foil over a baking dish or disposable aluminum pan, reserving the cooking liquid.

   Lightly dust all sides of the racks with the remaining seasoning blend and place, meat side up, in the cooker for 45 minutes.
8. Meanwhile, strain all of the juices and solids from the pan through a fine-mesh strainer set over a measuring cup. Discard the solids. Allow the fat to come to the top in the measuring cup, pour off, and discard. Pour the remaining liquid back in the pan to keep warm.
9. Remove the roasts from the cooker, wrap in plastic wrap, and let rest for 30 minutes.
10. Drizzle the olive oil on the board, add about 2 tablespoons of the defatted liquid, along with the parsley, fleur de sel, and pepper. Unwrap the roast, place on top of the mixture, and slice perpendicular to the bone into 1/4-inch slices. Dredge the slices in the mixture and sprinkle with additional fleur de sel and pepper.

FLANKEN-STYLE RIBLETS

When I was growing up, this cut of short rib almost always wound up in the soup pot. But I barbecue it, because after all, what's better for a party than riblets? When butchers slice short ribs through the bones to make this special cut, they create more surface area—in other words, more opportunity to add flavor. And that's exactly what I do. Five hours in the smoker and a glossy BBQ sauce make these sexy as hell.

Eight 3-bone, flanken cut, plate short ribs, about 4 pounds total (see Note on Buying and Cutting Short Ribs, page 138)

Seasoning Blend
¼ cup mild chile powder, preferably Chimayo (see Sources page 378), Ancho, or Hatch
2 tablespoons garlic salt
1 tablespoon coarsely ground fresh black pepper

About ¼ cup canola or vegetable oil

Wrapping Mixture
1 cup honey
3 tablespoons apple juice
1 tablespoon (½ ounce) unsalted butter or margarine, melted
1 tablespoon Japanese soy sauce
1 tablespoon Worcestershire sauce

Finishing Sauce
½ cup APL BBQ Sauce (page 362), or your favorite BBQ sauce
1 tablespoon apple cider vinegar

Fleur de sel

1. Preheat an indirect barbecue with a drip pan and hardwood (preferably hickory, oak, or pecan), a ceramic cooker with deflector plate and hardwood (preferably hickory, oak, or pecan), or a charcoal or gas grill with a box or packet of hardwood (preferably hickory, oak, or pecan) to 250°F.
2. Combine the seasoning blend ingredients and sprinkle evenly on all sides of the ribs.

    Using your hands or a brush, evenly, but lightly, coat the ribs with canola oil.
3. Place in the cooker uncut, smooth bone side down, and cook for 4 hours.
4. Meanwhile, about 30 minutes before the completion of the cooking, choose a baking dish or disposable aluminum pan, preferably a 13½ × 9⅝ × 2¾-inch lasagna pan that will hold the ribs in a single layer and fit into the cooker. If necessary, use more than one pan.

    Combine the wrapping mixture ingredients and pour into the pan(s).
5. Remove the ribs from the cooker and place in the pan(s) with the wrapping mixture. Turn to coat on all sides and finish with the ribs meat side down.

    Cover the pan(s) with heavy-duty aluminum foil, return to the cooker, stacking the pan(s) and rotating from top to bottom halfway through if using two pans. Cook for 1 hour.
6. Remove the pan(s) from the cooker. Let the ribs rest in the pan(s), still covered, for 45 minutes.
7. Transfer the ribs to a tray and reserve the liquid.

    Strain all of the juices from the pan(s) through a fine-mesh strainer set over a measuring cup. Discard any solids. Allow the fat to come to the top, pour off, and discard. Combine ¼ cup of the beef liquid with the barbecue sauce and the vinegar. Set aside.
8. Sprinkle the remaining seasoning blend on all sides of the ribs and place back in the cooker, uncut, smooth bone side down, for 45 minutes.
9. Coat all sides of the ribs with the reserved sauce and cook for an additional 15 minutes.
10. Paint a cutting board with some of the remaining sauce, top with ribs, and let rest for 10 minutes.
11. Cut the ribs into individual riblets, dredging them in the sauce. Season lightly with fleur de sel.

LONG COOK BEEF SHANK WITH SLIVERED AND MELTING GARLIC

SERVES 6 TO 8

Nothing reduces your friends to stuttering awe like a whole shank in a dark, spice-flecked crust. Without question, it's one of my most impressive-looking dishes—think lamb shank times six, Fred Flintstone cooking for Captain Caveman. And your guests will be wowed again when they dig in, because the shank is practically built for barbecue, its tough collagen just waiting for low heat to transform it into that luscious, stick-to-your-ribs kind of texture. Look for the shank in Asian markets—Vietnamese cooks use it to make soups—or ask a good butcher, who can place a special order for almost anything.

1 beef shank, silverskin removed
12 garlic cloves, peeled and thinly sliced

Seasoning Blend
¼ cup mild chile powder, preferably Chimayo (see Sources page 378), Ancho, or Hatch
1½ tablespoons coarsely ground fresh black pepper
1 tablespoon water
1 tablespoon garlic salt
1½ teaspoons crushed hot red pepper flakes
1½ teaspoons Worcestershire sauce
1½ teaspoons Dijon mustard
1½ teaspoons beef paste in paste form, such as Better Than Bouillon (see Sources page 378)

½ cup Apple Juice Spray (page 364)

Wrapping Mixture
½ cup honey
1 tablespoon apple juice
1 tablespoon (½ ounce) unsalted butter or margarine, melted

½ cup APL BBQ Sauce (page 362), or your favorite BBQ sauce
1 recipe Melting Garlic (page 335), held in the oil with the herbs
3 tablespoons coarsely chopped flat-leaf parsley
Fleur de sel

1. Using the point of a paring knife make 20 incisions, each about 1 inch deep, no wider than a paring knife, and 2 inches apart from each other on the surface of the shank. Press the sliced garlic into the incisions.

   Using kitchen twine, tie the shank at 2-inch intervals.

   Combine the seasoning blend ingredients and spread on all sides of the meat.

   Place in an extra-large resealable plastic bag. Squeeze out any excess air from the bag and close. Refrigerate for at least 12 hours, or up to 24.

2. Preheat an indirect barbecue with a drip pan and hardwood (preferably hickory, oak, or pecan), a ceramic cooker with deflector plate and hardwood (preferably hickory, oak, or pecan), or a charcoal or gas grill with a box or packet of hardwood (preferably hickory, oak, or pecan) to 275°F.

3. Remove the roast from the bag.

   Place in the cooker, spraying with apple juice spray every 15 minutes after the first 2½ hours. Cook for a total of 4 hours.

4. Meanwhile, combine the wrapping mixture ingredients.

   Lay out a double layer of heavy-duty aluminum foil large enough to encase the shank.

5. Remove the shank from the cooker and place on the foil. Cover with the wrapping mixture and securely wrap in the foil.

   Place back in the cooker and cook for 2 hours.

6. Remove from the cooker and let the shank rest, wrapped for 1 hour.

7. Carefully unwrap the shank over a baking dish or disposable pan, reserving the liquid.

   Place the meat back in the cooker and cook for 30 minutes.

8. Meanwhile, strain all of the juices from the pan through a fine-mesh strainer set over a measuring cup. Allow the fat to come to the top, pour off, and discard. Combine ¼ cup of the beef liquid with the barbecue sauce.

9. Remove the shank from the cooker and coat on all sides with the sauce.

   Return to the cooker and cook for 20 minutes.

   Place the pan with the melting garlic in its oil in the cooker.

10. Paint the board with the fortified sauce and sprinkle the parsley and fleur de sel over the top.

    Place the shank on the cutting board and let rest for 10 minutes.

11. Stand up the shank and slice on an angle, against the grain, perpendicular to the bone, into ¼-inch slices. Dredge the meat in the sauce and season with additional fleur de sel. Serve with the melting garlic on the side.

TEXAS-STYLE CHILI, AKA BOWL O'RED

There are no beans in this chili because this is a classic bowl o'red, a beef-focused Texas specialty that's so easy to make and delivers a rich, complex flavor. In my version, hand-cut chunks of chuck get marinated overnight in a paste of chiles, brown sugar, and cumin, and then bubble away until they fall apart. Cooking this chili in the barbecue means that it absorbs lots of smokiness and acquires a sort of 3-D depth of flavor that you just can't get in an oven or on the stovetop.

One 4-pound chuck roast, cut into 1-inch cubes

1 pound whole pod dried chiles, preferably New Mexican (see Sources page 378), stems and seeds removed (see Note)

4 cups boiling water

2 tablespoons dried oregano, preferably Mexican

1 tablespoon ground cumin

½ cup plus 2 to 4 tablespoons firmly packed dark brown sugar

2 tablespoons kosher salt, plus additional for seasoning

2 cups thinly sliced sweet white onion

10 garlic cloves, peeled, halved, germ removed, and grated on a Microplane grater

4 cups low-sodium chicken stock

1½ to 3 tablespoons apple cider vinegar

8 cups cooked white rice

16 flour tortillas, warm

½ cup thinly sliced raw chiles, preferably serrano or jalapeño

½ cup cilantro leaves

NOTE: When working with dried or fresh chiles it is important to avoid any contact with your eyes. Some stronger chiles can also leave a burning sensation on the skin, so wearing gloves is recommended.

Strain the pepper mixture through a medium strainer to remove any small pieces of pepper and/or skin. Let cool.

3. Place the onions, garlic, and meat in an extra-large resealable plastic bag and roll to combine. Add the chile paste, squeeze out any excess air from the bag, close, and roll again to thoroughly combine.

   Refrigerate for at least 12 hours, or up to 1 day.

4. If using an indirect cooker, preheat to 275°F. If using a charcoal or gas grill, preheat the grates to high and leave another off for indirect cooking.

5. Place the meat and the bag's contents in a small roasting pan or deep baking dish or pan that can take a direct flame. The pan should have about a 15-cup capacity. Add the chicken stock and stir to combine.

   Place the roasting pan over medium-high to high heat over two burners on the stovetop or directly on the grate and bring to a simmer.

   Carefully remove from the direct heat and place into the preheated cooker or, if using the grill, move to the indirect heat and keep the internal grill temperature at 275°F.

   Cook for 3 to 3½ hours, or until the beef is fork-tender.

6. Remove from the cooker and season with the remaining 2 to 4 tablespoons brown sugar, and the vinegar, and salt to taste.

   Serve with white rice, flour tortillas, chiles, and cilantro.

1. Place the chiles in a large glass bowl, pressing lightly with your hands so that the chiles fit. Pour the water over the top. The water will come only about one-third of the way up the chiles, but the steam will help to soften them all. Cover the top of the bowl with plastic wrap to form a tight seal. Let sit, covered, to steam for 30 minutes.

2. Using a slotted spoon place all of the chiles in a food processor. Reserve 1 cup of the liquid. Pour the remaining liquid in the processor. Add the oregano, cumin, ½ cup of the dark brown sugar, and 2 tablespoons of the salt. Blend until smooth, adding additional liquid only as necessary to make a smooth paste.

LAMB

Quick-Cook Sliceable Lamb Shanks (page 209)

WHAT IS LAMB?

When I haul a rack of lamb to the table, my guests know that it's not their average barbecue. Coated with dark, tasty spices, bones sticking up like fingers on a hand giving a high five, it emerges from the cooker rosy pink inside, with a whisper of smokiness.

Lamb knows the grill well—just think of those insanely good chops and kebabs cooked over charcoal—but slower cooking with smoke? Not so much. Sure, versions of its ribs occasionally pop up—a restaurant in Kansas City, a spot in Texas—and mutton (meat from sheep that are more than a year old) reigns in the barbecue of western Kentucky. But really, the meat has never joined beef, pork, and chicken in the public's Southern-barbecue imagination—especially not a seemingly fancy cut like the rack. It's time for that to change, and these recipes are how I'll make my case. Of course, as much as I love how smoke and lamb join forces, I also offer plenty of ways to explore lamb's affinity for direct-heat cooking.

THE "LAMB IS GAMY" MYTH

Some people adore the intense, almost feral flavor of mutton; some like lamb that has an undercurrent of what people call gaminess. I say, eat what you like. But to me, the tragedy is when people assume all lamb is like this and end up avoiding it altogether. Lamb acquired this reputation for good reason. Lamb from abroad (in other words, a large majority of lamb on the American market) tends to have a stronger flavor profile. Domestic lamb did, too, when the animal's wool was more valuable than its meat, and so ranchers chose shearing them for a few extra months over an earlier slaughter. And all else equal, this older lamb

has a stronger flavor than younger lamb. But now many ranchers are raising sheep for meat, not wool, and are choosing breeds that don't need to be sheared, whose meat has a lovely mild flavor.

To me, the best lamb is not gamy, but instead is packed with the meat's distinctive character—the toothsome texture and a full flavor that is reminiscent of beef along with a hard-to-define, subtle something else.

GRAIN VERSUS GRASS

Just like with beef, lamb's marbling and flavor is determined by a host of things. What the animal eats is one of those factors. Corn and grain, like oats and barley, not only help the animal grow quickly and contribute to the development of some truly lovely marbling, but they also seem to take the edge off lamb's flavor: You often get less gaminess, just clean, well-balanced flavor. Yet because age is also a major factor in the flavor, younger lamb (like baby lamb and spring lamb), even if it's not finished on grain, will have a lovely mild flavor and delicate meat. Traditionally slaughtered after it dines on the lush grasses of the season, spring lamb is now available year-round.

MARBLING

Lamb has a lot in common with beef—a similarly toothsome texture and deep, rich taste—but when it comes to marbling, I think about it more like I think about pork. That is, the marbling, although extremely important, is level with other factors (the animal's age, its breed, the feed) when it comes to determining the lamb's taste and texture. Still, good marbling is generally an indicator of tender, juicy, flavorful lamb.

SELECTION

BUY AMERICAN. Seek out meat from lambs raised in the United States, especially from local sources. A majority of the lamb that shows up in supermarkets is imported from New Zealand and Australia. "So what?" you say. "Pineapples aren't exactly sprouting on trees in Arkansas." But wait, ranchers are raising amazing lamb right here—in Colorado and Idaho and Texas and elsewhere. And not only that, on the whole, it blows most of the foreign stuff out of the water: It tends to have better marbling, sweeter fat, and meat with a cleaner, more buttery flavor. It's also significantly more expensive.

TRUST YOUR SENSES. Pick lamb that's a burgundy color, and avoid any that's excessively pale or dark.

KNOW YOUR FAT. Choose lamb with white fat, and avoid any with fat that looks yellowish. You don't want meat with a ton of external fat, not just because you're better off spending your money on meat than on something you'll probably just trim off, but also because I've found that lamb fat can cause excessive and aggressive flare-ups.

NEAT OR MEAT. Asking your butcher to french lamb (that is, trim the meat and fat from its bones) might give you a neater, more elegant presentation, but it also means discarding some truly delicious meat and fat. The decision is yours.

OH, BABY. If you can't stop fantasizing about cooking a whole baby lamb, a Greek or Halal market is the place to get it.

BUG YOUR BUTCHER. Color and marbling are pretty good indications of quality, but as I mentioned earlier, with lamb, there are other important factors. So find out as much about the lamb you buy as you can: Where was it raised? What was it fed? How old was it when it was slaughtered?

DOUBLE LAMB CHOPS INFERNO

My cooking buddy Steve Brourman, a hand surgeon who I suspect wishes he could spend every minute cooking, makes the most amazing lamb chops as an appetizer whenever he throws an outdoor party. Judging from the especially deep, dark crust—all that carbon flavor cutting into the rich, tasty fat—I think I know his secret: fire. In fact, he cooks the lovely little chops with such high heat that crusting them with spices would be an invitation for burning. For my version, then, I just add salt and pepper before I toss them on the grill. A basting butter spiked with herbs adds color and an extra blast of flavor. Since these are double chops (two bones, one extra-thick chop), the inside stays rosy red, just like I like it.

Basting Butter
16 tablespoons (8 ounces) unsalted butter
1/2 cup extra virgin olive oil
4 garlic cloves, peeled, halved, germ removed, and grated on a Microplane grater
1 tablespoon granulated sugar
2 tablespoons fresh marjoram leaves
2 tablespoons fresh mint, cut in chiffonade (see Note)
2 tablespoons coarsely chopped flat-leaf parsley
1 teaspoon dried oregano, preferably Mexican
1 teaspoon crushed hot red pepper flakes

Eight double lamb chops (cut with 2 bones per chop), 5 to 6 ounces each
About 2 tablespoons kosher salt
About 1 tablespoon finely ground fresh black pepper, plus additional for seasoning

About 1/2 cup canola or vegetable oil

1 bunch thyme, tied in an Herb Bundle (page 365)

Juice of 1 lemon
4 lemons, halved and seeds removed
Fleur de sel

NOTE: To chiffonade the mint, stack the leaves and roll as tightly as possible into a cylinder. Cut across the roll so that when unrolled, the mint will be in thin ribbon-like strips.

1. Preheat one area of a well-oiled charcoal or gas grill to high and another to medium.

2. Combine all of the basting butter ingredients together in a medium saucepan, place over medium heat, and bring to a simmer. Stir to thoroughly combine as the butter melts. Remove from the heat.

3. Season the lamb chops generously on both sides with salt and pepper.

   Using your hands or a brush, evenly, but lightly, coat the chops with canola oil.

4. Look at each of the chops and determine which is the presentation, or top side, of the chop. It is the side that looks the nicest and should be the one with the two bones closest to it.

5. It is preferable that the chops be moved to a clean area of the grate every time they are flipped.

   Place the chops presentation side down on the high grate. Close the lid and grill, without moving them, until well marked and lightly charred, about 2 minutes. Flip, brush with the butter mixture using the herb bundle, close the lid, and repeat on the second side, grilling for about 2 minutes.

   From here on out, flip, jockey, and stack as necessary. Flip again to the presentation side, still on the high grate. Brush with the butter mixture using the herb bundle, close the lid, and grill the chops, without moving them, for 2 minutes. Flip, still on the high grate, brush with the butter mixture using the herb bundle, close the lid, and grill without moving for 2 minutes. (Total grilling at this point is 8 minutes, 4 minutes on each side.)

   Brush the chops again with the butter using the herb bundle, and move to the medium area of the grate. Continue to grill, presentation side up, with the lid open, until you reach the desired doneness, brushing with the lemon juice during the last minute of cooking. Cook about 2 minutes per side for rare, about 3 to 4 minutes for medium rare to medium, about 5 minutes for medium well, and about 6 to 7 minutes for well-done.

6. Spread some of the remaining butter on a cutting board, squeeze over some lemon juice, and sprinkle with fleur de sel. Place the chops on the board and let rest for 5 minutes.

POUNDED LAMB CHOPS WITH SEASONED BREAD CRUMBS

SERVES 8

Here's a recipe that's great for getting out your aggression: You lay out a bunch of little lamb chops and WHAM! You whack them with a mallet (or even better, your fist) until they're almost completely flat. It's a technique I learned when I was studying the food of Sicily. You and your crew can eat them right off the grill, when they're still sizzling. (You'll quickly understand why Italians call this style of eating *scottadito*, which essentially means "burn your fingers.") As if the awesome char-to-flesh ratio isn't enough, I add a bit of crunch: a coating of seasoned toasted bread crumbs—a Sicilian touch.

Tossing Mixture
½ cup extra virgin olive oil
8 tablespoons (4 ounces) unsalted butter
15 unpeeled garlic cloves, crushed
2 tablespoons fresh rosemary leaves
2 tablespoons fresh thyme leaves

Seasoning Blend
2 tablespoons kosher salt
2 tablespoons coarsely ground fresh black pepper
1 tablespoon pimentón (see Sources page 378), or other smoked paprika
1 tablespoon crushed hot red pepper flakes (optional)

1 cup toasted Dried Bread Crumbs (page 367)
½ cup finely chopped flat-leaf parsley
24 lamb rib chops, about 2½ to 3 ounces each

4 lemons, cut into quarters and seeds removed
Fleur de sel

1. Preheat all grates of a well-oiled charcoal or gas grill to medium-high.

2. Place all of the tossing mixture ingredients in a medium saucepan over medium heat, stirring to combine as the butter melts. Remove from the direct heat, keep in a warm spot, and allow the flavors to develop by letting the mixture stand for 15 minutes. It should cool until just warm to the touch.

3. Combine all of the seasoning blend ingredients and sprinkle on all sides of the chops.

   Combine the bread crumbs and the parsley in a small bowl.

   Lightly dredge the chops in the butter mixture, allowing any residual butter to remain in the pan.

   Working with a couple chops at a time, season on all sides with the seasoning blend and place between two sheets of plastic wrap. Using a meat tenderizer/pounder (see Sources page 378), pound the meat to ¼-inch thickness.

   Using your hands to help them adhere, press a thin even layer of bread crumbs on both sides of the chops.

4. Place the chops on the grate, close the lid, and grill without moving, until the bread crumbs are toasted and showing some marks, about 4 minutes. Flip, close the lid, and repeat on the second side, grilling for about 4 minutes.

5. Remove the chops from the grill. Squeeze lemon juice over the top, season with fleur de sel, and serve immediately.

LAMB TENDERLOINS GLAZED WITH ORANGE BLOSSOM HONEY AND THYME

SERVES 8

To a lot of chefs, cuts like tenderloin are cop-outs, a sad sacrifice of flavor in exchange for tenderness. For others, tenderness is everything. I say every cut has its place. The mild flavor of this one will appeal to those put off by lamb's distinctive taste, but I make sure that no one will be left yearning for flavor. The slightly sticky honey glaze takes care of that. Plus it helps prevent the lean meat from drying out by creating a tasty barrier that stops steam from escaping.

Flavor Paste
1½ teaspoons crushed hot red pepper flakes
1 tablespoon boiling water
1 tablespoon kosher salt
10 garlic cloves, peeled, halved, and germ removed
1 teaspoon fresh thyme leaves
1 tablespoon granulated garlic
1 tablespoon coarsely ground fresh black pepper
½ cup extra virgin olive oil

8 lamb tenderloins, 4 to 5 ounces each, trimmed as needed

Glaze
1 cup honey, preferably orange blossom
½ cup sherry vinegar
½ cup finely chopped flat-leaf parsley
2 teaspoons finely chopped fresh thyme

About 3 tablespoons canola or vegetable oil.

Fleur de sel

1. Place the pepper flakes in a small bowl and pour the boiling water over them. Let sit for 1 to 2 minutes to rehydrate the flakes.

   Meanwhile, place the salt, garlic, thyme, granulated garlic, and black pepper in the bowl of a small food processor and blend until well combined and a paste consistency. Add the pepper flakes and their soaking water and blend until evenly distributed in the paste. Gradually add the olive oil, blending until thoroughly combined.

   Place the tenderloins in an extra-large resealable plastic bag (or divide between two large bags). Add the paste, squeeze out any excess air from the bag, and close. Roll the bag to coat the tenderloins evenly with the paste. Refrigerate for at least 2 hours, or up to 12.

2. Preheat all grates of a well-oiled charcoal or gas grill to high.

3. Place all of the glaze ingredients in a jar with a tight-fitting lid and shake to combine. Pour into a baking dish or disposable aluminum pan, preferably a 13½ ×9⅝ × 2¾-inch lasagna pan.

4. Remove the tenderloins from the bag, letting any excess blend remain in the bag. Lightly pat dry with paper towels.

   Using your hands or a brush, evenly, but lightly, coat the tenderloins with canola oil.

5. Place the tenderloins on the grates, and cook, turning once, until well marked and charred, about 1 minute on each of the 4 sides.

   Transfer the tenderloins to the pan with the glaze, turning to coat on all sides.

   Reduce the heat of the grates to low. Scrape the grates and re-oil as needed.

   Let the tenderloins rest in the glaze while the heat decreases, about 15 minutes.

6. Place the tenderloins back on the grates, occasionally dipping and rolling in the glaze and turning to caramelize, until you reach the desired doneness. Cook about 2 to 3 minutes for medium rare, about 4 minutes for medium, and about 5 minutes for well-done.

7. Drizzle some of the glaze on a cutting board, top with the tenderloins, and let rest for 5 minutes before serving.

8. Serve whole, or slice on the diagonal into ½-inch medallions, dredging them in the sauce. Sprinkle with the fleur de sel.

QUICK-COOK SLICEABLE LAMB SHANKS

SERVES 8

Everyone loves slow-cooked lamb shanks: the luscious meat falling off the big bone with just a prod from a fork. But just wait until you try this. Instead of braising it, I cook it high and hot, so they're really tender but retain a toothsome bite. Lots of red chiles enliven the seasoning blend, and a bit of fresh chile in the honey-lemon glaze adds another delicious dimension of spice.

8 lamb shanks, about 1 pound each, trimmed of any sinew or excess fat

Seasoning Blend
2 tablespoons dried oregano, preferably Mexican
2 tablespoons freshly ground coarse black pepper
2 tablespoons kosher salt
1 tablespoon crushed hot red pepper flakes

About ½ cup extra virgin olive oil

Packet Ingredients
40 unpeeled garlic cloves, crushed
16 marjoram sprigs
8 thyme sprigs
About ½ cup water

Glaze
1 cup honey
½ cup freshly squeezed lemon juice
2 garlic cloves, peeled, halved, germ removed, and grated on a Microplane grater
1 serrano, Thai bird, or other small hot chile of choice, thinly sliced
2 tablespoons (1 ounce) unsalted butter, melted

8 tablespoons (4 ounces) unsalted butter, softened at room temperature
½ bunch thyme and ½ bunch marjoram, tied in an Herb Bundle (page 365)

Finishing Dressing
½ cup extra virgin olive oil
Juice of 2 lemons
¼ cup finely chopped chives
16 large mint leaves, cut into a thin chiffonade (see Note)
Fleur de sel

NOTE: To chiffonade the mint, stack the leaves and roll as tightly as possible into a cylinder. Cut across the roll so that when unrolled, the mint will be in thin, ribbon-like strips.

1. This recipe utilizes a combination of direct and indirect cooking. It is best to read the recipe all the way through before beginning to set up your cooker(s) accordingly.

2. Preheat all grates of a charcoal or gas grill to high.

   If using a separate cooker for the slow cook and smoke, preheat an indirect barbecue with a drip pan and hardwood (preferably hickory, oak, or pecan), or a ceramic cooker with deflector plate and hardwood (preferably hickory, oak, or pecan) to 400°F.

3. Tear off 16 squares of heavy-duty aluminum foil, large enough to wrap the shanks.

   Combine all of the seasoning blend ingredients and season the shanks on all sides.

   Using your hands or a brush, evenly, but lightly, coat the shanks with olive oil.

   Place 5 garlic cloves, 2 marjoram sprigs, and 1 thyme sprig in the center of a foil square. Top with a shank and add 2 tablespoons of water. Wrap completely in the foil to seal. Wrap in a second sheet of foil. Repeat with the remaining shanks.

4. Place the wrapped shanks on the high grate and cook, with the lid closed, turning once halfway through, for 1 hour.

5. If continuing to cook in the charcoal or gas grill, add a box or packet with hardwood (preferably hickory, oak, or pecan), and adjust the temperature to 400°F, leaving one area off for the indirect cooking of the shanks.

   If using a separate indirect cooker for the slow cook, transfer the shanks, still wrapped, to that cooker. If continuing on the grill, transfer to the indirect area. Cook for 1 hour.

6. Meanwhile, place all of the glaze ingredients in a jar with a tight-fitting lid and shake to combine.

7. Remove the shanks from the cooker, carefully unwrap, and place back over direct high heat. Turn to crisp on all sides, brushing with butter using the herb bundle throughout the cooking, about 20 minutes.

   Give the glaze a quick shake to reincorporate any ingredients that may have settled and, using the same herb brush, brush the shanks on all sides with the glaze. Cook to tighten the glaze for about 10 minutes.

8. Drizzle the olive oil and the lemon juice on the board. Sprinkle with the chives, mint, and fleur de sel. Place the shanks on the board and let rest for 15 minutes.

9. Slice the meat into 1/4-inch slices, dredging them in the dressing. Sprinkle with additional fleur de sel, to taste.

LAMB KEBABS

These are all about quick-cooked, charred goodness. I mix a bunch of fresh garlic, oregano, and marjoram into hunks of meat from the shoulder or leg, and then skewer them. Then it's on to a blazing-hot grill (gas is great for this—charcoal's even better). This kicks butt as a snack and becomes a whole meal with some rice pilaf or grilled polenta.

Seasoning Blend
1 cup extra virgin olive oil
10 garlic cloves, peeled, halved, germ removed, and grated on a Microplane grater
3 tablespoons fresh marjoram leaves
3 tablespoons fresh thyme leaves
1 tablespoon dried oregano, preferably Mexican
1 tabespoon mild chile powder, preferably Chimayo (see Sources page 378), Ancho, or Hatch
1 tablespoon garlic salt
1 tablespoon coarsely ground fresh black pepper
Two .18-ounce packets Goya Sazón Azafrán (see Note)
2 teaspoons cayenne pepper

3 pounds of lamb, cut in 1½-inch pieces, preferably from the shoulder or leg
4 large sweet onions

Basting Butter
8 tablespoons (4 ounces) unsalted butter
¼ cup finely chopped flat-leaf parsley
4 garlic cloves, peeled, halved, germ removed, and grated on a Microplane grater

1 tablespoon freshly squeezed lemon juice

Glaze
½ cup freshly squeezed lemon juice
¼ cup water
¼ cup granulated sugar
1 tablespoon coarsely chopped fresh thyme leaves
1 tablespoon coarsely chopped fresh marjoram leaves
1 tablespoon serrano, Thai bird, or other small, hot chile of choice, thinly sliced

½ bunch thyme and ½ bunch rosemary, tied in an Herb Bundle (page 365)

¼ cup extra virgin olive oil
2 tablespoons coarsely chopped flat-leaf parsley
Fleur de sel
Coarsely ground fresh black pepper

NOTE: Goya Sazón Azafrán contains MSG. If you want to avoid it, substitute a combination of ¾ teaspoon each chili powder, cumin, garlic salt, and turmeric. The lamb will not have quite the punch or color as it would with the Sazón.

1. Combine the seasoning blend ingredients.

   Place the lamb in an extra-large resealable plastic bag (or divide between two large bags). Add the seasoning blend and roll to coat the meat evenly. Squeeze out any excess air from the bag and close. Refrigerate for at least 1 hour and up to 4.
2. Cover 8 long wooden skewers with water and let soak for 1 hour (or plan on using metal skewers).
3. Preheat one grate of a well-oiled charcoal or gas grill to high and another to medium.
4. Cut the onion into quarters and then cut each quarter, crosswise, into 2 or 3 pieces, depending on the size of the onion, to make 1½-inch pieces (about the same size as the lamb pieces).

   Put all of the basting butter ingredients in a small saucepan, and stir to combine as the butter melts.

   Place all of the glaze ingredients in a jar with a tight-fitting lid and shake to combine, being sure that the sugar has completely dissolved.
5. Assemble the kebabs by alternating between meat and onion on the skewers, leaving about 2 inches at each end.
6. Place the kebabs on the high grate and do not move the kebabs until they are well marked and lightly charred, about 3 minutes. Brush with the butter using the herb brush—just enough to moisten the meat.

(Excessive butter can cause flare-ups, so throughout the cooking, flip, jockey, and stack as needed to allow for char, but do not let the meat burn. Pay particular attention to the skewers if using wooden ones. If they begin to burn, move them so that the wood is over indirect heat or extending outside of the cooker.)

Turn and continue to grill until the meat is well marked and lightly charred, basting lightly with each turn on each of the remaining 3 sides, grilling for about 3 minutes on each side without moving.

Move the kebabs to the medium grate. Give the glaze a quick shake to reincorporate any ingredients that may have settled and brush the kebabs on all sides using the same herb bundle. Grill to tighten the glaze, for about 2 minutes.

7. Remove the kebabs from the grill and brush lightly on all sides with the butter using the herb brush. Place on a serving platter. Stir the oil and the parsley together and drizzle over the meat. Season with fleur de sel and pepper.

LAMB T-BONES WITH LEMON, MINT, AND OREGANO

This is one of those best-of-both-worlds cuts—you get the silky, yielding texture of the tenderloin and the toothsome meatiness of the loin back. All I do to make it shine is add an herb-packed rub that includes (believe me, you'll love this) dried mint. Some basting butter and a good squeeze of lemon at the end makes this one a real winner.

TIP: For this dish, the thickness of the lamb T-bones is more important than the weight. Make sure they're about, but no less than, 1¼ inches thick.

Seasoning Blend

2 tablespoons dried mint
2 tablespoons granulated sugar
1 tablespoon coarsely ground fresh black pepper
1 tablespoon kosher salt
1 teaspoon fresh thyme leaves
1 teaspoon dried oregano, preferably Mexican

Basting Butter

16 tablespoons (8 ounces) unsalted butter
1 small, or half a large, shallot, peeled, and grated on a Microplane grater
2 garlic cloves, peeled, halved, germ removed, and grated on a Microplane grater
1 teaspoon crushed hot red pepper flakes

1 bunch thyme, tied in an Herb Bundle (page 365)

Eight 1¼-inch-thick lamb T-bones, about 5 ounces each (see Note)
About ½ cup canola or vegetable oil

Juice of ½ lemon
2 lemons, halved and seeds removed
¼ cup extra virgin olive oil
3 tablespoons coarsely chopped flat-leaf parsley
Fleur de sel
Finely ground fresh black pepper

1. Preheat all grates of a well-oiled charcoal or gas grill to medium.

2. Combine all the seasoning blend ingredients in a small food processor or coffee grinder that has been designated for spices and pulse until the mint leaves are completely broken down and the mixture is well combined.

   Put all of the basting butter ingredients in a small saucepan, and stir to combine as the butter melts.

   Season the lamb chops on all sides with the blend.

   Using your hands or a brush, evenly, but lightly, coat the chops with canola oil.

3. It is preferable that the chops be moved to a clean area of the grate every time they are flipped.

   Place the chops on the grill, close the lid, and do not move the chops until they are well marked and lightly charred, about 2 minutes. Flip, brush with the butter using the herb bundle, close the lid, and repeat on the second side, grilling for about 2 minutes.

   Flip again and continue to cook with the lid down, opening occasionally to brush the chops with the butter and lemon juice using the herb bundle during the last minute of cooking. Flipping, jockeying, and stacking as needed, cook 3 minutes per side for medium rare, 4 minutes per side for medium, 5 minutes per side for medium well, and 7 to 8 minutes per side for well-done.

4. Remove the chops from the heat, brush again with butter, and squeeze the lemon halves over the top. Stir the olive oil and the parsley together and drizzle over the meat. Season with fleur de sel and black pepper.

MARINATED BONELESS LAMB LOIN WITH GRATED JALAPEÑO AND MARJORAM

SERVES 8

You are probably familiar with the boneless beef loin, but the lamb version is also a truly great cut, with beautiful marbling, a wonderful tender texture, and a thickness that makes it real fun to cook. You get this mean crust, which looks even more gorgeous after a last-minute, honey-vinegar glaze.

Marinade

1 teaspoon crushed hot red pepper flakes
1 tablespoon boiling water
2 cups canola or vegetable oil
1 cup white wine vinegar
¼ cup finely chopped shallots
8 garlic cloves, peeled, halved, germ removed, and grated on a Microplane grater
2 tablespoons fresh thyme leaves
2 tablespoons prepared yellow mustard
1 tablespoon granulated sugar
1 tablespoon dried oregano, preferably Mexican
1 tablespoon garlic salt
1 tablespoon lemon pepper

3 boneless lamb top loins, about 16 ounces each, any fat trimmed to about ⅛ inch

Seasoning Blend

¼ cup mild chile powder, preferably Chimayo (see Sources page 378), Ancho, or Hatch
2 tablespoons sweet paprika
2 tablespoons firmly packed dark brown sugar
1½ teaspoons dry mustard
¾ teaspoon garlic salt
¾ teaspoon coarsely ground fresh black pepper
¾ teaspoon kosher salt
½ teaspoon Old Bay Seasoning (see Sources page 378)

Basting Butter

8 tablespoons (4 ounces) unsalted butter

6 garlic cloves, peeled, halved, germ removed, and grated on a Microplane grater

Glaze

½ cup honey, preferably orange blossom

¼ cup red wine vinegar

Juice of 1 lemon

2 tablespoons flat-leaf parsley leaves

1 tablespoon fresh thyme leaves

1 tablespoon fresh marjoram leaves

Zest of half of a lemon, grated on a Microplane grater

¼ jalapeño chile, grated on a Microplane grater, stopping short of the seeds

¼ to ½ cup canola or vegetable oil

½ bunch rosemary and ½ bunch thyme, tied in an Herb Bundle (page 365)

Finishing Dressing

¼ cup of extra virgin olive oil

Juice of 1 lemon

Fleur de sel

1. Place the pepper flakes in a small bowl and pour the boiling water over them. Let sit for 1 to 2 minutes to rehydrate the flakes. Combine all of the remaining marinade ingredients in a blender, or in a bowl using an immersion/stick blender. Stir in the pepper flakes and the soaking water.

   Place the lamb loins in an extra-large resealable bag (or divide between two large bags). Pour over the marinade, squeeze out any excess air from the bag, and close. Refrigerate for at least 2 hours and up to 4.

2. Preheat one grate of a well-oiled charcoal or gas grill to medium-high and another to medium-low.

3. Combine the seasoning blend ingredients.

   Put the butter and garlic in a small saucepan and place over medium heat, stirring to combine as the butter melts.

   Place all of the glaze ingredients except the lemon zest and the jalapeño in a jar with a tight-fitting lid and shake to combine.

4. Remove the lamb from the bag and lightly pat dry with paper towels.

   Season the meat on all sides with the seasoning blend.

   Using your hands or a brush, evenly, but lightly, coat the loins with canola oil.

5. Place the loins on the grate, fat side down, and keeping the lid open, cook without moving them until well marked and lightly charred, about 3 minutes. Flip to the second side, brush with the butter using the herb bundle, and repeat on the second side, grilling, with the lid open, for about 3 minutes.

   Meanwhile, give the jar a quick shake to reincorporate any ingredients that may have settled.

   Move the loins to the medium-low area of the grill. Brush with the butter using the herb bundle throughout, flipping, jockeying, and stacking as needed. Brush with the glaze during the last minute of cooking. Cook about 3 minutes on each side for rare, about 5 minutes on each side for medium, about 7 minutes on each side for medium well, and about 9 minutes on each side for well-done.

6. Drizzle some of the remaining glaze on the cutting board. Add the reserved lemon zest and jalapeño. Drizzle over the oil and the lemon juice, and sprinkle with fleur de sel. Top with the chops and let rest for 5 minutes.

7. Slice the meat straight down into 1-inch slices. Season with additional fleur de sel.

BONELESS BUTTERFLIED LEG OF LAMB

SERVES 8

This recipe is a nice break: little work, big results. You can buy the leg already butterflied, although it's pretty easy to do yourself. You marinate it in red wine vinegar, thyme, shallots, a lot of garlic, and go to sleep. The next day, when you're ready to cook, you rub on a seasoning blend and toss it on the grill. Because the big, honking leg has been transformed into a thin, even piece of meat, it cooks quickly and evenly, and there's even more exterior to become crispy and caramelized when it's kissed by those flames.

One 5-pound boneless leg of lamb

Marinade
2 cups extra virgin olive oil
½ cup red wine vinegar
1½ teaspoons fresh rosemary leaves
1 tablespoon granulated sugar
30 garlic cloves, peeled, halved, and germ removed
5 medium shallots, peeled and thinly sliced
2 teaspoons fresh thyme leaves

Seasoning Blend
¼ cup mild chile powder, preferably Chimayo (see Sources page 378), Ancho, or Hatch
2 tablespoons garlic salt
2 tablespoons coarsely ground fresh black pepper
1 teaspoon ground cumin
1 teaspoon cayenne pepper

Glaze
½ cup honey
2 tablespoons red wine vinegar
¼ cup coarsely chopped flat-leaf parsley

½ cup extra virgin olive oil
1 lemon, cut in half and seeds removed
Fleur de sel
Finely ground fresh black pepper

1. Before you begin preparations, make room in your refrigerator for a half sheet pan.
2. Butterfly the lamb (see Note page 221).
3. Unroll a piece of cheesecloth that is about 3 feet long. Look at the number of layers of cloth; usually there are four. If there are less than four, unroll more cheesecloth and fold over so you have a 3-foot piece with four layers.

   Cut the 3-foot piece of cheesecloth from the roll, unwrap completely to a single layer, then fold into a double layer that is about 16 inches by 3 feet.

   Keeping all of the lamb in a single layer, flattening with your hands as needed, place it on one side of the cheesecloth. Fold the cheesecloth over to cover the lamb.
4. Combine all of the marinade ingredients in a food processor, blender, or in a large bowl using an immersion/stick blender. Blend until completely smooth.

   Pour half of the marinade onto a half sheet pan and spread in an even layer. Position the wrapped lamb on the marinade and then pour the remaining marinade over the top. Cover the sheet pan tightly with plastic wrap or aluminum foil. Place 2 firebricks (Sources page 378) wrapped in heavy-duty aluminum foil on the lamb to weigh it down. Refrigerate for at least 6 hours, or up to 24.
5. Preheat one grate of a well-oiled charcoal or gas grill to medium and leave another off for indirect heat. Depending on the size of your grill, you may need to turn all burners to medium for the initial grilling and then turn the heat off under part of an area for finishing.
6. Combine the seasoning blend ingredients.

   Place the glaze ingredients in a jar with a tight-fitting lid and shake to combine.

7. Lift off the bricks, and remove the lamb from the pan.

   Peel off the cheesecloth, and lift out the lamb, letting any excess marinade remain in the pan.

   Transfer the lamb to a clean sheet pan, or other work surface, and rub all sides with the seasoning blend.
8. Place the meat, fat side down, on the medium area of the grate, top with 2 firebricks wrapped in clean, heavy-duty aluminum foil, and cook until nicely charred, 10 to 15 minutes. Remove the bricks, flip to the second side, top with the bricks again, and grill until nicely charred, 10 to 15 minutes.

   Give the glaze a quick shake to reincorporate any ingredients that may have settled, and brush the lamb on the top side with the glaze.

   Keep the meat moving between the medium and the indirect grates. Do not be afraid of flame, but flip, jockey, and stack as needed.

   After 2 to 3 minutes flip and brush the second side with the glaze. Continue to cook, moving between medium and indirect heat, until the meat is nicely caramelized on all sides, 2 to 3 minutes more. At this point the meat should be medium rare in the center. Cook for slightly longer, 6 to 8 minutes for well-done, if desired.
9. Drizzle the olive oil on a large cutting board and squeeze lemon juice over the top. Sprinkle the fleur de sel and pepper over the mixture. Place the lamb on the board and let rest for 10 minutes.
10. Divide the lamb into more manageable pieces and then slicing against the grain, cut ¼-inch slices from each. Season with additional fleur de sel to taste.

NOTE: STEP-BY-STEP FOR BUTTERFLYING LAMB

When butterflying the leg, the goal is to finish with one large piece of meat that is even in thickness, about $1^1/2$ inches.

Here is how to do it: Lay the leg on a large work surface. Trim the exterior of any excess fat or sinew, leaving a $^1/8$- to $^1/4$-inch layer of fat.

You will notice that there are two distinct sections of the leg: A larger portion and a smaller one. Turn the leg of lamb so that the larger portion is closest to you. In the center of this section, you'll notice a large area of fat. Inside this fat is a flat, gray, semi-hard object (a lymph node). Remove this by slicing around it and discard.

Keep the blade of the knife parallel to the work surface and slice through the meat, as you gently and gradually peel back the meat with the other hand. Continue to cut and unfold, but stop short of the end. Keep the end intact and press slightly so that the meat lays flat and opens like a book. Remove any large pieces of fat or sinew from the newly exposed surface.

Repeat with the smaller section, continuing to cut and peel back as needed until you have the desired $1^1/2$-inch-thick piece.

MOROCCAN-SPICED HONEY LAMB SHANKS

SERVES 6

Some barbecue chefs say spices like turmeric, nutmeg, and cinnamon shouldn't come in contact with smoke. But I'm crazy about these staples of Moroccan cooking, so of course I couldn't help but try rubbing them on lamb shanks that I was about to barbecue. And guess what? The result was stunning. It proves that going against the pack can pay off—big-time. As long as you're laying on only a little smoke, the tender, luscious meat takes on an exotic flavor, not an off-putting one. And the turmeric adds to the wicked color of the bark.

Seasoning Blend
1 tablespoon ground allspice
1 tablespoon freshly grated nutmeg
1 tablespoon ground cinnamon
1 tablespoon ground cardamom
1 tablespoon ground ginger
1 tablespoon turmeric
1 tablespoon finely ground fresh black pepper
1 tablespoon kosher salt

8 whole lamb shanks, about 1 pound each
Water, in a spray bottle

Pan Ingredients
12 tablespoons (6 ounces) unsalted butter, cut into chunks
3/4 cup honey
3/4 cup finely chopped sweet white onion
12 unpeeled garlic cloves, crushed
1 1/2 cups dark raisins
4 cups water
1 tablespoon kosher salt

1/2 cup sliced almonds
1 cup dark raisins
1/2 cup coarsely chopped flat-leaf parsley

1. Combine the seasoning blend ingredients.

   Spray the lamb shanks with water. Place in an extra-large resealable plastic bag (or divide between two large bags). Pour over the seasoning blend, squeeze out any excess air from the bag, and close. Roll the bag to evenly coat all of the meat. Refrigerate for at least 2 hours, but preferably up to 12.

2. Preheat an indirect barbecue with a drip pan and fruitwood (preferably apple), a ceramic cooker with deflector plate and fruitwood (preferably apple), or a charcoal or gas grill with a box or packet of fruitwood (preferably apple) to 325°F.

3. Divide the butter and scatter in the bottom of two baking dishes or disposable aluminum pans, preferably 13½ × 9⅝ × 2¾-inch lasagna pans. Divide the honey, onion, garlic, raisins, and water between the two pans. Sprinkle the salt evenly over the tops of the mixtures.

   Arrange 4 shanks in each pan. They should be in an even layer, but it is OK if they are touching.

   Cover the tops tightly with heavy-duty aluminum foil, crimping the edges to seal.

   Place in the cooker, stacking the pans if needed, rotating the pans from top to bottom halfway through cooking, and cook for 3½ hours.

4. Carefully remove the covered pans from the cooker and let the shanks rest, still covered, for 30 minutes.

5. Meanwhile, spread the almonds on a double sheet of heavy-duty aluminum foil and place in the cooker to toast until golden, 5 to 7 minutes. Set the nuts aside.

6. Line a sheet pan with a double layer of heavy-duty aluminum foil.

   Remove the shanks from the pans and place on the foil. Cover, tented, with another piece of aluminum foil.

7. Strain all of the juices and solids from the pan through a fine-mesh strainer set over a liquid measuring cup. Discard the solids. Allow the fat to come to the top in the measuring cup, pour off, and discard. Pour the liquid into one baking dish or disposable pan that will hold the shanks. Add the raisins and the shanks to the pan with the juices.

8. Place the pan in the hottest part of the cooker to plump the raisins and to thicken the pan juices. If using a ceramic cooker, carefully remove the cooking grate and place on the deflector plate.

   Cook until the liquid has reduced to a syrupy consistency, about 30 minutes.

9. Remove the pan from the heat.

   Arrange the shanks on a serving platter. Spoon the pan liquid over the shanks and around the platter. Sprinkle the parsley and toasted almonds over the top.

RACK OF LAMB CRUSTED WITH GRAIN MUSTARD AND CHILI POWDER

SERVES 8

Barbecue's fundamental purpose has always been turning cheap cuts of meat like shoulder and brisket into something profoundly delicious. But that doesn't mean regal cuts don't belong in the smoker. In fact, the magic of smoke can work wonders for expensive cuts. Rack of lamb is a fancy one, for sure, so you might decide to reserve this dish only for celebratory occasions. Or you may be so taken with it that it becomes a more common luxury. I cooked countless racks during my days (and nights) in French kitchens and one thing I've learned is that I prefer to cook them slower than most people do, so the meat stays rosy pink from just beneath the crust to the center. For the crust I pack on plenty of chili powder, tangy mustard, and salt to spark each bite.

4 racks of lamb, not frenched, about 1½ pounds each

Seasoning Blend
¼ cup chili powder
2 tablespoons sweet paprika
2 tablespoons firmly packed dark brown sugar
¾ teaspoon garlic salt
¾ teaspoon coarsely ground fresh black pepper
¾ teaspoon kosher salt
½ teaspoon cayenne pepper

Mustard Moisturizer
½ cup whole-grain mustard

¼ cup water
1 tablespoon Worcestershire sauce
1 tablespoon thyme leaves

About ¼ cup canola or vegetable oil
Fleur de sel

Herb Dressing
⅔ cup extra virgin olive oil
2 tablespoons freshly squeezed lemon juice
½ cup finely chopped flat-leaf parsley
¼ cup finely chopped chives
¼ cup fresh marjoram leaves
1 teaspoon finely chopped lemon zest
1 teaspoon kosher salt

1. Preheat an indirect barbecue with a drip pan and fruitwood (preferably apple), a ceramic cooker with deflector plate and fruitwood (preferably apple), or a charcoal or gas grill with a box or packet of fruitwood (preferably apple) to 250°F.

2. Using a paring knife, make a straight cut between each of the bones, starting from the top of the rack where the bones are exposed and cutting down to just before the top of the meat.

   Combine the seasoning blend ingredients.

   Combine the mustard moisturizer ingredients.

   Stir the seasoning blend into the moisturizer and then rub on all sides of the meat.

   Using your hands or a brush, evenly, but lightly, coat the racks with canola oil.

   Insert a remote thermometer into the center of one of the racks.

3. Place the racks, fat side down, in the cooker.

   Cook to desired doneness; for rare (120°F) about 30 minutes, for medium rare (125°F) about 35 minutes, for medium (130°F) about 40 minutes, for medium well (140°F) about 50 minutes, and well-done (150°F) about 1 hour.

4. Meanwhile, place all of the dressing ingredients in a jar with a tight-fitting lid and shake to combine.

5. Remove the racks from the cooker and let rest for 15 minutes.

   At this point, the racks can be dressed and served (skip the next step of charring), they can be charred, or they can rest for up to 1 hour before charring.

   If charring, remove the deflector plate of the ceramic cooker or preheat a well-oiled charcoal or gas grill to medium-high.

6. To char the racks, place the racks on the grate, fat side down, and cook without moving them, with the lid open, until well marked and lightly charred, about 2 minutes. Flip, and with the lid open, repeat on the second side, grilling for about 2 minutes.

7. Give the dressing a quick shake to reincorporate any ingredients that may have settled. Drizzle some of the dressing on a cutting board. Top with the racks and let rest for 10 minutes.

8. Cut the lamb into individual chops and dredge in the dressing on the board. Sprinkle with fleur de sel and serve.

SIX-HOUR LEG OF LAMB "MECHOUI"

SERVES 8

When I visited Morocco as a chef, my first item of business was lamb, specifically the Moroccan specialty called *mechoui*, which is slowly cooked until it's tender enough to be cut with a plate. Not only do I love slow-cooked lamb—it's hard not to—but I'm blown away by the spice blends used in Morocco. With all the fusion cuisine happening nowadays, it's rare to find flavors that really epitomize a particular country. But when you taste this lamb, you'll just know it's Moroccan. And after it gets a good dose of indirect heat, man, will you love it!

TIP: Ask the butcher to remove the aitchbone. Otherwise, carving will be more of a challenge.

One 7- to 7½-pound leg of lamb, trimmed of any excess fat and sinew, aitchbone removed
10 garlic cloves, peeled, cut into thirds, and germ removed

Seasoning Blend
2 tablespoons mild chile powder, preferably Chimayo (see Sources page 378), Ancho, or Hatch
¾ teaspoon ground allspice
¾ teaspoon freshly grated nutmeg
¾ teaspoon ground cinnamon
¾ teaspoon ground ginger
¾ teaspoon turmeric
¾ teaspoon ground cumin
¾ teaspoon crushed hot red pepper flakes
¾ teaspoon finely ground fresh black pepper

¾ teaspoon kosher salt

¼ to ½ cup water
½ cup Apple Juice Spray (page 364)

Wrapping Mixture
2 tablespoons (1 ounce) unsalted butter or margarine, melted
½ cup honey
1 cup water

1 cup dried apricots, cut in ½-inch slices
¾ cup freshly squeezed orange juice

Preserve Blend
½ cup apricot preserves
1 tablespoon lemon juice

½ cup extra virgin olive oil
¼ cup coarsely chopped flat-leaf parsley
Fleur de sel
Coarsely ground fresh ground black pepper

1. Using the point of a paring knife, make 30 incisions, each about 1 inch deep, the width of a paring knife, and about 2 inches apart from each other, on the surface of the lamb. Insert the pieces of garlic.

   Combine the seasoning blend ingredients.

   Moisten the lamb with water and rub the seasoning blend into the meat, being sure to work it into the incisions. Wrap in plastic wrap and refrigerate for at least 2 hours, but preferably overnight.

2. Preheat an indirect barbecue with a drip pan and hardwood (preferably hickory, pecan, or oak), a ceramic cooker with deflector plate and hardwood (preferably hickory, pecan, or oak), or a charcoal or gas grill with a box or packet of hardwood (preferably hickory, pecan, or oak) to 250°F.

3. Unwrap the meat from the plastic and place in the cooker. Cook for 4 hours, spraying with the apple juice spray on the hour at 2, 3, and 4 hours.

4. Meanwhile, combine the wrapping mixture ingredients.

   Lay out a double sheet of heavy-duty aluminum foil large enough to wrap the lamb.

5. Remove the lamb from the cooker.

   Transfer the lamb to the center of the foil, cover with the wrapping mixture, and securely wrap in the foil.

   Place back in the cooker for 1 hour.

6. Remove the lamb from the cooker. Let rest, still wrapped, for 30 minutes.

7. Meanwhile, lay two sheets of heavy-duty aluminum foil, each about 8 inches square, on top of each other, and fold up the sides, creating a bowl shape with a rounded base. Put the apricots and orange juice in the bowl. Gather the sides of the foil bowl, bringing them together to create a rounded packet.

8. Carefully unwrap the lamb.

   Stir together the preserves and lemon juice. Reserve half for the cutting board. Brush over the entire surface area of the lamb with the other half.

   Place the apricot packet in the hottest part of the cooker. If using a ceramic cooker, carefully lift the cooking grate and place on the deflector plate. Replace the grate.

   Place the lamb back in the cooker on the grate. Cook for 30 minutes.

9. Brush half of the reserved preserve blend on a cutting board, drizzle on the olive oil, and sprinkle with the parsley. Top with the lamb. Remove the apricot packet from the meat and set aside. Spray the lamb with the apple juice spray and let rest for 10 minutes.

10. Slice the lamb, against the grain, into ¼-inch slices, dredging to coat in the blend and adding additional preserve blend as needed. Season with fleur de sel and pepper, and arrange the apricots over the board. Serve directly from the board.

LAMB BLADE CHOPS WITH SLIVERED GARLIC AND MARJORAM

SERVES 8

Remember when I showed you how to make unbelievably quick pulled pork by using blade chops instead of the whole shoulder (page 82)? The same goes for lamb, though I add a special rub, an herb dressing, and some honey—don't even get me started on how amazing honey tastes with lamb—that go perfectly with the, well, lambiness of the meltingly tender meat. Tuck a mound of this into a soft, grilled pita or serve it over jasmine rice.

Seasoning Blend
¼ cup sweet paprika
¼ cup firmly packed dark brown sugar
1½ teaspoons garlic salt
1½ teaspoons dried oregano, preferably
    Mexican
1½ teaspoons coarsely ground fresh black
    pepper
1½ teaspoons kosher salt

Eight ¾- to 1-inch-thick lamb blade chops
    (see Note)

Wrapping Mixture
8 tablespoons (4 ounces) unsalted butter or
    margarine, melted
½ cup honey
10 garlic cloves, peeled, halved, germ
    removed, and very thinly sliced
2 tablespoons fresh marjoram leaves

Herb Dressing
6 tablespoons finely chopped flat-leaf parsley
¼ cup finely chopped chives
1 serrano or other small hot chile of choice,
    thinly sliced and seeds removed (optional)
1 lemon
½ cup extra virgin olive oil

Fleur de sel
8 pieces pita bread, warmed

NOTE: Blade chops are cut from the lamb shoulder and include a piece of the bone.

1. Preheat an indirect barbecue with a drip pan and hardwood (preferably hickory, pecan, or oak), a ceramic cooker with deflector plate and hardwood (preferably hickory, pecan, or oak), or a charcoal or gas grill with a box or packet of hardwood (preferably hickory, pecan, or oak) to 275°F.

2. In a small bowl, combine the seasoning blend ingredients and sprinkle on all sides of the chops.

3. Place the chops in the cooker and cook for 1½ hours.

4. Meanwhile, combine the wrapping mixture ingredients. Pour into a baking dish or disposable aluminum pan, preferably a 13½ × 9⅝ × 2¾-inch lasagna pan.

   Lay out 4 double layers of heavy-duty aluminum foil, each large enough to wrap 2 chops in.

5. Remove the chops from the cooker, toss in the wrapping mixture, and wrap, 2 chops per packet, in a double layer of foil.

   Place back in the cooker for 1½ hours.

6. Remove and let rest, still wrapped, for 30 minutes.

7. Carefully unwrap the chops over a disposable pan, reserving the juices.

   Pour the reserved cooking juices through a fine-mesh strainer into a large liquid measuring cup. Discard any solids. Allow the fat to come to the top, pour off, and discard.

   Place the chops back in the cooker for 40 minutes, basting halfway through with the defatted liquid.

8. Meanwhile, for the herb dressing, combine the parsley, chives, and chile, if using, in a small bowl. Using a Microplane grater, zest the lemon over the top, squeeze in the juice, and mix in the oil.

9. Serve the chops whole, or shred the meat.

   If serving whole, arrange on a serving platter and spoon the dressing over the top. If serving shredded, drizzle some dressing on the board, shred the meat, and dredge in the dressing as the meat is being shredded.

   Sprinkle with fleur de sel and serve inside the pita bread.

LEG OF LAMB—
BONED, ROLLED, AND TIED

SERVES 8

Bless the butcher. He kindly removes the big bone from a leg of lamb, rolls it up, and tidily ties it for you. With the heavy lifting taken care of, you and I just have to add some flavor. So I unroll it and stuff a ton of delicious stuff inside, and then try to package it as nicely as he did.

One 4½-pound boneless leg of lamb, trimmed of any excess fat or sinew

Internal Roast Seasoning
½ cup extra virgin olive oil
¼ cup thinly sliced garlic
¼ cup flat-leaf parsley leaves
2 tablespoons fresh marjoram leaves
1 tablespoon fresh thyme leaves
1 tablespoon dried oregano, preferably Mexican
1 tablespoon dry mustard
1 tablespoon mild chile powder, preferably Chimayo (see Sources page 378), Ancho, or Hatch
1 tablespoon coarsely ground fresh black pepper
1 tablespoon kosher salt
1 teaspoon crushed hot red pepper flakes

Flavor Paste
¼ cup Dijon mustard
¼ cup firmly packed dark brown sugar
¼ cup canola or vegetable oil
2 tablespoons water
2 tablespoons sweet paprika
2 tablespoons chili powder
1 tablespoon garlic salt
1 tablespoon dried oregano, preferably Mexican

Glaze
½ cup honey, preferably orange blossom
¼ cup red wine vinegar
Juice of 1 lemon
2 tablespoons flat-leaf parsley leaves
1 tablespoon fresh thyme leaves
1 tablespoon fresh marjoram leaves

Finishing Dressing
About ¼ cup extra virgin olive oil
1 lemon, halved and seeds removed
Fleur de sel

1. Preheat an indirect barbecue with a drip pan and hardwood (preferably hickory, oak, or pecan), a ceramic cooker with deflector plate and hardwood (preferably hickory, oak, or pecan), or a charcoal or gas grill with a box or packet of hardwood (preferably hickory, oak, or pecan) to 250°F.

2. Open the leg of lamb and place the internal side, facing up, on a sheet pan.

   Combine all of the internal roast seasoning ingredients in a large resealable plastic bag. Squeeze to remove any excess air from the bag, close the top, and, using a dowel or wine bottle, roll over the contents of the bag about 10 times.

   Pour the blend on the internal side of the leg of lamb.

   Roll up the roast and tie with kitchen twine at 2-inch intervals up the roast, folding in the sides as needed to keep in the seasoning ingredients. You may need to run a piece of kitchen twine down the length of the roast and tie to secure.

   Combine all of the flavor paste ingredients in a blender, or in a bowl, using an immersion/stick blender.

   Coat the exterior of the roast with the paste.

   Place all of the glaze ingredients in a jar with a tight-fitting lid and shake to combine. Set aside.

   Insert a remote thermometer into the thickest part of the meat.

3. Place the lamb in the cooker. Finishing times will vary depending on preferred degree of doneness. In order to have the meat perfectly glazed on the outside and just how you like it on the inside, give the glaze a quick shake and then glaze when the internal temperature is 10 degrees less than your preferred doneness (see below).

   For rare, glaze the meat when the internal temperature reaches 110°F. Total cooking time for rare (120°F) is about 2 hours.

   For medium rare, glaze the meat when the internal temperature reaches 115°F. Total cooking time for medium rare (125°F) is about 2 hours and 15 minutes.

   For medium, glaze the meat when the internal temperature reaches 120°F. Total cooking time for medium (130°F) is about 2 hours and 30 minutes.

   For medium well, glaze the meat when the internal temperature reaches 130°F. Total cooking time for medium well (140°F) is about 3 hours.

   For well-done, glaze the meat when the internal temperature reaches 140°F. Total cooking time for well-done (150°F) is about 3 hours and 30 minutes.

4. Drizzle olive oil on a cutting board, squeeze the lemon over the top, and sprinkle with fleur de sel. Place the lamb on the board and let rest for 15 minutes.

5. Remove the twine and slice the lamb into ¼-inch slices. Dredge the slices in the dressing, and arrange on a serving platter.

HERB STUDDED CRACKED LAMB SHORT LOIN

SERVES 8

It's happened to everyone who spends a ton of time cooking outdoors. A buddy shows up with some six-packs and a cut of meat you've never cooked before. That's how I felt when a major haul of cracked loin fell into my lap. I thought, What am I going to do with these? So I started tinkering, and came up with a killer method: The cut is almost like a roast, so I treat it like one. First, though, I jam fresh thyme in the cracks to add a kiss of herbaceousness.

TIP: You might have to ask the butcher for this cut. Tell him it's the loin and the tenderloin still attached to the bone that's been cut through at $1\frac{1}{2}$- to 2-inch intervals.

Marinade
$\frac{1}{4}$ cup finely chopped shallots
8 garlic cloves, peeled, halved, germ removed, and grated on a Microplane grater
2 tablespoons prepared yellow mustard
2 tablespoons fresh thyme leaves
2 tablespoons dried oregano, preferably Mexican
1 tablespoon garlic salt
1 tablespoon lemon pepper
1 tablespoon firmly packed dark brown sugar
1 teaspoon crushed hot red pepper flakes
1 cup white wine vinegar
2 cups canola or vegetable oil

2 lamb short loins, cut through the bone at $1\frac{1}{2}$- to 2-inch intervals, each loin about 10 inches long and $2\frac{3}{4}$ pounds

Seasoning Blend
$\frac{1}{4}$ cup mild chile powder, preferably Chi-

mayo (see Sources page 378), Ancho, or Hatch
2 tablespoons sweet paprika
2 tablespoons firmly packed dark brown sugar
1 tablespoon garlic salt
1 tablespoon chili powder
$1\frac{1}{2}$ teaspoons lemon pepper
$1\frac{1}{2}$ teaspoons dry mustard
$\frac{3}{4}$ teaspoon coarsely ground fresh black pepper

Glaze
$\frac{1}{4}$ cup red wine vinegar
2 garlic cloves, peeled, halved, germ removed, and grated on a Microplane grater
2 teaspoons crushed hot red pepper flakes
$\frac{1}{2}$ cup honey

$\frac{1}{2}$ cup canola or vegetable oil
About 16 thyme sprigs

Finishing Dressing
$\frac{1}{2}$ cup extra virgin olive oil
3 tablespoons freshly squeezed lemon juice
3 tablespoons finely chopped chives
Fleur de sel
Coarsely ground fresh black pepper

1. Place the shallots, garlic, mustard, thyme, oregano, garlic salt, lemon pepper, sugar, pepper flakes, and vinegar in the blender or in a large bowl and let sit for 10 minutes to allow the flavors to develop.

   Blend to combine in the blender, or in a bowl using an immersion/stick blender. Slowly add the oil and blend until thoroughly combined.

   Place the lamb in an extra-large resealable plastic bag (or divide between two large bags) and pour over the marinade. Squeeze out any excess air from the bag, seal to close, and refrigerate for at least 1 hour and up to 2.

2. Preheat an indirect barbecue with a drip pan and hardwood (preferably hickory, oak, or pecan), a ceramic cooker with deflector plate and hardwood (preferably hickory, oak, or pecan), or a charcoal or gas grill with a box or packet of hardwood (preferably hickory, oak, or pecan) to 300°F.

3. Combine all of the seasoning blend ingredients.

   Combine the vinegar, garlic, and pepper flakes for the glaze in a jar with a tight-fitting lid and let sit for 10 minutes to allow the flavors to develop.

   Add the honey to the jar and shake to combine. Set aside.

4. Remove the short loins from the marinade and lightly pat dry with paper towels.

   Sprinkle the seasoning blend over the entire roast, outside and inside areas.

   Using your hands or a brush, evenly, but lightly, coat the roast with canola oil.

   Place a few thyme sprigs into each crack in the bone.

   Insert a remote thermometer into the thickest part of the loin (as opposed to the thickest part of the tenderloin).

5. Place the short loins in the cooker, bone side down. Finishing times will vary depending on the preferred degree of doneness. In order to have the meat perfectly glazed on the outside and just how you like it on the inside, give the glaze a quick shake and then glaze when the internal temperature is 10 degrees less than your preferred doneness (see below).

   For rare, glaze the meat when the internal temperature reaches 110°F. Total cooking time for rare (120°F) is about 1 hour.

   For medium rare, glaze the meat when the internal temperature reaches 115°F. Total cooking time for medium rare (125°F) is about 1 hour and 5 minutes.

   For medium, glaze the meat when the internal temperature reaches 120°F. Total cooking time for medium (130°F) is about 1 hour and 10 minutes.

   For medium well, glaze the meat when the internal temperature reaches 130°F. Total cooking time for medium well (140°F) is about 1 hour and 30 minutes.

   For well-done, glaze the meat when the internal temperature reaches 140°F. Total cooking time for well-done (150°F) is about 1 hour and 45 minutes.

6. Drizzle olive oil on a cutting board. Pour the lemon juice over the top and sprinkle on the chives, fleur de sel, and pepper. Place the lamb on the board and let rest for 10 minutes.

7. Cut through the meat where the cracks in the bones are for individual chops and dredge in the dressing. Season with additional fleur de sel and pepper.

SPIT-ROASTED SPRING LAMB

SERVES 10 TO 15 PEOPLE

Cooking like this is rare nowadays. Sure, it takes serious time and a couple of items you won't come across at your local supermarket. But when you're manning the spit (see Sources page 378) with friends gathered around, laying on a sweet-and-sour glaze and cranking up the heat to crisp the skin, you'll be so glad you made the effort.

SPECIAL ITEMS TO PURCHASE:

Spit (see Sources page 378)
About 60 pounds brick charcoal
Fire Starters
Rake

Large ash can
Fireproof gloves
Fire extinguisher

One 20- to 30-pound spring lamb

Basting Butter
4 pounds unsalted butter
1 sweet white onion, coarsely chopped
5 heads of garlic, cut in half horizontally
6 thyme sprigs
4 sage sprigs
2 rosemary sprigs

Seasoning Blend
1/2 cup mild chile powder, preferably Chimayo (see Sources page 378), Ancho, or Hatch
1/2 cup sweet paprika
1/4 cup garlic salt
1/4 cup light brown sugar
1/4 cup dried oregano, preferably Mexican
2 tablespoons turmeric
2 tablespoons finely ground fresh black pepper
1 teaspoon cayenne pepper
1 cup water

Herb Bundle
1 bunch thyme
1 bunch sage
1 bunch marjoram
1 bunch rosemary

Glaze
1 cup honey
Juice of 1 lemon
1 tablespoon red wine vinegar
1/4 cup coarsely chopped flat-leaf parsley
2 tablespoons fresh marjoram leaves
4 garlic cloves, peeled and grated on a Microplane grater

About 1/4 cup kosher salt
About 1/4 cup finely ground fresh black pepper
About 1 cup canola or vegetable oil

1. Set up your spit.
2. If it has not been done by the butcher, remove the head, any internal organs, and cut off the shanks (bottom of the legs), stopping 2 inches before the thicker leg and shoulder muscles.

   Position the lamb on the spit according to the manufacturer's instructions.
3. Combine all of the basting butter ingredients in a baking dish or disposable pan and place under the lamb on the spit to catch any drippings.

   Combine the seasoning blend ingredients.

   Tie together all of the herbs using kitchen twine and attach to a dowel, about 3 feet long and ½ inch in diameter.

   Place all of the glaze ingredients in a jar with a tight-fitting lid and shake to combine. Set aside.

   If the skin of the lamb is dry, moisten it with water, using your hands. Season generously with salt and pepper. Then, again using your hands, coat generously with canola oil.
4. Spread about 18 pounds of charcoal approximately 2½ feet away from, but parallel to, the lamb. The coals should be in a mound next to the lamb.

   Using anything but lighter fluid, light the coals.
5. To know that the coals are properly placed to cook the lamb, watch the lamb. The skin should begin to sweat very lightly and start to render fat. If the sweating or rendering is too aggressive, using a rake, move the coals about 6 inches away from the lamb. Conversely, if the lamb is not sweating, use the rake to move the pile closer to the lamb.
6. During the cooking time, you will be adding about 9 pounds of coals per hour, but the time frame will vary based on weather conditions. Coals should be added when the charcoal is almost completely ashed over and is not letting off as much heat. Do not wait too long to add new coals.
7. After 1 hour, with your hands, smear the seasoning blend over the meat, covering all areas as best you can.

   After smearing with the blend, brush with the butter, using the herb bundle, every 30 minutes.

   Cook the lamb until the internal temperature in the thickest part of the shoulder is 170°F, about 4 hours. (Calculate the appoximate cooking time from the time the coals are hot and positioned correctly next to the lamb.)

   Brush with the glaze, using the herb brush, and continue to cook for 30 minutes to tighten the glaze.
8. Cut the meat directly from the spit and serve. Or give knives to all of your guests.

MOROCCAN LAMB STEW

Sometimes, when I tell people I cook stew on the barbecue, they look at me a little funny. Isn't the barbecue for, well, barbecue? they ask. Sure, but it also brings awesome smoke flavor to this lamb stew, which is already an ambrosial pot of melting lamb goodness thanks to lots of Moroccan spices and slow, steady heat.

Seasoning Blend
2 tablespoons ground allspice
2 tablespoons freshly grated nutmeg
2 tablespoons ground cinnamon
2 tablespoons ground cardamom
2 tablespoons ground ginger
2 tablespoons turmeric
2 tablespoons finely ground fresh black
    pepper
2 tablespoons kosher salt

½ cup firmly packed dark brown sugar

4 pounds of lamb, preferably from the
    shoulder or leg, cut in 1½-inch pieces

Pan Ingredients
16 tablespoons (8 ounces) unsalted butter
6 cups thinly sliced sweet white onion
10 unpeeled garlic cloves, crushed
1 cup honey
1 cup low-sodium chicken broth
¼ cup roughly chopped flat-leaf parsley
2 tablespoons fresh thyme leaves
2 tablespoons fresh marjoram leaves

1 cup cilantro leaves
½ cup roughly chopped flat-leaf parsley
2 lemons, halved and seeds removed
Fleur de sel
Coarsely ground fresh black pepper
8 pieces flat bread or pocketless pita bread,
    warmed
8 lemon wedges, seeds removed

1. Preheat an indirect barbecue with a drip pan and hardwood (preferably hickory, oak, or pecan), a ceramic cooker with deflector plate and hardwood (preferably hickory, oak, or pecan), or a charcoal or gas grill with a box or packet of hardwood (preferably hickory, oak, or pecan) to 225°F.

2. Combine all of the seasoning blend ingredients, followed by the sugar, in an extra-large resealable plastic bag (or divide between two large bags). Add the lamb and toss to coat. Refrigerate for 2 hours, or up to 4.

3. Arrange the lamb on a sheet pan or in a baking dish that will hold the pieces in a single layer.

   Place in the cooker for 1 hour.

4. Transfer the meat to a pot, small roasting pan, or deep baking dish with high sides that can take a direct flame (if necessary the ingredients can be split between two pans, stacked, and rotated halfway through the cooking). Add all of the pan ingredients and stir to combine. Top with a tight-fitting lid or with heavy-duty aluminum foil, crimping tightly to seal.

   Place the pan(s) in the cooker and cook until the meat is fork-tender, about 3 hours.

5. Remove the pan(s) from the cooker and let cool slightly, about 10 minutes.

   Skim off any fat from the surface and stir in the cilantro and parsley. Squeeze in the lemon juice, and season with fleur de sel and pepper to taste.

6. Transfer to a large serving bowl, or serve directly from the pan with flatbread and lemon wedges on the side.

SMOKED LAMB GYRO

This hyperseasoned crowd-pleaser is my take on the Middle Eastern classic, which once marked the end of every great late night when I was in school. If the word "gyro" suggests something too complicated for you, just think of it as lamb meatloaf. I add tons of flavor by smoking it. You can eat it right out of the barbecue, or do like I do: Wait until the next day, slice it, and char each piece over on the grill.

TIP: If ground lamb from the shoulder or leg is not available at the store, ask the butcher to grind it for you, or do it at home. Run the meat through the grinder once using the larger die and then a second time using the smaller die.

Extra virgin olive oil

Gyro Meatloaf
3/4 cup Fresh Bread Crumbs (page 367)
1 1/2 tablespoons plus a pinch of kosher salt
3/4 cup water
1 medium sweet white onion, peeled
3 tablespoons finely chopped garlic
1 1/2 tablespoons dried oregano, preferably Mexican

2 1/2 teaspoons fresh rosemary
2 1/2 teaspoons finely ground fresh black pepper
3 pounds ground lamb from the shoulder or leg
1/3 cup coarsely chopped flat-leaf parsley
Sliced garlic
Flat-leaf parsley leaves
About 4 tablespoons (2 ounces) unsalted butter
8 pieces of flatbread or pocketless pita bread, warmed on the grill
1 recipe Yogurt Sauce (page 369)
1/2 cup thinly sliced red onion
1 recipe Marinated Tomatoes (page 349)
1 cup crumbled feta cheese

1. Preheat an indirect barbecue with a drip pan and hardwood (preferably hickory, oak, or pecan), a ceramic cooker with deflector plate and hardwood (preferably hickory, oak, or pecan), or a charcoal or gas grill with a box or packet of hardwood (preferably hickory, oak, or pecan) to 325°F.

2. Oil a meatloaf pan (see Sources page 378) or standard loaf pan, about 9 × 5 × 3 inches, with olive oil. (A meatloaf pan isn't essential, but it does prevent the meatloaf from sitting and cooking in residual fat.)

3. Place the bread crumbs, tossed with a pinch of salt, in a large bowl. Add the water and let stand.

4. Grate the onion on a box grater. Place in a clean dish towel and squeeze over the sink to extract the juices.

    Place the onion, garlic, oregano, rosemary, remaining 1½ tablespooons of the salt, and pepper in the bowl of a food processor. Pulse to combine. Add the lamb, one-third at a time so as not to overwork the machine, and process to form a smooth paste, stopping as necessary to scrape down the sides to ensure even mixing. Depending on the size of your food processor, this may need to be done in batches.

    If you don't have a food processor, mix by hand. The flavor will still be great, but the texture will not be as smooth.

5. Transfer the meat mixture to the large bowl with the soaked bread crumbs. Top with the chopped parsley. Using your hands, fold the meat into the soaked bread crumbs along with the parsley.

Spoon the mixture into the prepared loaf pan, mounding slightly. Using the back of a chef's knife, score the top in a crosshatch pattern.

Place the loaf pan in the center of a baking dish or disposable baking pan or on a small sheet pan and insert a remote thermometer into the center of the loaf.

6. Place the meatloaf in the cooker and cook until the internal temperature registers 150°F, 1 hour and 15 minutes to 1 hour and 30 minutes.

7. Remove the loaf pan from the cooker and, if not using a meatloaf pan, carefully pour off any residual liquid.

    Brush the top with olive oil.

8. If eating right away, let cool to warm and slice. Serve as is, or grill to char (see below). The meatloaf can also be refrigerated, then sliced the next day and grilled to char.

    If charring, place a griddle over one area of a well-oiled charcoal or gas grill and preheat to high.

    Once the meat has cooled, slice it into ½-inch slices. For every slice of meatloaf, thinly slice 1 garlic clove and have on hand 6 parsley leaves. Melt 2 tablespoons of the butter on the griddle. Arrange the slices on the griddle and brown on both sides, about 2 minutes per side, adding additional butter as needed. Toward the end of the browning, add the garlic and parsley to the griddle to soften the garlic and wilt the parsley slightly. Top the slices with the garlic and parsley.

    Serve with pita, yogurt sauce, onion, marinated tomatoes, and crumbled feta.

Bacon-Wrapped Skinless Drumsticks with Sage and Garlic (page 271)

CHICKEN
AND
TURKEY

WHAT IS CHICKEN?

The lid goes up and I pull out a whole chicken, the crackling skin mottled with golds and caramelized browns, the flesh juicy and bursting with the flavors of garlic and thyme. It's all here—the luscious leg and thigh meat, the chewy-crispy wings, and the delicate breast meat. This is what comes to mind when I think of chicken cooked outdoors, at least until my mind drifts to flash-grilled breasts with gorgeous grill marks or drumsticks slightly sticky from a sweet-tart glaze.

In other words, I'm really into chicken (and turkey, for that matter). I love its mild flavor, which lets you treat it as a canvas for the flavors you're craving that night. Spices and sauces might complement beef, pork, and lamb, but I like to think that chicken complements whatever you add to it. I especially love how Asian ingredients, like soy sauce, chiles, and ginger, make the meat shine, though I also often tend to layer on the same sorts of flavors that go well with pork—sweet-tart fruit preserves, honey, apple cider vinegar . . . My mouth's already watering!

But for me, chicken is as much about distinct texture as it is about flavor. And to get perfectly succulent meat, you have to recognize that cooking chicken is a whole different ball game from cooking beef. On the whole, it's made up of a higher proportion of protein and water relative to fat. Take a look at a piece, even a relatively fatty one like the thigh, and you won't see any of the marbling you do on even the lean filet mignon. Most likely, all you'll notice is a bit of external fat, which won't assist you in your quest for tasty, juicy chicken. Have no fear: As usual, each of my recipes is geared to perfecting the cut in question—from boneless, skinless breasts to skin-on thighs. So not only will each one give you a stunning, I-gotta-make-this-again dish, but it'll also help guide you

when you decide to take on the cut using your own favorite glaze, sauce, or spice blend.

AIR-CHILLED

Most chicken that shows up on the shelves has been what's called water-chilled. That is, it's been plunged into a giant cold water bath (unfortunately, there's often chlorine in there, too) to bring it down to a safe temperature. The problem is that the meat absorbs some of that water, diluting the wonderful chicken flavor. "Chicken flavor?" you ask. "Chicken tastes pretty mild to me." Just wait until you try air-chilled chicken. This chicken is chilled by cold air instead of water, which might not sound revolutionary but makes a big difference. The meat is still mild in that lovely way chicken is, but it has so much more character. A few large companies have added air-chilled birds to their repertoire (see Sources page 378), so it's no longer as difficult to find. It's more expensive, sure, but not only do you get more flavorful meat and better texture, you get the satisfaction of not paying for water.

FREE RANGE

The term "free-range" is bandied about a lot, but it's no assurance of high quality or a cruelty-free life. So you must ask a lot of questions when you're buying chicken—do some research, or visit a farmers' market, where you can speak directly with the people who actually raise the chickens.

THE DARK AND THE LIGHT

Just as beef has its rib eye and its brisket, the meat on a chicken can't be treated as just one thing. Keeping a whole bird juicy presents a different challenge than, say, making perfectly luscious thighs or making sure boneless, skinless breasts come out like heaven, not like cardboard. That's because different parts of the chicken have different amounts of connective tissue and fat. Dark meat has more than light meat (and therefore can achieve a deeper, richer flavor and more succulent texture), so as you might guess, you have to treat the two differently when you're cooking. For example, thighs (a dark meat lover's dream) can stand up to higher heat and longer cooking than their lighter counterparts. My Competition Thighs (page 279), for example, take just over two hours and emerge from the barbecue unbelievably tender and moist. Try that same method with the much leaner protein of the breast, on the other hand, and you get something dry and chewy. So how to treat the breasts? I cook them relatively quickly, but because they are so lean, I rarely use the very high heat I might use for steaks. A nice brine will keep them moist, add flavor, and enhance grill marks while a glaze adds extra protection against excessive moisture loss.

SKIN AND BONES

Everywhere you look, you see boneless and skinless chicken. And although I'm perfectly happy cooking it—add a brine, a marinade, or a coat of bacon (a great skin stand-in), and you can have a juicy, flavorful dish—I do love what the bone and the skin offer the cook. Both help keep the meat juicy, and the skin can give you that crunchy-as-a-potato-chip texture.

Crispy, caramelized skin is not always my goal—My Competition Thighs feature skin that's terrifically tender, not crackling—but when it is, here's how I get it:

- Make sure you dry the skin thoroughly with paper towels before you cook.
- Direct, relatively high heat is key to rendering the fat and repelling any moisture so the skin can crisp.
- Finishing with butter helps make skin even more golden and delicious.

SELECTION

SIZE MATTERS. Chickens come in different sizes. Here's a rundown of what you'll typically see.

Poisson (baby chickens) weigh about a pound
Fryers weigh about 2.5 pounds
Broilers weigh about 3.5 to 4 pounds
Roasters weigh about 7 to 9 pounds

BANG FOR YOUR BUCK. I've found that when you move from a 2.5-pound chicken to one around 3.5 pounds, you get a similarly sized frame but more meat. So if you're looking for a meaty bird, a chicken at the higher end of that range will be a better value.

CHICKEN LABELS OFTEN SPECIFY WHETHER THE MEAT HAS BEEN FROZEN OR NOT. I prefer fresh, but chicken is more tolerant to freezing than, say, pork. Note that bones that look especially dark or purplish near the joint suggest that the chicken has been frozen.

THE FRESHER THE BETTER. Look at the sell-by date and ask the butcher if there's fresher chicken available that he hasn't yet put in the meat case.

TRUST YOUR SENSES. Look for chicken that's pretty firm to the touch and avoid any that feels too soft. Avoid chicken that looks excessively wet or has excessive liquid in the package. A little fat on the surface of skinless meat is inevitable. You can just trim it off.

WHERE TO SHOP. To find air-chilled or antibiotic-free chickens, and birds raised on organic feed, try your local gourmet market or butcher shop. For birds raised on small farms, your best bet is your local farmers' market.

PINEAPPLE-AND-APRICOT– GLAZED, BONELESS, SKINLESS CHICKEN BREASTS

SERVES 8

Bring on the flavor! Boneless, skinless chicken breasts are an outdoor staple, but they rarely come out right: They're either too bland or dried out. Not in my hands. To do justice to this popular but mild-mannered cut, I brine it and then whip up a glaze with pineapple and apricot preserves, which is all sweet and tangy and gives the chicken this wicked color. Soy and ginger give it a bit of an edge, and all is right in the boneless, skinless world.

Brine

6 cups water

3 tablespoons kosher salt

2 tablespoons granulated sugar

2 tablespoons honey

1½ teaspoons Japanese soy sauce

3 thyme sprigs

4 garlic cloves, peeled and crushed

1 seranno or other small, hot chile of choice, grated on a Microplane grater, stopping before the seeds

8 large boneless, skinless chicken breasts, tender removed and trimmed of any excess fat, 7 to 8 ounces each

Glaze

½ cup APL BBQ Sauce (page 362), or your favorite BBQ sauce

½ cup water

½ cup pineapple preserves

¼ cup apricot preserves

¼ cup honey

1 tablespoon Japanese soy sauce

1 tablespoon grated fresh ginger

2 garlic cloves, peeled, halved, germ removed, and grated on a Microplane grater

¼ cup chopped scallions, white and green portions

3 tablespoons black sesame seeds

1 tablespoon finely ground fresh black pepper

¼ to ½ cup canola or vegetable oil

Fleur de sel

1. In a large bowl, combine all of the brine ingredients, whisking to dissolve the salt and sugar.

   Place the chicken in an extra-large resealable plastic bag (or divide between two large bags). Pour over the brine, squeeze out any excess air from the bag, and close. Refrigerate for at least 3 hours, or up to 6 hours.

2. Preheat one grate of a well-oiled charcoal or gas grill to medium-high, leaving another off for indirect cooking.

3. Place the BBQ sauce, water, both preserves, honey, soy sauce, ginger, garlic, 2 tablespoons of the scallions, and 1 tablespoon of the sesame seeds in a jar with a tight-fitting lid. Shake to combine. Pour into a disposable aluminum pan, preferably a 13½ × 9⅝ × 2¾-inch lasagna pan.

4. Remove the breasts from the brine and lightly pat dry with paper towels.

   Season the breasts on both sides with the pepper, and using your hands or a brush, evenly, but lightly, coat with canola oil.

5. Place the chicken breasts, presentation side (rounded, top side of the breast) down, on the medium-high grate, keeping the lid open, and do not move the breasts until they are well marked and have a light char, about 4 minutes. Flip, and keeping the lid open, repeat on the second side, grilling for about 4 minutes. Return to the presentation side and grill for 4 minutes. Then, flip a final time and grill for 4 minutes, for a total of 16 minutes of grilling.

6. Dredge each of the breasts in the glaze, coating on all sides.

   Place, presentation side up, on the indirect area of the grate, close the lid, and cook for 8 minutes.

7. Transfer the chicken breasts to a serving platter and top with the remaining 2 tablespoons of the scallions and remaining 2 tablespoons of the sesame seeds. Sprinkle with fleur de sel.

POUNDED BONELESS CHICKEN BREASTS

SERVES 8

Here's another antidote to the typically blah boneless, skinless preparations: Pound them and make cutlets. That way, they'll cook quickly and stay juicy. Plus pounding gives you a lot of surface area (an opportunity to add lots of spices and herbs). If you crank up the heat and resist the temptation to move the cutlets around a lot, you'll end up with enviable grill marks. Serve these with a salad that's not shy, like one with peppery arugula (see page 348) or a wedge of iceberg topped with plenty of my Blue Cheese Dressing (see page 368).

Seasoning Blend
1½ tablespoons garlic salt
1½ tablespoons thyme salt (see Note)
1½ tablespoons freshly ground black pepper
1½ tablespoons dried oregano, preferably
   Mexican
1½ tablespoons crushed hot red pepper
   flakes (optional)
¾ cup canola or vegetable oil

8 whole boneless, skinless chicken breasts,
   tender removed and trimmed of any
   excess fat, 7 to 8 ounces each
1 recipe Herb Sauce (page 371)

Finishing Dressing
¼ cup extra virgin olive oil
1 tablespoon freshly squeezed lemon juice
¼ cup finely chopped chives

4 lemons, halved and seeds removed

NOTE: To make thyme salt, combine ½ cup kosher salt with 1 tablespoon fresh thyme leaves in a spice mill or coffee grinder dedicated to spices. Blend until you have a uniform powder. Store in an airtight container at room temperature.

1. Preheat all grates of a well-oiled charcoal or gas grill to high.
2. Combine the garlic salt, thyme salt, black pepper, oregano, pepper flakes, if using, and canola oil and pour into a disposable aluminum pan, preferably a $13\frac{1}{2} \times 9\frac{5}{8} \times 2\frac{3}{4}$-inch lasagna pan.
3. To butterfly each chicken breast, place on the work surface and look at the thickness of the meat. Make an incision midway through the breast and parallel to the work surface on one of the longer sides of the breast. Continue to slice through the breast along that longer side and then on the two shorter sides, stopping just short of the other long side. Open up the breast like a book.

   Place the breasts into the seasoning blend as they are each butterflied, dredging to coat evenly on all sides.
4. Working with one breast at a time, place between two sheets of plastic wrap, and using a meat tenderizer/pounder (see Sources page 378) pound to about $\frac{1}{8}$-inch thick. Repeat with additional plastic wrap and the remaining chicken breasts.
5. Peel off the top layer of plastic wrap from each of the chicken breasts. Then one at a time, slap directly onto the grate, immediately removing the remaining plastic wrap.

   If you notice the breasts curling slightly around the edges, or want to intensify the char, use a grill press(es) or a firebrick(s) (see Sources page 378) wrapped in heavy-duty aluminum foil to weigh them down.

   Grill the chicken breasts, with the lid open, without moving them, until well marked and lightly charred, about 4 minutes. Flip, and keeping the lid open, repeat on the second side, grilling for about 4 minutes.
6. Meanwhile, spread the Herb Sauce on a serving platter or on individual plates.
7. Remove the chicken breasts from the grill and place on the herb sauce.

   Combine the olive oil, lemon juice, and chives, and drizzle over the top.

   Serve with the lemon halves for squeezing over the top, and additional sauce on the side.

STICKY DRUMSTICKS

This is one of those dishes that smell so insanely good while you're cooking that your friends will start getting giddy and crowding around you, asking again and again, "Are they done yet?" I know the feeling well. My dad lives in Thailand, and when he takes me to the markets, these are the aromas that waft all around me: the sharp smell of chiles, the fresh punches of basil, browning chicken, and garlic—so much garlic. It takes control of me, and I think, "I have to eat—now!" That's the feeling I have re-created here by combining bright flavors and using the grill to intensify them. This dish is the perfect starter, and one of the best ways there is to treat underused, underappreciated drumsticks.

Marinade

9 tablespoons fish sauce
6 tablespoons freshly squeezed lime juice
6 tablespoons freshly squeezed orange juice
6 tablespoons granulated sugar
3 tablespoons Japanese soy sauce
3 tablespoons chile paste, preferably Sriracha or sambal
9 garlic cloves, peeled and crushed

16 chicken drumsticks
4 tablespoons (2 ounces) unsalted butter
1/4 cup water
16 basil leaves, preferably Thai basil

Glaze

12 garlic cloves, peeled, halved, germ removed, and grated on a Microplane grater
6 tablespoons toasted sesame oil
3 tablespoons soy sauce
3 tablespoons fish sauce

6 tablespoons lightly packed dark brown sugar
6 tablespoons mirin
6 tablespoons apricot preserves
1 medium jalapeño chile, thinly sliced
1 1/2 tablespoons chile paste, preferably Sriracha or sambal

15 basil leaves, preferably Thai basil, cut into 1/4-inch chiffonade (see Note)
Coarsely ground fresh black pepper

NOTE: To chiffonade the basil, stack the leaves and roll as tightly as possible into a cylinder. Cut across the roll so that when unrolled, the basil will be in thin, ribbon-like strips.

1. Combine all of the marinade ingredients in a medium bowl.

    Place the drumsticks in an extra-large resealable plastic bag (or divide between two large). Pour over the marinade, squeeze out any excess from the bag, and close. Refrigerate for at least 1 hour, or up to 8.

2. Position two heavy-duty aluminum foil–wrapped firebricks (see Sources, page 378) on one area of the grate, and preheat all areas to medium-high.

3. Lightly butter the bottom of two baking dishes or two disposable aluminum pans (using 2 tablespoons in each), preferably 13½ × 9⅝ × 2¾-inch lasagna pans, then divide the water between the two pans.

4. Remove the drumsticks from the marinade letting any excess run off and remain in the bag.

    Place the drumsticks in the prepared pans, skin side down. The drumsticks will be touching, but should be in an even layer in the pan.

    Lightly bruise the basil leaves using the back of a chef's knife and arrange evenly across the drumsticks. Cover the tops of the pans with heavy-duty aluminum foil and crimp to seal.

5. Stack the pans on the bricks, close the lid, and cook, rotating the pans from top to bottom once halfway through cooking. Cook for 20 minutes.

6. Meanwhile, place all of the glaze ingredients in a jar with a tight-fitting lid and shake to combine.

7. Remove the pans from the grill.

    Carefully, because the steam can burn, peel back the foil. Turn all of the drumsticks over. Cover the pan and seal. Place back on the bricks, close the lid, and cook, rotating the pans once halfway through cooking, for 20 minutes.

8. Remove the pans from the grill.

    Arrange an even layer of paper towels on a sheet pan or work surface. Place the drumsticks on the towels, turning to dry on all sides. At this point the drumsticks should rest for at least 15 minutes, up to 2 hours, or can be cooled and refrigerated for up to 1 day.

9. When ready to finish, give the glaze ingredients a quick shake and pour into a baking dish or disposable aluminum pan, preferably a 13½ × 9⅝ × 2¾-inch lasagna pan.

    Dredge the drumsticks in the glaze and place on the grate, flipping, jockeying, stacking, reglazing, and turning occasionally until all sides are well marked and lightly charred, about 15 minutes.

    Roll the drumsticks in the glaze a final time and sprinkle with the basil chiffonade and the black pepper.

    At this point the drumsticks can be held on the bricks on low in a covered grill for 30 minutes, or transferred to a serving platter.

GREEN (OR RED) HATCH CHILE BONE-IN CHICKEN BREASTS

SERVES 8

I fell in love with the grassy overtones and vibrant fruity flavor of green Hatch chiles while I was in New Mexico, and this is an awesome way to feature them. Not only does the chicken get this killer greenish hue, but since the chiles aren't all fire, the flavor just explodes. There's no need to brine the chicken, because I cook it slowly and because the skin and the bone help keep it moist during the cooking process.

TIP: You've got to try green Hatch chiles at least once. If you must, use red Hatch or another chile powder like Ancho. The result will be different but no less delicious.

Pan Ingredients
6 tablespoons (3 ounces) unsalted butter
12 unpeeled garlic cloves, crushed
2 tablespoons water

Seasoning Blend
9 tablespoons New Mexican Hatch green
   chile powder (see Sources page 378)
1 tablespoon ground coriander
1 tablespoon dried oregano, preferably
   Mexican
1 tablespoon kosher salt
2 teaspoons finely ground fresh black pepper

8 bone-in, skin-on chicken breasts, trimmed
   of excess skin

Dressing
1/4 cup extra virgin olive oil
2 tablespoons freshly squeezed lemon juice
2 tablespoons coarsely chopped flat-leaf
   parsley
Kosher salt
Finely ground fresh black pepper

1. Preheat an indirect barbecue with a drip pan and hardwood or fruitwood (preferably hickory or apple), a ceramic cooker with deflector plate and hardwood or fruitwood (preferably hickory or apple), or a charcoal or gas grill with a box or packet of hardwood or fruitwood (preferably hickory or apple) to 325°F.

2. In two disposable aluminum pans, preferably 13½ × 95/8 × 23/4-inch lasagna pans, that will hold the breasts in a single layer, spread the butter (3 tablespoons in each) in the bottom. Divide the garlic and the water between the two pans.

   Combine 5 tablespoons of the chile powder with the rest of the seasoning blend ingredients.

   Sprinkle the seasoning blend generously on all sides of the chicken, and place the chicken, skin side down, in the pans. Cover with heavy-duty aluminum foil, and crimp the top to seal.

3. Place the chicken in the cooker, stacking the pans if needed, and rotating halfway through the cooking. Cook for 45 minutes.

4. Remove the pans from the cooker, peel back the foil, and turn the chicken over to be skin side up. Rotate the pans, baste the chicken with the pan juices, and return to the cooker for 25 minutes.

5. Meanwhile preheat all grates of a well-oiled charcoal or gas grill to medium-high. (Or, if using a ceramic cooker, remove the deflector plate when ready to direct grill.)

6. Remove the chicken from the pans and place, skin side up, on a sheet pan. Sprinkle the remaining 4 tablespoons of the chile powder evenly on the skin side of the breasts.

   Strain all of the juices from the pans through a fine-mesh strainer set over a measuring cup. Discard any solids. Allow the fat to come to the top, pour off, and discard.

   Stir the oil, lemon juice, and parsley into the pan juices, and season to taste with salt and pepper.

   Spoon the seasoned pan sauce onto a platter.

7. Grill the breasts, skin side down, with the lid open, until well marked and lightly charred, about 3 minutes. Flip, and repeat on the other side, grilling for about 3 minutes.

   Place the chicken on top of the sauce on the platter.

CHICKEN TENDER SATAY

SERVES 8

It's hard to think of a better appetizer to pass around before a big meal. I cook these skewers just like street vendors do in Southeast Asia, using big flavors to add spark to the mild tenders, and grilling the skewers quickly with high heat so the lean meat stays juicy. Lime juice, fish sauce, and the char brought by the grill go a long way toward re-creating the street food feeling.

Marinade

½ cup water

2 tablespoons fish sauce

2 tablespoons Japanese soy sauce

2 tablespoons firmly packed light brown sugar

2 tablespoons freshly squeezed lime juice

2 tablespoons toasted sesame oil

3 medium shallots peeled and grated on a Microplane grater, about 2 tablespoons

1 tablespoon grated fresh ginger

6 garlic cloves, peeled, halved, germ removed, and grated on a Microplane grater

1 serrano, or other small, hot chile of choice, grated on a Microplane grater, stopping before the seeds

24 chicken tenders

Glaze

Juice of 2 limes

¼ cup firmly packed light brown sugar

2 garlic cloves, peeled, halved, germ removed, and grated on a Microplane grater

About 1 tablespoon toasted sesame oil

15 basil leaves, preferably Thai basil, cut into ¼-inch chiffonade (see Note)

¼ cup thinly sliced scallions, white and green portions

2 tablespoons black sesame seeds, lightly toasted, if desired

¼ cup finely chopped peanuts, lightly toasted, if desired

NOTE: To chiffonade the basil, stack the leaves and roll as tightly as possible into a cylinder. Cut across the roll so that when unrolled, the basil will be in thin, ribbon-like strips.

1. Combine all of the marinade ingredients in a blender, or in a large bowl using an immersion/stick blender.

    Place the tenders in a large resealable plastic bag, pour the marinade over the top, squeeze out any excess air from the bag, and close. Roll the bag to evenly coat all of the tenders in the marinade. Refrigerate for at least 3 hours, or up to 6.

2. Cover 24 long wooden skewers with water and let soak for 1 hour (or plan on using metal skewers).

3. Preheat one grate of a well-oiled charcoal or gas grill to high, leaving another off for indirect cooking.

4. Place the glaze ingredients in a jar with a tight-fitting lid and shake to combine.

5. Keeping the tenders as flat as possible, place each one on a skewer, leaving enough room at one end for turning the skewers.

6. Place the chicken directly over the high grates, keeping the exposed end of the skewer over the indirect portion. Grill for 3 minutes on the first side without moving the skewers. Flip to the second side and grill, without moving, for 3 minutes. Flip, brush with the glaze, and grill for 3 minutes. Flip again, brush with the glaze, and grill for 3 minutes more.

    Turn the skewers to lightly toast the exposed wood portion of the skewers, cooking off any raw chicken residue that may have accumulated, about 1 minute on each side.

7. Remove the skewers from the grill, arrange on a serving platter, drizzle with sesame oil, and sprinkle with basil, scallions, sesame seeds, and peanuts.

ADOBO BONE-IN, SKIN-ON CHICKEN BREAST

SERVES 8

Adobo has different meanings in Mexico and the Philippines, but here it just means flavor. I combine a bunch of ingredients found in both cuisines—don't worry, this ain't fusion, this just makes sense—in a seasoning blend and a brine. After the chicken has picked up all those great grill flavors, I take it off the heat and let it lounge in *escabèche*, a trick you'll see in Spain and Jamaica that I just think of as a vinaigrette for cooked meat.

Brine
12 cups water
6 tablespoons kosher salt
¼ cup granulated sugar
¼ cup honey
1 tablespoon Japanese soy sauce
5 thyme sprigs
7 garlic cloves, peeled and crushed

8 bone-in, skin-on chicken breasts, about 12 ounces each

Seasoning Blend
Two .18-ounce packets Goya Sazón Azafrán (see Sources page 378) (see Note)
1 tablespoon granulated garlic or garlic powder
1 tablespoon coarsely ground fresh black pepper
2 teaspoons crushed hot red pepper flakes

Adobo Spray
½ cup water
¼ cup mirin
¼ cup Japanese soy sauce

About 6 tablespoons canola or vegetable oil

Escabèche
6 tablespoons extra virgin olive oil
¼ cup finely chopped shallots
1½ tablespoons finely diced jalapeño chile, seeds removed
4 garlic cloves, peeled, halved, germ removed, and grated on a Microplane grater
1 bay leaf
1 teaspoon kosher salt
1 teaspoon finely ground fresh black pepper
½ cup rice wine vinegar
2 tablespoons finely chopped cilantro leaves
2 tablespoons finely chopped flat-leaf parsley leaves

Fleur de sel

NOTE: Goya Sazón Azafrán contains MSG. If you want to avoid it, substitute a combination of ¾ teaspoon each chili powder, cumin, garlic salt, and turmeric. The chicken will not have quite the punch or color as it would with the Sazón.

1. In a large bowl, combine all of the brine ingredients, whisking to dissolve the salt and sugar.

   Place the breasts into an extra-large resealable plastic bag (or divide between two large bags). Pour over the brine, squeeze out any excess air from the bag, and close. Refrigerate for at least 3 hours, but preferably up to 24.

2. Preheat all grates of a well-oiled charcoal or gas grill to medium-high.

3. Combine all of the seasoning blend ingredients.

   Combine all of the adobo spray ingredients in a spray bottle.

   Remove the breasts from the brine and lightly pat dry with paper towels.

   Season on all sides with the seasoning blend.

   Using your hands or a brush, evenly, but lightly, coat the breasts with canola oil.

4. Place the chicken on the grill, skin side down, close the lid, and do not move the chicken until it is well marked and lightly charred, 4 to 5 minutes.

   Flip, close the lid, and, keeping the lid closed as much as possible, flip, jockey, stack, and spray aggressively with adobo spray. Cook the breasts for 30 minutes.

5. Transfer the chicken to a platter and let rest while preparing the sauce.

6. To prepare the *escabèche*, pour 2 tablespoons of the oil in a small saucepan and place over medium heat. Add the shallots, jalapeño, garlic, bay leaf, salt, and black pepper. Sauté until the onions are translucent, 3 to 5 minutes.

   Remove from the heat and stir in the remaining ¼ cup of the oil and the rice wine vinegar. Stir in the cilantro and parsley.

   Pour over the chicken on the platter, and sprinkle with fleur de sel.

HONEY-GLAZED SPATCHCOCKED CHICKEN

SERVES 8 TO 10

What an awesome way to cook whole birds on the grill. Spatchcocking chickens—basically butterflying them so they lay flat—lets you give the direct heat to the entire thing. I cook them slowly with bricks on top of the chickens, so the meat stays juicy and the skin becomes crackly crisp. A layer of compound butter and a simple honey glaze provide the final spark.

Two 3½-pound chickens, spatchcocked (see Note)
Kosher salt
Finely ground fresh black pepper
¼ to ½ cup canola or vegetable oil

Glaze
2 tablespoons honey
Juice of 1 lemon
2 tablespoons apple cider vinegar
1 tablespoon coarsely chopped flat-leaf parsley leaves
3 serrano, or other small, hot chiles of choice, thinly sliced and seeds removed (optional)

½ recipe Compound Butter (page 366)
1 bunch thyme, tied in an Herb Bundle (page 365)
Fleur de sel

1. Place the chickens on a sheet pan and season all sides with salt and pepper.

   Using your hands or a brush, evenly, but lightly, coat the chickens with canola oil.

   Refrigerate for 30 minutes.

2. Preheat all grates of a well-oiled charcoal or gas grill to medium.

3. Place the glaze ingredients in a jar with a tight-fitting lid and shake to combine. Set aside.

4. Place the chickens, skin side down, on the grate, and top with a sheet pan, followed by two heavy-duty aluminum foil–wrapped firebricks (see Sources page 378) to weigh down the chickens. Grill until the skin is a medium to rich golden, about 15 minutes. (Alternately, you can eliminate the sheet pan, and place the clean wrapped bricks directly on the chicken, being sure the weight is equally distributed.)

   Carefully lift off the bricks and tray, turn both chickens skin side up, and brush generously with the butter using the herb bundle (but too much at this point could cause a flare-up). Replace the tray and bricks, and grill until the internal temperature registers 165°F in the thigh and 155°F in the breast using an instant-read thermometer, about 8 minutes.

   Remove the bricks and tray, brush the chicken with the butter, and then brush with the glaze using the herb bundle. Continue to cook, flipping, jockeying, and stacking, until the internal temperature registers 175°F in the thigh and 165°F in the breast, 5 to 10 minutes.

5. Spread some of the butter on a cutting board, and then drizzle some of the remaining glaze on top. Remove the chickens from the grill and place on the board. Sprinkle with fleur de sel and black pepper. Let rest for 5 minutes.

6. Cut the chicken into quarters or individual serving pieces (thighs, drumsticks, wings, and half breasts) and transfer to a serving platter.

HOW TO SPATCHCOCK CHICKENS:

Place one of the chickens breast side down. Using poultry shears, cut along one side of the backbone through the ribs. Turn the bird around (for ease of cutting) and repeat on the other side of the backbone. Remove and discard the backbone.

Next, remove the wishbone and the keel bone. Turn the chicken so that the wishbone is facing you. Cut out the wishbone using the poultry shears or by running a boning knife along all sides of it until it loosens and pulls out easily. Once the wishbone is removed, the keel bone is easier to see. (It is a darker bone that runs the length of the cavity.) Using poultry shears or by running a boning knife along it, remove the keel bone and its connecting cartilage.

Turn the chicken breast side up, pushing so that the bird lies flat.

PULLED CHILE CHICKEN LEGS

SERVES 8

My sweet-and-sour chile glaze might be the highlight here if I were brushing it on chicken breasts. But the leg—the thigh plus the drum—has such moist, tasty meat that by the time these come out of the cooker, tinged with smoke, the glaze is just a background player. The meat, pulled into tender strands, is the star. Serve it like you would pulled pork, on a bun with slaw or on a platter surrounded by sides.

Brine

12 cups water

6 tablespoons kosher salt

¼ cup granulated sugar

¼ cup honey

1 tablespoon Japanese soy sauce

5 thyme sprigs

½ head of garlic, about 7 cloves, peeled and crushed

1 serrano, or other small, hot chile of choice, grated on a Microplane grater, stopping before the seeds

8 skinless chicken legs

Seasoning Blend

¼ cup mild chile powder, preferably Chimayo (see Sources page 378), Ancho, or Hatch

2 tablespoons sweet paprika

2 tablespoons firmly packed dark brown sugar

½ tablespoon dry mustard

¾ teaspoon garlic salt

¾ teaspoon coarsely ground fresh black pepper

¾ teaspoon kosher salt

Sweet-and-Sour Chile Glaze

1 cup water

½ cup apple cider vinegar

½ cup granulated sugar

½ cup honey

¼ cup thinly sliced assorted chiles, such as serrano, jalapeño, and Thai Bird

1 garlic clove, peeled, halved, germ removed, and grated on a Microplane grater

1 teaspoon finely ground fresh black pepper

¼ to ½ cup canola or vegetable oil

½ cup Apple Juice Spray (page 364)

Finishing Dressing

½ cup extra virgin olive oil

½ lemon, seeds removed

¼ cup finely chopped chives

Fleur de sel

1. In a large bowl, combine all of the brine ingredients, whisking to dissolve the salt and sugar.

   Place the chicken in an extra-large resealable plastic bag (or divide between two large bags). Pour over the brine, squeeze out any excess air from the bag, and close. Refrigerate for at least 4 hours, but preferably up to 12.

2. Preheat an indirect barbecue with a drip pan and fruitwood (preferably apple), a ceramic cooker with deflector plate and fruitwood (preferably apple), or a charcoal or gas grill with a box or packet of fruitwood (preferably apple) to 300°F.

3. Combine the seasoning blend ingredients.

   Place all of the glaze ingredients in a jar with a tight-fitting lid and shake to combine. Pour into a disposable aluminum pan, preferably a $13\frac{1}{2} \times 9^{5}/8 \times 2^{3}/4$-inch lasagna pan. Set aside.

4. Remove the legs from the brine, letting any excess remain in the bag, and lightly pat dry with paper towels.

   Generously coat the legs with the seasoning blend.

   Using your hands or a brush, evenly, but lightly, coat the legs with canola oil.

5. Place the chicken in the cooker, spraying every 15 minutes with apple juice spray, for a total of 45 minutes.

6. Meanwhile, during the last 20 minutes of cooking, preheat one grate of a well-oiled charcoal or gas grill to medium and leave another off for indirect cooking (or plan on removing and then replacing the deflector plate on a ceramic cooker).

7. Remove the legs from the smoker and place, presentation side (the plumper, outer side) down, on the grate, close the lid, and grill until well marked and lightly charred, about 3 minutes. Flip, close the lid, and repeat on the second side, grilling for about 3 minutes.

   Dip each of the legs in the glaze and dredge to coat on all sides.

   Place, presentation side up, on the indirect area of the grill. Using a slotted spoon, lift out the chiles and mound them on the tops of each of the legs. Cook for 10 minutes more.

8. Drizzle a cutting board with the olive oil, squeeze the lemon over the top, and sprinkle with fleur de sel. Remove the legs from the grill and place on the board.

   Pull the meat off the bones to shred, dredging in the dressing. Transfer to a serving platter.

BACON-WRAPPED SKINLESS DRUMSTICKS WITH SAGE AND GARLIC

SERVES 8

I love chicken skin: Treat it right and it becomes crispy, salty, and irresistible. So when I'm craving this flavor-packed crunch, but I have skinless chicken, I look to bacon. Wrapping it around drumsticks is such an easy way to pump up the flavor and to keep the chicken really moist and juicy. It also it has another cool purpose. It acts as a kind of porky shield, preventing the heat from burning the delicate sage and garlic and helping their woodsy flavors permeate the meat.

TIP: Wrapping in plastic helps the bacon adhere to the drumsticks and intensifies the deliciousness, because it prevents the flavors from going anywhere but into the meat. And no, the plastic won't melt!

Marinade
1/4 cup extra virgin olive oil
1 tablespoon dried oregano, preferably Mexican
1 tablespoon coarsely ground fresh black pepper
1 tablespoon garlic salt
1 tablespoon sweet paprika
1 tablespoon thinly sliced serrano chile, seeds removed (optional)
10 garlic cloves, peeled and thinly sliced
Juice of 2 lemons

16 skinless drumsticks

32 fresh sage leaves
16 slices smoked bacon, not thick-cut
1 cup water

Glaze
1 teaspoon crushed hot red pepper flakes
1 tablespoon boiling water
1/2 cup firmly packed dark brown sugar
Juice of 2 lemons

About 1/4 cup canola or vegetable oil
1/2 bunch thyme and 1/2 bunch sage, tied in an Herb Bundle (page 365)
1/4 cup coarsely chopped parsley
Extra virgin olive oil
Fleur de sel
Finely ground fresh black pepper

1. Combine the marinade ingredients in a large bowl.

   Place the drumsticks in an extra-large resealable plastic bag (or divide between two large bags). Pour over the marinade, squeeze out any excess air from the bag, and close. Refrigerate for at least 2 hours, but preferably up to 24.

2. Preheat an indirect barbecue with a drip pan and fruitwood (preferably apple), a ceramic cooker with deflector plate and fruitwood (preferably apple), or a charcoal or gas grill with a box or packet of fruitwood (preferably apple) to 250°F. If using the charcoal or gas grill, leave one area off for indirect heat.

3. Working with one drumstick at a time, remove from the marinade, and do not wipe off any excess. Place a sage leaf on both sides of the meat.

   Lay the largest portion of the drumstick on the end of one slice of bacon. Wrap the bacon once around the top of the drumstick so that there is a full circle of bacon that won't unravel. Then continue to roll the bacon, keeping it taut, down the length of the meat. At the bottom, carefully tuck the end under to keep the bacon from unraveling.

   Wrap the drumstick in food-safe plastic wrap. Repeat with the remaining drumsticks.

4. Lay all of the drumsticks in a baking dish or pan that will hold them in a single layer without crowding, preferably dividing them between two disposable $13\frac{1}{2} \times 9\frac{5}{8} \times 2\frac{3}{4}$-inch lasagna pans.

   Pour ½ cup of water into each pan, cover the top with heavy-duty aluminum foil, and crimp to seal.

5. Place the drumsticks in the cooker in the indirect area. Depending on the size of the cooker, you may need to stack the pans on top of each other and rotate them from top to bottom halfway through the cooking. Cook for 50 minutes.

6. Remove the pans from the cooker and let the drumsticks rest in the pans, covered, for 30 minutes.

   If grilling right away, preheat one area of the grill to medium-high and leave another off for indirect cooking (or plan on removing and then replacing the deflector plate on a ceramic cooker).

7. Meanwhile, place the pepper flakes in a jar with a tight-fitting lid and pour the boiling water over them. Let sit for 1 to 2 minutes to rehydrate the flakes. Add the remaining glaze ingredients and shake to combine.

8. Carefully remove the drumsticks from the plastic wrap. At this point the drumsticks can be finished, or refrigerated up to 24 hours.

9. Lightly brush the drumsticks with oil and place them, bacon-seam-side down, on the medium-high section of the grill. Do not move them for 2 minutes, or until the bacon is at the desired crispness. Roll a quarter-turn at a time and continue to grill until all of the bacon is at the desired crispness.

   Move the drumsticks to the indirect portion of the grill. Give the glaze a quick shake to reincorporate any ingredients that may have settled, and brush on the chicken using the herb bundle. Close the lid and cook for 3 minutes. Turn to the other side, brush with the glaze, and cook for 3 minutes.

10. Transfer to a serving platter, sprinkle with parsley, drizzle generously with olive oil, and season with fleur de sel and pepper.

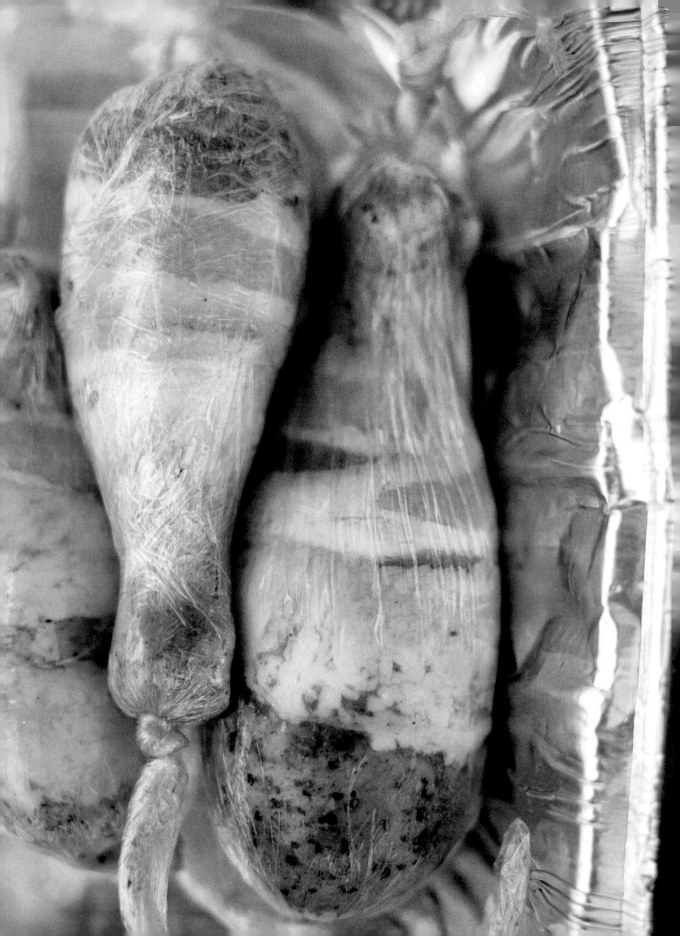

HOT WINGS

Think of every great hot wing you've ever had and say a final goodbye—these Buffalo-style beauties are about to become your go-to wings. I don't change the classic recipe too much—don't you worry, the winning combination of butter and Frank's Red Hot Sauce is here—but I add a chile seasoning blend, some scallions and chives, and even grated garlic and jalapeño. Add some mild wood while you're cooking for yet another layer of flavor.

24 whole, fully intact chicken wings (tips still attached)

Seasoning Blend
1/4 cup mild chile powder, preferably Chimayo (see Sources page 378), Ancho, or Hatch
2 tablespoons sweet paprika
2 tablespoons firmly packed dark brown sugar
1 1/2 teaspoons dry mustard
1 1/2 teaspoons cayenne pepper
3/4 teaspoon garlic salt
3/4 teaspoon coarsely ground fresh black pepper
3/4 teaspoon kosher salt
1/2 teaspoon Old Bay Seasoning (see Sources page 378)

4 tablespoons (2 ounces) unsalted butter
1 cup water

Hot Sauce Blend
1 cup Frank's Red Hot Sauce (see Sources page 378), or other hot sauce
4 tablespoons (2 ounces) unsalted butter cut into 1/4-inch cubes
1/4 cup thinly sliced scallions, white and green portions
1/4 cup finely chopped chives

4 garlic cloves, peeled, halved, germ removed, and grated on a Microplane grater
1 jalapeño chile, grated on a Microplane grater, stopping before the seeds
1 bunch thyme, tied in an Herb Bundle (page 365)
1/4 to 1/2 cup canola or vegetable oil
Kosher salt
Coarsely ground fresh black pepper
1 recipe Blue Cheese Dressing (page 368)

1. Preheat an indirect barbecue with a drip pan and fruitwood (preferably apple), a ceramic cooker with deflector plate and fruitwood (preferably apple), or a charcoal or gas grill with a box or packet of fruitwood (preferably apple) to 350°F.

2. Combine all the ingredients for the seasoning blend.

   Using poultry shears or a chef's knife, cut the tip off the end of each of the wings and discard. Separate the drumette from the wingette by cutting through the joint.

   In two disposable aluminum pans, preferably 13½ × 9⅝ × 2¾-inch lasagna pans that will hold the wings in a single layer, spread the butter (2 tablespoons in each) in the bottom, and divide the water between the pans.

   Place the wings in a large bowl and toss with the seasoning blend to coat evenly on all sides.

   Arrange the wings in an even layer in the two pans. Top each with heavy-duty aluminum foil, and crimp to seal.

3. Place the wings in the cooker, stacking the pans on top of each other, if needed to fit, and rotating them from top to bottom halfway through the cooking. Cook for 45 minutes.

4. Meanwhile, during the last 20 minutes of cooking, if you have not been using a charcoal or gas grill or a ceramic cooker up to this point, preheat your direct cooker to medium-low, adding hardwood (preferably hickory, oak, or pecan) to smoke, if desired.

   Pour the hot sauce into a medium saucepan and bring to a simmer over medium heat. Add the butter and swirl the pan until the butter is completely incorporated. Add the scallions and chives.

Remove from the direct heat, but keep in a warm spot.

5. Transfer the chicken wings to a sheet pan or work surface and lightly pat dry with paper towels.

   Reserve 1 cup of the cooking liquid and combine with the garlic and grated jalapeño.

   Using your hands or a brush, evenly, but lightly, coat the wings with canola oil.

6. Place the wings on the grates and cook until well marked and lightly charred on the first side, about 10 minutes. Flip all of the wings, brushing with the garlic and jalapeño cooking juices using the herb bundle. Cook until the second side is well marked and lightly charred, 5 to 10 minutes. (The reason for the 5 minute variance of time is based on just how long it will take you to flip over all of the wings.)

7. Remove the wings from the cooker and immediately toss in a large bowl with the hot sauce. Season with salt and pepper.

   Transfer to a clean bowl, if desired, and serve with blue cheese dressing on the side.

CHICKEN WINGS WITH COARSELY GROUND SPICES

Here's another wing that'll have you licking your fingers. The magic here comes from the seasoning blend, which is a bit coarser than usual so you get these big pops of flavor. I can think of nothing better to eat while you're outside with a cold beer.

Seasoning Blend

¼ cup mild chile powder, preferably Chimayo (see Sources page 378), Ancho, or Hatch

¼ cup sweet paprika

1 tablespoon dehydrated onion flakes

1 tablespoon dehydrated garlic flakes or dehydrated garlic slivers

1 tablespoon coriander seeds, crushed with the bottom of a pan

1 tablespoon black pepper corns, crushed with the bottom of a pan

1 teaspoon crushed hot red pepper flakes

¼ cup Sugar in the Raw (see Sources page 378), or other turbinado sugar

1 tablespoon dried oregano, preferably Mexican

24 whole, fully intact chicken wings (tips still attached)

BBQ Sauce

1½ cups APL BBQ Sauce (page 362), or your favorite BBQ sauce

¼ cup hot sauce

1 teaspoon Japanese soy sauce

2 tablespoons honey, preferably orange blossom

2 tablespoons apple cider vinegar

1. Preheat an indirect barbecue with a drip pan and a combination of hardwood and fruitwood (preferably hickory and apple), a ceramic cooker with deflector plate and a combination of hardwood and fruitwood (preferably hickory and apple), or a charcoal or gas grill with a box or packet with a combination of hardwood and fruitwood (preferably hickory and apple) to 275°F.

2. Combine all of the seasoning blend ingredients in a large bowl. Add the wings and toss to coat.

Combine the BBQ sauce ingredients and set aside.

3. Place in the cooker and cook for 1 hour and 15 minutes.

4. Remove from the cooker, place in a large bowl, toss with half of the sauce, and place back in the cooker for 25 minutes.

5. Remove from the cooker, toss with the remaining sauce, and place back in the cooker for 25 minutes.

6. Serve immediately.

MY COMPETITION THIGH RECIPE

Barbecue judges wisely take just a bite or two of each entry—otherwise, how could they eat through hundreds of them—so as a competitor, you have to impress them right away, which is why I go all out and hit them with an especially intensely flavored seasoning blend and BBQ sauce. This strategy works just as well in the contest for backyard bragging rights. An added bonus: My method gives you skin that's not only packed with flavor, but is also super tender, meaning a neat piece comes off with each bite of juicy meat.

16 bone-in, skin-on chicken thighs
2 cups bottled Italian salad dressing

Seasoning Blend
3/4 cup mild chile powder, preferably Chimayo (see Sources page 378), Ancho, or Hatch
3/4 cup sweet paprika
1/2 cup Sugar in the Raw (see Sources page 378), or other turbinado sugar
2 tablespoons garlic salt
2 teaspoons dried oregano, preferably Mexican
2 teaspoons Old Bay Seasoning (see Sources page 378)

Pan Ingredients
4 tablespoons (2 ounces) unsalted butter
1/4 cup water
2 teaspoons kosher salt
2 teaspoons Accent (see Sources page 378), (optional) (see Note)

BBQ Sauce
2 1/4 cups APL BBQ Sauce (page 362), or your favorite BBQ sauce
3 tablespoons apricot preserves
3 tablespoons pineapple preserves
3 tablespoons honey, preferably orange blossom
3 tablespoons apple cider vinegar
1 1/2 teaspoons Japanese soy sauce
1 1/2 teaspoons Accent (see Sources page 378) (optional)

NOTE: You'll notice that I call for Accent (see Sources page 378), which contains MSG. Although monosodium glutamate has acquired a bad reputation, numerous studies have concluded that it has no effect on most people—well, unless you count happiness, because of the extra blast of deliciousness it offers. Still, if you're skeptical, leave it out of this dish. It'll be great either way.

1. Place the thighs in an extra-large resealable plastic bag (or divide between two smaller bags) and pour the dressing over the top. Squeeze out any excess air from the bag, and roll to coat all of the meat. Refrigerate for 3 hours.

2. Preheat an indirect barbecue with a drip pan and a combination of hardwood and fruitwood (preferably hickory and apple), a ceramic cooker with deflector plate and a combination of hardwood and fruitwood (preferably hickory and apple), or a charcoal and gas grill with a box or packet with a combination of hardwood and fruitwood (preferably hickory and apple) to 300°F.

3. Combine the seasoning blend ingredients and grind in a coffee or other small grinder that is dedicated to spices. Depending on the size of the grinder, it may need to be done in batches.

   In two baking dishes or two disposable aluminum pans, preferably $13^{1}/_{2} \times 9^{5}/_{8} \times 2^{3}/_{4}$-inch lasagna pans that will hold the thighs in a single layer, spread the butter (2 tablespoons in each) in the bottom. Divide the water, salt, and Accent, if using, between the pans.

4. Remove the chicken from the dressing, letting any excess remain in the bag, and lightly pat dry with paper towels.

   Place the chicken, skin side down, in the pans, keeping in a single layer.

   Using about 1 teaspoon of the seasoning blend on each thigh, sprinkle the top flesh side with the blend. Cover each pan with heavy-duty aluminum foil, and crimp the edges to seal.

5. Place the thighs in the cooker, stacking the pans on top of each other, if needed, to fit in the cooker, and rotate them from top to bottom halfway through the cooking. Cook for 45 minutes.

6. Remove the thighs from the cooker and let rest in the pans, covered, for 15 minutes.

7. Transfer the thighs to a sheet pan or work surface and lightly pat dry with paper towels. Season on all sides with the seasoning blend; there may be some unused blend.

   Place back in the cooker, skin side up, and cook for an additional 45 minutes.

8. Meanwhile, combine all of the ingredients for the BBQ sauce. Pour into a baking dish or disposable aluminum pan, preferably a $13^{1}/_{2} \times 9^{5}/_{8} \times 2^{3}/_{4}$-inch lasagna pan.

9. Remove the thighs from the cooker and carefully dip each one in the sauce, dredging to coat on all sides and making sure the skin side, especially, is evenly coated.

   Being sure to tuck the skin under to make the skin taut, place the thighs back in the cooker, skin side up, for 30 minutes.

10. Transfer to a platter and serve.

JERK DRUMSTICKS

SERVES 8

Between living in New York City and working as a private chef in the Caribbean, I've come across a lot of different recipes for jerk chicken, some so wildly aromatic that they call for five whole cloves of nutmeg! When I started cooking the dish myself, I took the qualities I admired most in each version and created a recipe that showcased them all—the almost fruity presence of habañeros, the warm flavors of allspice and nutmeg, and the bright flavor of cilantro.

Marinade
1 cup white vinegar
½ cup freshly squeezed orange juice
½ cup Japanese soy sauce
½ cup canola or vegetable oil
Juice of 1 lime
1 cup finely chopped shallots
¼ cup chopped scallions, white and green
    portions
5 garlic cloves, peeled, halved, germ removed,
    and grated on a Microplane garlic
2 habañero (Scotch bonnet) peppers, cut in
    quarters, seeds removed
3 tablespoons firmly packed dark brown
    sugar
2 tablespoons thyme leaves
1 tablespoon ground allspice
1 tablespoon finely ground fresh black pepper
1 teaspoon freshly grated nutmeg
1 teaspoon ground cinnamon

16 skin-on drumsticks

Pan Ingredients
4 tablespoons (2 ounces) unsalted butter
2 tablespoons water

¼ to ½ cup canola or vegetable oil
½ cup cilantro leaves
½ cup chopped scallions, white and green
    portions
Juice of 2 limes
½ cup extra virgin olive oil
Kosher salt

1. In the blender, or in a medium to large bowl using an immersion/stick blender, combine all of the marinade ingredients and blend until smooth.

   Place the drumsticks in an extra-large resealable plastic bag (or divide between two large bags). Pour the marinade over the top, squeeze out any excess air, and close. Roll the bag to coat all of the meat. Refrigerate for at least 2 hours, but preferably for 4.

2. Preheat an indirect barbecue with a drip pan and fruitwood (preferably apple), a ceramic cooker with deflector plate and fruitwood (preferably apple), or a charcoal or gas grill with a box or packet of fruitwood (preferably apple) to 325°F.

3. In two baking dishes or disposable aluminum pans, preferably $13\frac{1}{2} \times 9\frac{5}{8} \times 2\frac{3}{4}$-inch lasagna pans that will hold the drumsticks in a single layer, spread the butter (2 tablespoons in each) in the bottom. Divide the water between the pans.

   Remove the drumsticks from the marinade, letting any excess remain in the bag, and divide between the pans. Cover with heavy-duty aluminum foil and crimp the edges to seal.

4. Place the pans in the cooker, stacking the pans on top of each other, if needed, to fit in the cooker, and rotate them from top to bottom halfway through the cooking. Cook for 50 minutes.

5. Meanwhile, after about 30 minutes of cooking, preheat all grates of a well-oiled charcoal or gas grill to medium-high (or plan on removing the deflector plate on a ceramic cooker).

6. Reserving the cooking juices, transfer the chicken to a sheet pan or work surface and lightly pat dry with paper towels.

   Using your hands or a brush, evenly, but lightly, coat the drumsticks with canola oil.

   Strain all of the juices from the pan through a fine-mesh strainer set over a measuring cup. Discard any solids. Allow the fat to come to the top, pour off, and discard.

   Place the liquid in a medium bowl and whisk in the cilantro, scallions, lime juice, and olive oil. Season to taste with salt and cover to keep warm.

7. Grill the drumsticks over direct medium heat, turning about every 2 minutes to brown on all sides. Cook for a total of about 10 minutes.

8. Pour the sauce onto a serving platter and arrange the drumsticks on top.

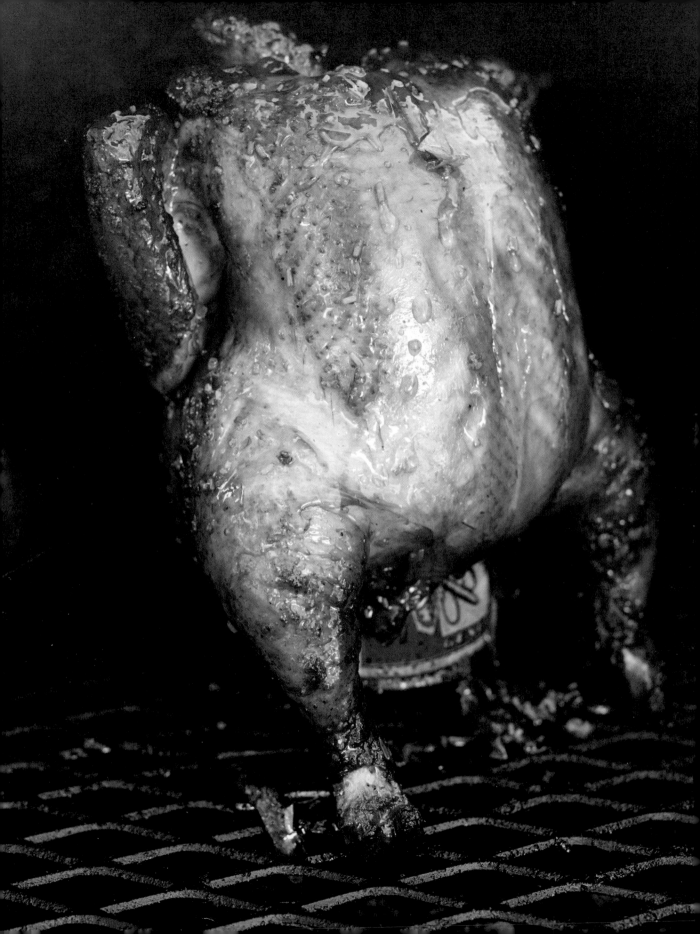

WHOLE BEER-CAN CHICKEN

SERVES 8

Beer-can chicken is a barbecue classic: You stand a whole bird upright on a beer can, pop it in the barbecue, and about an hour and a half later, you pull out a smoky, unbelievably juicy version of an often dried-out dinner staple. I've never found that the specific beer (or soda) you use affects the meat, so you can also use a vertical roasting rack or a chicken sitter (see Sources page 378), a device that lets the chicken sit upright in the cooker.

Marinade

½ cup canola or vegetable oil

½ cup water

2 tablespoons Worcestershire sauce

2 tablespoons Japanese soy sauce

1 tablespoon cider vinegar

1 tablespoon prepared yellow mustard

1 tablespoon firmly packed dark brown sugar

1 tablespoon chili powder

1 tablespoon coarsely ground fresh black pepper

1 tablespoon kosher salt

6 garlic cloves, peeled, halved, germ removed, and grated on a Microplane grater

1 medium sweet white onion, coarsely chopped

1 serrano, Thai bird, or other small, hot chile of choice, sliced, seeds removed

Two 3- to 3½-pound chickens

Glaze

½ cup orange marmalade

¼ cup honey

2 tablespoons cider vinegar

1 tablespoon freshly squeezed lemon juice

1 tablespoon coarsely chopped chives

1 tablespoon coarsely chopped parsley

Two 12-ounce cans of beer

½ bunch thyme and ½ bunch marjoram, tied in an Herb Bundle (page 365)

8 tablespoons (4 ounces) unsalted butter, melted

Finishing Dressing

1 tablespoon finely chopped flat-leaf parsley

1 tablespoon finely chopped chives

1 lemon

¼ cup extra virgin olive oil

Fleur de sel

1. In the blender, or in a medium to large bowl using an immersion/stick blender, combine all of the marinade ingredients and blend until smooth.

   Place each of the chickens in a large to extra-large resealable plastic bag. Pour the marinade over the top, squeeze out any excess air from the bags, and close. Roll the bags to evenly coat the chicken. Refrigerate for at least 8 hours, or up to 24.

2. Preheat an indirect barbecue with a drip pan and fruitwood (preferably apple), a ceramic cooker with deflector plate and fruitwood (preferably apple), or a charcoal or gas grill with a box or packet of fruitwood (preferably apple) to 300°F.

3. Place the glaze ingredients in a jar with a tight-fitting lid and shake to combine.

4. Remove the chickens from the bags, letting any excess marinade remain in the bags, and lightly pat dry with paper towels.

   If using beer cans, open the cans, pour out (or drink) about an inch from each of the cans. Place the chickens on the cans or on a chicken sitter (see Sources page 368) or other stand for beer-can chicken.

   Position a remote thermometer in the thickest part of one of the chickens' thighs—or one in the thigh and one in the breast if you have two remote thermometers.

5. Place the chickens in the cooker, basting occasionally during the cooking with the herb bundle dipped in the butter. Cook until the internal temperature registers 165°F in the thigh and 155°F in the breast, about 1 hour and 15 minutes.

6. Give the glaze a quick shake and, using the herb brush, brush the chickens completely with the glaze. Place back in the cooker and cook until the internal temperature of the thigh is 175°F and the breast is 165°F, about 15 to 20 more minutes.

7. Remove the chickens from the cooker and let rest upright on the can or on the stand for 30 minutes.

8. Meanwhile, combine the parsley and chives in a small bowl. Using a Microplane grater, zest the lemon over the top, squeeze in all of the juice, and mix in the olive oil. Pour onto a cutting board or other work surface.

9. Place both chickens on top of the dressing and cut each chicken into quarters or individual serving pieces (thighs, drumsticks, wings, and half-breasts), dredging the pieces in the dressing.

   Arrange on a serving platter and sprinkle with fleur de sel.

PAELLA

Traditionally, this Spanish rice dish is cooked over an open fire, but it turns out great in a paella pan set on the grill. I add plump shrimp, briny clams, and some smoky marinated chicken, and the rice gets infused with saffron and cooked so it develops this lovely crispy crust on the bottom. It's so beloved that the Spanish have a name for it: *soccarat*.

Seasoning Paste

6 garlic cloves, peeled, halved, germ removed, and grated on a Microplane grater
1 tablespoon fresh thyme leaves
1 tablespoon kosher salt
2 teaspoons finely ground fresh black pepper
1 tablespoon pimentón (see Sources page 378), or other smoked paprika
1 teaspoon cayenne pepper
1 tablespoon firmly packed light brown sugar
Juice of 2 lemons
2 tablespoons red wine vinegar
¼ cup extra virgin olive oil

One 3½- to 4-pound chicken, cut into 8 pieces

Shrimp

4 cups cold water
2 tablespoons kosher salt
2 tablespoons granulated sugar
Eight 8 to 12 count unpeeled shrimp (this means shrimp that come 8 to 12 to a pound)

Pan Ingredients

1 teaspoon saffron, preferably Spanish (see Sources page 378)
2 tablespoons boiling water
¼ cup extra virgin olive oil

4 tablespoons (2 ounces) unsalted butter
5 garlic cloves, peeled and grated on a Microplane grater
1 cup finely chopped sweet white onion
½ cup scallions, white and green portions
1 habañero pepper, quartered, seeds removed, and finely chopped (optional)
1 to 2 pieces cooked chorizo, preferably Spanish (see Sources page 378), cut into ½-inch dice (½ to ¾ cup)
2 teaspoons pimentón (see Sources page 378), or other smoked paprika
2 Roasted Marinated Peppers (page 331)
1 tablespoon kosher salt
3 cups Bomba, Calasparra, or other short-grained Spanish rice (see Sources page 378)
½ cup dry white wine, such as Sauvignon Blanc
8 Littleneck clams
6 cups low-sodium chicken stock
2 tablespoons finely chopped flat-leaf parsley

1 lemon, halved and seeds removed
½ cup extra virgin olive oil
3 tablespoons coarsely chopped flat-leaf parsley
Fleur de sel
Coarsely ground fresh black pepper

NOTE: Invest in a real-deal paella pan (this dish is perfect in a 17-inch pan) to ensure that the rice is cooked evenly and can develop that irresistible crust (see Sources page 378).

Bomba rice (see Sources page 378) is also worth the effort to get. Because it's a bit starchier than regular short-grain rice, you get a slightly creamier texture and a better bite.

1. Combine all of the seasoning paste ingredients in a blender, or in a large bowl using an immersion/stick blender.

   Place the chicken pieces in an extra-large resealable plastic bag (or divide between two large bags). Pour over the seasoning paste, squeeze out any excess air in the bag, and close. Refrigerate for at least 2 hours, or up to 4.

2. Preheat all grates of a well-oiled charcoal or gas grill to high.

3. Combine the water, salt, and sugar for the shrimp, whisking to dissolve the salt and sugar.

   For each of the shrimp, using a paring knife, cut along the curve of the back of the shrimp, and remove the vein, keeping the shells intact. Cut the feet off using small scissors.

   Place the shrimp in the brine and refrigerate for 1 hour.

4. Meanwhile place the saffron in a small bowl and cover with the boiling water.

5. Remove the chicken from the seasoning paste, scraping off any excess.

6. Place the paella pan directly on the grates and let heat for 1 to 2 minutes.

   Add the olive oil and butter to the pan. Just as the butter begins to melt, add the chicken, skin side down, and cook until golden, about 10 minutes. Remove from the pan and place in a baking dish or a disposable aluminum pan next to the grill.

   Add the garlic, onion, scallions, habañero, if using, chorizo, paprika, roasted peppers, and salt to the paella pan, stirring

to combine, and cook until the onions are translucent, 3 to 5 minutes.

   Stir in the rice and continue to stir until the rice is lightly toasted, about 5 minutes.

   Pour in the wine, deglazing the pan and scraping it to loosen any bits that may have stuck to the bottom or sides. Cook until the wine has completely evaporated. Stir in the saffron and saffron water.

   Pour in the chicken stock and parsley, stirring well to evenly distribute all of the ingredients.

   Arrange the chicken, skin side up, around the pan on top of the rice, leaving about 2 inches between the pieces.

   Bring the liquid up to a simmer. At this point you may have to close the lid to increase the temperature of the grill. (For the remainder of the cooking the temperature of the grill should be maintained at 325°F.) Simmer for 20 minutes.

   Position the shrimp and the clams around the pieces of chicken, nudging into the chicken slightly, without disrupting the rice too much.

   Close the lid and cook until the shrimp are pink and cooked through and the clams have opened, about 10 minutes.

7. Remove the pan from the grill and let rest for 10 minutes.

8. Squeeze the lemon over the top, drizzle with the olive oil, and sprinkle with the parsley. Season with fleur de sel and black pepper.

   Serve immediately directly from the pan.

SMOKED CHICKEN LIVERS

I grew up eating and loving chopped liver, that rich, creamy Jewish staple that my family spread on matzoh and, sometimes, spooned right into their mouths. So when I was cleaning chickens during a barbecue competition in Huntsville, Alabama, and had a bunch of livers, I decided to smoke them and make my own version. I added some cream, fresh thyme, and bourbon, and the result blew me away. After you've tried it, perhaps spread on bagel chips or toasted pita, you won't believe that people typically toss this tasty chicken part.

2 pounds chicken livers, cleaned (see Note)

3 cups whole milk

1 tablespoon kosher salt, plus additional for seasoning

1 tablespoon coarsely ground fresh black pepper, plus additional for seasoning

3 tablespoons (1½ ounces) unsalted butter

2 cups thinly sliced shallots

6 garlic cloves, peeled, halved, germ removed, and grated on a Microplane grater

1 tablespoon fresh thyme leaves

1 tablespoon fresh marjoram leaves

¾ cup bourbon or brandy

2 cups heavy cream

4 tablespoons (2 ounces) unsalted butter, softened at room temperature

About ¼ cup finely chopped flat-leaf parsley

Extra virgin olive oil

Fleur de sel

Coarsely ground fresh black pepper

NOTE: Cut out any sections that are greenish in color—this is natural, but should be removed—and trim off the white connective pieces.

1. Place the chicken livers in a storage container and cover with the milk. Refrigerate for at least 8 hours, or up to 24. Soaking in the milk will clean the livers by drawing out some of the residual blood.

2. Preheat an indirect barbecue with a drip pan and fruitwood (preferably apple), a ceramic cooker with deflector plate and fruitwood (preferably apple), or a charcoal or gas grill with a box or packet of fruitwood (preferably apple) to 225°F.

3. Remove the livers from the milk, discard the milk, and pat the livers dry on paper towels.

    Season the livers on all sides with salt and pepper. Place in a disposable pan that will hold them in a single layer; a 9- or 10-inch square will work well. Some overlap is OK. Set aside.

4. Place the butter in a medium sauté pan (it will later go in the cooker) over medium heat. Just as it begins to melt, add the shallots and continue to cook, stirring occasionally, until golden, 8 to 10 minutes. Stir in the garlic, thyme, marjoram, 1 tablespoon of salt, and 1 tablespoon of pepper. Cook for an additional 2 minutes, stirring as needed to keep from getting too dark.

    Pour in the brandy, and deglaze the pan, scraping the pan to loosen any bits that may have stuck to the bottom or sides. Cook until the brandy has almost completely evaporated and the shallots are nicely glazed, about 8 minutes.

    Stir in the cream and bring to a boil. Remove from the heat.

5. Position the pan with the cream and the pan with the livers in the cooker. Cook for 30 minutes.

6. Stir the chicken livers and any residual liquid into the cream mixture and cook for an additional 20 minutes.

7. Remove from the cooker and let cool slightly, about 10 minutes.

8. Pour everything in the pan into a food processor and pulse until well combined. Add the butter and continue to process until the butter is completely incorporated and the mixture is smooth.

    Pour into a serving bowl or bowls (nice to separate and have at opposite ends of the table). Let cool to room temperature and then refrigerate for at least 6 hours, but preferably overnight. The livers definitely taste better the next day.

9. Serve the livers cold or at room temperature. Just before serving, garnish the top with parsley, drizzle with olive oil, and sprinkle with fleur de sel and black pepper.

WHOLE TURKEY WITH LIGHT SALT BRINE

SERVES 12 TO 15

One Thanksgiving a while back, I told my family that I was going to barbecue our turkey, and they insisted I roast a back-up in the oven, in case they didn't like it. But surprise, surprise, the smoke-blasted turkey was a tremendous hit, both that night and in a phenomenal turkey salad the next day.

TIP: This method works beautifully with a smaller bird and even one that weighs up to 25 pounds.

One 12- to 14-pound turkey (see Tip)

Brine
1 tablespoon crushed hot red pepper flakes
2 tablespoons boiling water
18 cups water
½ cup kosher salt
1 tablespoon granulated sugar
4 thyme sprigs, bruised with the broad side of a knife
2 tablespoons black peppercorns, crushed with a dowel or bottom of a heavy pot
Three .18-ounce packets Goya Sazón Azafrán (see Sources page 378) (see Note)

About ½ cup canola or vegetable oil

Seasoning Blend
3 tablespoons garlic salt
1½ tablespoons chili powder
1½ tablespoons coarsely ground fresh black pepper

8 tablespoons (4 ounces) unsalted butter, melted
½ bunch thyme and ½ bunch sage tied in an Herb Bundle (page 365)

Finishing Dressing
½ cup extra virgin olive oil
6 tablespoons finely chopped chives
Fleur de sel
Finely ground fresh black pepper

NOTE: Goya Sazón Azafrán contains MSG. If you want to avoid it, substitute a combination of 1 teaspoon chile powder, 1 teaspoon cumin, 1 teaspoon garlic salt, and 1 teaspoon turmeric. The turkey will not have quite the punch or color as it would with the Sazón.

1. Place the pepper flakes in a small bowl and pour the boiling water over them. Let sit for 1 to 2 minutes to rehydrate the flakes. Combine all the brine ingredients, including the pepper flakes and the soaking water in a large bowl and stir to dissolve the salt and sugar. Let sit at room temperature for 24 hours to allow the flavors to develop.

2. Strain the brine and discard the solids.

3. For easier carving, remove the wishbone from the turkey by carefully running a boning knife underneath the skin along all sides of the wishbone to loosen and then remove it without damaging the skin. (The wishbone can be smoked alongside the bird and later traditionally broken.)

    Place the turkey into a jumbo-size resealable bag (some manufacturers make storage bags that are up to 2 feet square), a brining bag, or an unscented garbage bag that can be sealed with a plastic tie. Pour over the brine, squeeze out any excess air from the bag, and close. Place into another bag, for insurance against leaking, and seal again. Refrigerate for at least 12 hours, or up to 24. (If you don't have room in your refrigerator the turkey can be stored in a small cooler with ice or frozen ice packs.)

4. Preheat an indirect barbecue with a drip pan and hardwood (preferably hickory, oak, or pecan), a ceramic cooker with deflector plate and fruitwood (preferably hickory, oak, or pecan), or a charcoal or gas grill with a box or packet of hardwood (preferably hickory, oak, or pecan) to 275°F.

5. Remove the turkey from the bags. Rinse and lightly pat dry with paper towels.

Using your hands or a brush, evenly, but lightly, coat the turkey with canola oil.

Going under the skin, place a remote thermometer in the thickest part of the thigh—or one in the thigh and one in the breast, if you have two remote thermometers.

6. Place the turkey in the cooker and cook until the internal temperature of the thigh registers 165°F and the breast registers 155°F, about 3¾ hours to 4 hours and 15 minutes, depending on the size of the bird. (A 25-pound turkey will take about 7 to 7½ hours.)

7. Meanwhile, combine the seasoning blend ingredients.

8. Remove the turkey from the cooker, brush the skin with the melted butter using the herb bundle, and season all of the skin with the seasoning blend.

    Return the turkey to the cooker and cook until the internal temperature of the thigh registers 175°F and the breast registers 165°F, about 30 minutes to 1 hour more, depending on the size of the bird. (A 25-pound turkey will take about 2 more hours, for a total cooking time of 9 to 10 hours.)

9. Drizzle the olive oil on an extra-large cutting board. Top with the chives, fleur de sel, and pepper. Remove the turkey from the cooker, place on the board, and let rest for 15 minutes.

10. Slice the breast and dredge in the dressing. Pull all of the dark meat from the thighs into chunks and dredge in the dressing. Leave the drumsticks and wings whole. Arrange on a serving platter and sprinkle with fleur de sel and pepper.

HONEY-GLAZED WHOLE TURKEY BREAST

SERVES 8

Whether you include turkey breasts as part of a mixed barbecue feast or as a cool substitute for the whole bird on Thanksgiving, you'll have to contend with two headaches: this super-lean cut's big potential for drying out and for coming out bland. No worries: I inject it with a simple brine to keep it juicy and glaze the crispy skin with turkey-friendly flavors like thyme, honey, and mustard.

1 whole, bone-in and skin-on turkey breast, preferably about 8 pounds

Injection
2¼ cups water
1 tablespoon kosher salt
1¼ teaspoons granulated sugar

Seasoning Blend
¼ cup mild chile powder, preferably Chimayo (see Sources page 378), Ancho, or Hatch
2 tablespoons sweet paprika
2 tablespoons firmly packed dark brown sugar
1½ teaspoons dry mustard
¾ teaspoon garlic salt
¾ teaspoon coarsely ground fresh black pepper
¾ teaspoon kosher salt
½ teaspoon Old Bay Seasoning (see Sources page 378)

Glaze
½ cup apple cider vinegar
½ cup honey
2 tablespoons prepared yellow mustard
1 tablespoon fresh thyme leaves
1 tablespoon fresh marjoram leaves
2 teaspoons finely ground fresh black pepper

Finishing Dressing
½ cup extra virgin olive oil
1 tablespoon freshly squeezed lemon juice
1 tablespoon finely chopped chives
Fleur de sel
Finely ground fresh black pepper

1. For easier carving, remove the wishbone by carefully running a boning knife underneath the skin and along all sides of the wishbone to loosen and then remove it without damaging the skin. (The wishbone can be smoked alongside the bird and later traditionally broken.)

   Combine all the injection ingredients in a medium bowl and stir to dissolve the salt and sugar.

   Loosen the skin from the breast of the turkey. Going under the skin, and using approximately 2 cups of the liquid (depending on the size of the turkey you won't use it all), use an injecting needle (see Sources page 378) to inject the breast in a grid-like pattern.

   Place the turkey into an extra-large resealable bag, squeeze out any excess air from the bag, and close. Place into another bag for insurance against leaking, and seal again. Refrigerate for at least 12 hours, or up to 24.

2. Preheat an indirect barbecue with a drip pan and hardwood (preferably hickory, oak, or pecan), a ceramic cooker with deflector plate and hardwood (preferably hickory, oak, or pecan), or a charcoal or gas grill with a box or packet of hardwood (preferably hickory, oak, or pecan) to 250°F.

3. Combine all of the seasoning blend ingredients.

   Place all of the glaze ingredients in a jar with a tight-fitting lid and shake to combine.

   Remove the breast from the bag, lightly dry with paper towels, and season generously with the seasoning blend.

   Going under the skin, insert a remote thermometer into the thickest part of the breast.

4. Place the breast in the cooker and cook until the internal temperature registers 155°F, 2¼ to 2½ hours.

5. Remove the breast from the cooker.

   Give the jar a quick shake to reincorporate any ingredients that may have settled, and brush the breast with the glaze.

   Return the turkey breast to the cooker and cook until the internal temperature registers 165°F, 30 to 45 additional minutes.

6. Drizzle the olive oil on a cutting board. Top with the lemon juice, chives, fleur de sel, and pepper. Remove the turkey from the cooker, place on the board, and let rest for 20 minutes.

7. Slice off the bone into ¼-inch slices, and sprinkle with additional fleur de sel and pepper.

BACON-WRAPPED BONELESS SKINLESS TURKEY BREAST

SERVES 8

If you've given up on turkey breasts because they can come out dry and dull, a bite into these bacon-wrapped beauties will change your mind in an instant. A brine ensures these stay moist, and that bacon becomes crisp and salty, like the turkey skin of your dreams.

1 whole 5- to 6-pound, boneless, skinless turkey breast, split into 2 halves

Brine
14 cups water
6 tablespoons kosher salt
¼ cup granulated sugar

Marinade
1 teaspoon crushed hot red pepper flakes
1 tablespoon boiling water
¼ cup minced shallots
4 cloves garlic, peeled, halved, germ removed, and grated on a Microplane grater
2 tablespoons fresh thyme leaves
1 tablespoon granulated sugar
1 tablespoon dried oregano, preferably Mexican
1 tablespoon kosher salt
1 teaspoon lemon pepper
1 teaspoon Old Bay seasoning (see Sources page 378)
2 tablespoons prepared yellow mustard
1 cup white wine vinegar
2 cups canola or vegetable oil

Seasoning Blend
2 tablespoons mild chile powder, preferably Chimayo (see Sources page 378), Ancho, or Hatch

2 tablespoons sweet paprika
2 tablespoons firmly packed dark brown sugar
1½ teaspoons pimentón (see Sources page 378), or other smoked paprika
1½ teaspoons dry mustard
¾ teaspoon garlic salt
¾ teaspoon onion salt
¾ teaspoon coarsely ground fresh black pepper
½ teaspoon Old Bay Seasoning (see Sources page 378)

Glaze
¼ cup cider vinegar
¼ cup honey
1 tablespoon prepared yellow mustard
1½ teaspoons fresh thyme leaves
1½ teaspoons fresh marjoram leaves
1 teaspoon finely ground fresh black pepper

½ pound sliced bacon

½ bunch thyme and ½ bunch sage, tied in an Herb Bundle (page 365)
8 tablespoons (4 ounces) unsalted butter, melted

Fleur de sel

1. Combine all of the brine ingredients in a large bowl and stir to dissolve the salt and sugar.

2. Place the breast halves in an extra-large resealable plastic bag (or divide between two large bags). Pour over the brine, squeeze out any excess air from the bag, and close. Refrigerate for at least 12 hours and up to 24.

3. Place the pepper flakes in a small bowl and pour the boiling water over them. Let sit for 1 to 2 minutes to rehydrate the flakes. In a large bowl, or in the container of a blender, stir together the shallots, garlic, thyme, sugar, oregano, salt, lemon pepper, pepper flakes and their soaking water, Old Bay, mustard, and vinegar and let sit at room temperature for 10 minutes for the flavors to develop.

   Using an immersion blender or a traditional blender, blend the ingredients and slowly add the oil to emulsify.

4. Remove the breasts from the brine and dry lightly with paper towels.

   Place into a clean extra-large resealable plastic bag (or divide between two large bags), and pour over the marinade. Roll to coat, squeeze out any excess air from the bag, and close. Refrigerate for at least 2 hours and up to 4.

5. Preheat an indirect barbecue with a drip pan and hardwood (preferably hickory, oak, or pecan), a ceramic cooker with deflector plate and hardwood (preferably hickory, oak, or pecan), or a charcoal or gas grill with a box or packet of hardwood (preferably hickory, oak, or pecan) to 250°F.

6. Combine the seasoning blend ingredients.

   Place all of the glaze ingredients in a jar with a tight-fitting lid and shake to combine.

   Remove the turkey from the marinade, letting any excess marinade remain in the bag. Lightly pat dry with paper towels.

   Season generously on all sides with the seasoning blend.

   Insert a remote thermometer in the thickest part of the breast.

7. Place the turkey in the cooker and cook for 1 hour.

8. Remove the turkey from the cooker, and arrange the bacon slices over the top of each piece. The slices should be laid on an angle with each piece overlapping the next slightly.

   Place the turkey back in the cooker and continue to cook until the internal temperature registers 155°F, about 1 hour.

9. Remove the turkey from the cooker and brush with the glaze using the herb bundle.

   Return the turkey to the cooker and cook until the internal temperature registers 165°F, about 45 additional minutes.

10. Spread some of the butter on a cutting board, and drizzle some of the remaining glaze over the top. Remove the turkey from the cooker, brush with the melted butter using the herb bundle, and let rest for 15 minutes.

11. Slice into ¼-inch slices and sprinkle with fleur de sel.

BOURBON-GLAZED TURKEY LEGS

For lots of people, amusement parks and fairs bring up happy memories of funnel cakes and cotton candy. No offense to the sweet stuff (I certainly don't turn it down), but as a meat lover, what I remember most fondly is lugging around a massive turkey drumstick. It translates beautifully to your home table. The inexpensive drums, with my just-sweet-enough bourbon glaze, will have your guests feeling like Vikings.

Brine

1 tablespoon crushed hot red pepper flakes

$\frac{1}{4}$ cup boiling water

4 cups water

2 cups apricot nectar

2 cups apple juice, plus more for basting

$1\frac{1}{4}$ cups firmly packed dark brown sugar

$\frac{1}{4}$ cup granulated sugar

$\frac{1}{4}$ cup kosher salt

10 garlic cloves, peeled, halved, germ removed, and grated on a Microplane grater

$1\frac{1}{2}$ teaspoons Worcestershire sauce

Two .18-ounce packets Goya Sazón Azafrán (see Sources page 378) (see Note)

8 turkey drumsticks, about $\frac{3}{4}$ to 1 pound each

Seasoning Blend

$\frac{1}{2}$ cup chile powder, preferably Chimayo (see Sources page 378), Ancho, or Hatch

$\frac{1}{4}$ cup sweet paprika

$\frac{1}{4}$ cup firmly packed dark brown sugar

1 tablespoon dry mustard

$1\frac{1}{2}$ teaspoons garlic salt

$1\frac{1}{2}$ teaspoons coarsely ground fresh black pepper

$1\frac{1}{2}$ teaspoons kosher salt

$1\frac{1}{2}$ teaspoons lemon pepper

1 teaspoon Old Bay Seasoning (see Sources page 378)

Glaze

$\frac{1}{2}$ cup bourbon

$\frac{1}{2}$ cup honey

$\frac{1}{2}$ cup apple cider vinegar

4 garlic cloves, peeled, halved, germ removed, and grated on a Microplane grater

2 tablespoons thinly sliced scallions, white and green portions

1 tablespoon fresh thyme leaves

$\frac{1}{2}$ cup Apple Juice Spray (page 364)

8 tablespoons (4 ounces) unsalted butter, melted

$\frac{1}{2}$ bunch thyme and $\frac{1}{2}$ bunch sage, tied in an Herb Bundle (page 365)

2 tablespoons minced chives

NOTE: Goya Sazón Azafrán contains MSG. If you want to avoid it, substitute a combination of 3/4 teaspoon each chile powder, cumin, garlic salt, and turmeric. The chicken will not have quite the punch or color as it would with the Sazón.

1. Place the pepper flakes in a small bowl and pour the boiling water over them. Let sit for 1 to 2 minutes to rehydrate the flakes. Combine all the brine ingredients including the pepper flakes and the soaking water in a large bowl and stir to dissolve the salt and sugar. Let sit at room temperature for 24 hours to allow the flavors to develop.

2. Strain the brine and discard the solids.

   Place the drumsticks into an extra-large resealable bag (or divide between two large bags). Pour over the brine, squeeze to remove any excess air from the bag, and close. Refrigerate for at least 6 hours, or up to 12.

3. Preheat an indirect barbecue with a drip pan and hardwood (preferably hickory, oak, or pecan), a ceramic cooker with deflector plate and hardwood (preferably hickory, oak, or pecan), or a charcoal or gas grill with a box or packet of hardwood (preferably hickory, oak, or pecan) to 275°F.

4. Combine the seasoning blend ingredients in a small bowl.

   Place all of the glaze ingredients in a jar with a tight-fitting lid and shake to combine. Pour into a baking dish or disposable aluminum pan, preferably a $13^{1}\!/2 \times 9^{5}\!/8 \times 2^{3}\!/4$-inch lasagna pan.

5. Remove the drumsticks from the bag and dry lightly with paper towels.

   Season generously on all sides with the seasoning blend.

6. Place the drumsticks in the cooker and cook, spraying with apple juice spray every half hour after the first hour, until the internal temperature registers 165°F, 2 to 2½ hours.

7. Remove from the cooker and dredge the drumsticks in the glaze to evenly coat on all sides.

   Return the drumsticks to the cooker and cook until the internal temperature registers 175°F, about 30 additional minutes.

8. Remove the drumsticks from the cooker, brush with the butter using the herb bundle, sprinkle with the chives, and let rest for 15 minutes before serving.

9. Serve whole or pull the meat from the bones. If pulling the meat, spread some of the remaining butter on a cutting board, and drizzle with some of the glaze before shredding, dredging the meat in the mixture.

SIDES

Grilled Corn on the Cob (page 323)

THE CO-STAR

Barbecue sides are not just supporting actors, although they do provide indispensable contrast—a mellow or tart or crisp or cooling break from all that awesomely rich, in-your-face meat. No, they're stars in and of themselves. I see this every time my guests' eyes light up when I bring out a pot of baked beans, tinged with molasses and barbecue sauce and bobbing with bacon, and, sometimes, crispy burnt ends. They go just as crazy for my creamy, crunchy slaw and my buttery new potatoes, flecked with dill and Old Bay. So here are the recipes for perfect versions of my favorite sides, which I've tweaked so they won't have you running inside to the stove when you're supposed to be hanging out outside with a beer and your barbecue.

GRILLED SHRIMP COCKTAIL

SERVES 8

After these plump up from a quick brine, and cook in their shells, they'll eat more like peel-and-eat lobster tails than plain old shrimp. Serve this alongside grilled steak, and it'll be not only a great respite from the meat's richness, but it'll give you a surf-and-turf experience, which for me was one of the most exciting things to get at a restaurant when I was little.

Brine
8 cups water
¼ cup kosher salt
2 tablespoons granulated sugar
2 lemons
4 garlic cloves, peeled, and grated on a
    Microplane grater
3 cups ice

Twenty-four 8- to 12-count unpeeled shrimp
    (this means shrimp that come 8 to 12 to a
    pound)

⅓ cup canola or vegetable oil
½ cup extra virgin olive oil
Juice of 2 lemons
¼ cup minced chives
Kosher salt
Freshly ground coarse black pepper

1 recipe Amped-Up Cocktail Sauce (page 370)
2 lemons, each cut into 4 wedges

1. Combine all of the brine ingreients in a large bowl and stir to dissolve the salt and sugar. Cut the lemons in half, squeeze the juice into the brine, and add the whole lemons as well. Stir in the garlic, followed by the ice.

    For each of the shrimp, using a paring knife, cut along the curve of the back of the shrimp, and remove the vein, keeping the shells intact. Clip the feet off with a small pair of scissors.

    Place the shrimp in the brine and refrigerate for 1 hour.

2. Preheat all grates of a well-oiled charcoal or gas grill to medium.

3. Remove the shrimp from the brine and lightly pat dry with paper towels.

    In a bowl, toss the shrimp in the canola oil.

    In a separate bowl, combine the olive oil, lemon juice, and chives. Set aside.

4. Place the shrimp on the grate, close the lid, and grill for 4 minutes. Flip to the second side and grill for 4 minutes.

5. Remove from the grill and immediately place in the bowl with the olive oil mixture, tossing to coat. Season with salt and pepper and serve with cocktail sauce and lemon wedges on the side.

CORN GRIDDLE CAKES

This celebration of corn is a hybrid of a classic pancake and an arepa, a delicious, denser corn cake made by street vendors in Colombia. I use cornmeal to make a simple dough (better quality cornmeal will mean sweeter, tastier cakes) and mix in fresh kernels of corn, which give each bite a crunch and a burst of summery sweetness. Pair these with Caramel Smoked Bacon (page 108) and some fried eggs, and the ultimate brunch is born.

2 to 4 tablespoons canola or vegetable oil

2 cups stone-ground yellow cornmeal
(see Sources page 378)
1 cup all-purpose flour
1 tablespoon granulated sugar
1½ teaspoons kosher salt
1 teaspoon baking powder
1 teaspoon baking soda
1 cup buttermilk
1 cup heavy cream
1 cup canned creamed corn
5 tablespoons canola or vegetable oil
2 large eggs
2 large egg yolks
1 cup whole corn kernels, preferably fresh,
drained if canned, or thawed and drained
if frozen
3 thinly sliced scallions, white and green
portions
1 jalapeño chili, seeds removed, and minced

2 to 4 tablespoons (1 to 2 ounces) unsalted
butter cut into ¼-inch pieces
Whole parsley leaves (optional)
Coarsely chopped chives (optional)

1 stick of unsalted butter (8 tablespoons), at
room temperature
Jar of honey, for serving

1. Place a lightly oiled cast-iron griddle on one area of a charcoal or gas grill and preheat to medium.

2. In a large bowl, combine the cornmeal, flour, sugar, salt, baking powder, and baking soda.

   In a medium to large bowl using an immersion/stick or in a blender, combine the buttermilk, cream, creamed corn, oil, eggs, and egg yolks and blend until smooth.

   Slowly stir the wet ingredients into the dry, but do not overmix; there will be some lumps. Fold in the whole corn, scallions, and jalapeño.

3. Line a sheet pan with a Silpat or heavy-duty aluminum foil and tear off a second large piece of foil to use later as a top.

4. Using a ⅓-cup dry measuring cup, scoop and pour portions of batter on the griddle. Cook until the edges just start to turn light brown, about 1 minute. Scatter a few small pieces of butter around the edges of the cakes, and continue to cook on the first side until bubbles appear on the surface, 1½ to 2 minutes.

   Flip the cakes and cook until browned on the second side, about 2 minutes.

   Transfer to the sheet pan and cover with the foil.

   Re-oil the griddle if needed. Repeat with the remaining batter and butter, adjusting the heat as necessary to keep the griddle at a medium heat.

5. The cakes should stay warm under the foil, but if necessary, reheat slightly before serving. Top with parsley and chives if you like.

   Serve with butter and honey on the side.

TEXAS TOAST

MAKES 8 SLICES

When my Texan buddies first made me Texas toast, I knew I'd never go back to the garlic bread of my childhood—the kind toasted in the oven that comes out way too garlicky and greasy. After I spread on a thin layer of softened butter on both sides of the bread and toast it on the griddle, I rub each slice with garlic—you want to just feel the garlic, not be blown back by it. White bread works nicely, but I like to use eggy breads such as brioche or challah, which develop even more color and get especially chewy and crispy from the grill. The high heat perks up day-old bread, too, though if you use it, make sure your guests eat the toast right away.

TIP: Chill the bread beforehand, so it firms up and won't absorb too much butter.

1 unsliced rectangular loaf of egg bread, preferably brioche

16 tablespoons (8 ounces) unsalted butter, softened at room temperature
1 to 2 large garlic cloves, peeled
Kosher salt

1. Place a cast-iron griddle on a well-oiled charcoal or gas grill. Preheat all areas to medium.
2. Slice eight 1-inch-thick slices. Reserve the remaining bread for another use (or make more if you like, based on the size of the loaf; simply up the amount of the butter and garlic).

    Spread about 1 tablespoon of butter on each side of each slice.

3. Place as many slices as will fit on the griddle. Toast on each side until golden, about 3 minutes per side.
4. Remove the slices from the grill. Lightly rub on both sides with the garlic and sprinkle with salt immediately.
5. Repeat with the remaining slices.

GRILLED SWEET ONIONS

MAKES ABOUT 2 CUPS

I often have a ton of these sizzling next to whatever meats I have on the grill—especially if I'm cooking burgers, because to me, caramelized onions are as essential as ketchup. With a cast-iron griddle you can give the onions some bonus caramelization. I didn't think it was possible either, but yes, this improves on perfection.

3 to 4 sweet white onions, peeled
3 tablespoons extra virgin olive oil
1 tablespoon fresh thyme leaves
1 tablespoon granulated sugar
1 teaspoon kosher salt

1 teaspoon finely ground fresh black pepper
2 tablespoons (1 ounce) unsalted butter
6 garlic cloves, peeled, and grated on a
   Microplane grater
2 tablespoons red wine vinegar

1. Cut the onions through the root end and lay, cut side down, on the work surface. Cut across, each half, following the natural lines, to make perfectly even ⅛-inch slices. You will need 6 cups.
2. Place a cast-iron griddle on a well-oiled charcoal or gas grill. Preheat all areas to high.
3. Toss the onions with 2 tablespoons of the olive oil, thyme, sugar, salt, and pepper.
4. Pour the remaining 1 tablespoon of the oil on the griddle and let heat for about 1 minute.
   Spread the onions on the griddle and decrease the heat to medium. Close the lid and cook the onions, without stirring, for 10 minutes.

5. Move the onions to one side of the griddle. Melt the butter on the cleared space, add the garlic, and stir to coat in the butter. Cook until fragrant, about 1 minute.
   Stir the onions and garlic together and cook with the lid open until the onions are completely tender, about 3 minutes.
   Pour the vinegar right onto the griddle and mix into the onions.
6. Serve directly from the grill or transfer to a bowl.

RADISHES WITH ANCHOVY BUTTER

MAKES ABOUT 1 CUP

Radishes might not sound like your typical barbecue side. OK, they sound like the exact opposite of your typical barbecue side. But what's easier than this? Slice some fresh radishes. Blend butter with some fresh lemon juice, parsley, and anchovies, and be amazed as the awesomely salty punch of the anchovies mellow into this subtle sea tang. The soft, melting butter is an excellent foil to the crisp, sweet radishes with their trademark peppery tinge. No matter how much I put out for guests, I find the platter empty by the time the meat comes off the grill.

5 bunches red radishes, trimmed and washed well

16 tablespoons (8 ounces) high-quality, unsalted butter, softened at room temperature

10 salted anchovy fillets, rinsed and finely chopped

1 tablespoon freshly squeezed lemon juice

1 teaspoon finely ground fresh black pepper

1 tablespoon finely chopped flat-leaf parsley

1. Place the radishes in a bowl of ice water to chill while you prepare the butter.
2. Combine the butter, anchovies, lemon juice, and pepper in a small food processor, or in a medium bowl using an immersion/stick blender. Blend until well combined and smooth.

Stir in the parsley leaves and place in a small serving bowl. If the butter has softened beyond that of a spread, refrigerate just until firm enough to dip the radishes in.

3. Serve the butter surrounded by the radishes for easy dipping.

GRILLED ZUCCHINI AND SUMMER SQUASH WITH SHAVED PECORINO ROMANO

SERVES 8

The idea of marinating vegetables in orange juice and soy sauce seemed a bit wacky to me when a chef buddy made this, but I flipped when I saw the stunning grill marks and flipped again when I tasted the result. A drizzle of honey and dusting of pecorino (a combination made in heaven) make a good thing even better. Just don't let it sit for more than 1 hour in the marinade, and this will be a guaranteed crowd-pleaser.

4 medium zucchini, about 6 inches long and 7 ounces each
4 medium yellow squash, about 6 inches long and 7 ounces each

Marinade
1 cup freshly squeezed orange juice
½ cup extra virgin olive oil
Juice of 2 lemons
¼ cup honey
1 tablespoon soy sauce, preferably Japanese
5 garlic cloves, peeled and thinly sliced
3 tablespoons chopped scallions, white portion only, slice and reserve the green portion for garnish (see below)
2 tablespoons finely chopped shallots
1 tablespoon finely chopped fresh ginger

¼ cup extra virgin olive oil
Kosher salt
Coarsely ground fresh black pepper
1 block pecorino Romano cheese, about 6 ounces
⅓ cup chopped scallions, light and dark green portions only
¼ cup coarsely chopped chives
1 tablespoon honey

1. Trim the ends of the zucchini and yellow squash, split each one lengthwise, and place in an extra-large resealable plastic bag (or divide between two smaller bags).

   In the blender, or in a medium to large bowl using an immersion/stick blender, combine all of the marinade ingredients and blend until smooth. Pour over the zucchini and squash. Squeeze out any excess air from the bag and close. Roll the bag to evenly coat in the marinade. Refrigerate for 1 hour.

2. Preheat all grates of a well-oiled charcoal or gas grill to medium.

3. Remove the zucchini and squash from the bag, letting all excess run into the bag. Lightly pat dry with paper towels and place in a large bowl. Toss with the olive oil.

4. Place, cut side down, on the grate, close the lid, and grill until well marked, 5 to 7 minutes. Flip, close the lid, and grill on the second side until well marked, 5 to 7 minutes.

   If you notice the squash curling slightly around the edges or want to intensify the char, use a grill press(es) or a firebrick(s) (see Sources page 378) wrapped in heavy-duty aluminum foil to weigh them down.

5. Arrange the squash on a serving platter. Sprinkle with salt and pepper. Using a vegetable peeler, cut shavings of the cheese over the top; you will not use all of the cheese. Scatter the sliced scallions and chives over the top and drizzle with honey.

GRILLED PEACHES

When you're working with ripe peaches, which are nearly perfect already, you don't want to change the flavor and texture too much—you just want to take them to the next level. So instead of cooking the fruit, I use a hot griddle just to intensify the natural sweetness and tartness, and to maximize caramelization. They make a great partner for chicken and pork dishes, especially those with peaches in the sauce or glaze, or with some heat, like my Bone-In Pork Butt with Green Apple and Crushed Hot Red Pepper (page 74). Oh, and did I mention I add brandy and peach Jell-O?

TIP: A freestone peach is just a peach with a pit that pops out easily when you cut the fruit in half.

¼ cup brandy
½ cup peach Jell-O
½ cup granulated sugar

1 teaspoon cayenne pepper
8 large freestone peaches, halved and pitted
About ¼ cup canola or vegetable oil
1 stick of unsalted butter (8 tablespoons),
    cold and unwrapped
Fleur de sel

1. Place a cast-iron griddle on a well-oiled charcoal or gas grill. Preheat all areas to medium.
2. Pour the brandy into a shallow bowl.

   Combine the Jell-O, sugar, and cayenne and spread in the bottom of a sheet pan that will hold the peach halves in a single layer.

   For each of the halves, dip the cut side into the brandy, then place, cut side down, in the Jell-O mixture. Let the peaches sit in the mixture for 5 minutes.

   Lift up the peaches. There should be a thin, almost translucent layer of the mixture on the cut side. If any granules remain, lightly brush off with a clean pastry brush.

   Using a pastry brush, lightly blot the cut sides with canola oil.
3. Pour enough oil on the griddle to create a thin film, and let heat for about 5 minutes.

4. Place the peaches, cut side down, on the griddle. After about 3 minutes, lift gently to peek at the color; they should be light golden. If not, continue to cook, checking about every 30 seconds.

   Once golden, flip to the rounded side. Touch the stick of butter to the griddle just enough to begin to melt it and then use to lightly coat the cut side of all of the peaches.

   Flip back to be cut side down and continue to cook, adding additional butter and flipping as necessary to keep the cut side from getting too dark. Cook until the peaches are tender, 3 to 5 minutes.

   If at this point the peaches are cut side down, flip to be cut side up. Touch the butter to the griddle and fill each of the wells in the peaches with butter and sprinkle with fleur de sel.
5. Remove the peaches from the grill and arrange on a serving plate.

GRILLED ASPARAGUS WITH SHERRY-SHALLOT VINAIGRETTE

SERVES 8

Asparagus deserves to be treated simply, but that doesn't mean just a squirt of lemon will do. I love to lay on a vinaigrette first and then finish them with the brightness of lemon juice and some tarragon leaves. You can serve these hot or cold, but just be sure to dress them just before you serve them.

Sherry-Shallot Vinaigrette
1/4 cup sherry vinegar
1 tablespoon Dijon mustard
2 tablespoons thinly sliced shallots
1 teaspoon kosher salt
1 teaspoon freshly ground black pepper
1/2 cup extra virgin olive oil
1/4 cup canola or vegetable oil
2 tablespoons finely chopped chives

2 bunches pencil asparagus, about 1½ pounds total
1/4 to 1/2 cup extra virgin olive oil
1 lemon, halved
Kosher salt
Finely ground fresh black pepper
1/4 cup fresh tarragon leaves
Fleur de sel
2 lemons, each cut into 6 to 8 wedges

1. Preheat all grates of a well-oiled charcoal or gas grill to high.
2. In a small bowl, or in the container of a blender, stir together the vinegar, mustard, shallots, salt, and pepper and let sit at room temperature to allow 10 minutes for the flavors to develop.

   Using an immersion/stick blender or a traditional blender, blend the ingredients and slowly add the oils to emulsify. Set aside.
3. Cut off the tough ends of the asparagus, about 1 inch from each piece.

   Toss the asparagus with enough oil to coat, and squeeze the lemon juice over the top. Sprinkle with salt and pepper.
4. Grill, rolling the pieces to char moderately on all sides, about 8 minutes, depending on the thickness of the asparagus.

   To keep the asparagus in contact with the grate, use a grill press(es) or a firebrick(s) (see Sources page 378) wrapped in heavy-duty aluminum foil to weigh them down.
5. Transfer to a large bowl or long baking dish, and while still hot, toss with about three-quarters of the tarragon and season with the fleur de sel and pepper. Add enough vinaigrette to coat and toss again.

   Transfer the asparagus to a serving dish and sprinkle with the remaining tarragon leaves. Serve any remaining vinaigrette and lemon wedges on the side.

GRILLED CORN ON THE COB

SERVES 8

This one's a backyard party classic that I've put a new spin on. To protect those delicate, sugar-sweet kernels, I grill each cob in its husk. Then toward the end of cooking, I peel the husk back and let the corn develop just a bit of tasty char. As if this weren't lovely enough, I bring it all up a notch with a cilantro pesto (use basil or parsley if you prefer) and plenty of butter.

8 ears of unhusked corn

Cilantro Pesto
½ cup cilantro leaves, large stems removed
2 tablespoons freshly squeezed lime juice
1 garlic clove, peeled, and grated on a
    Microplane grater
1 teaspoon kosher salt
1 teaspoon finely ground fresh black pepper

¼ cup canola or vegetable oil
¼ cup extra virgin olive oil

4 limes, each cut into 4 to 6 wedges
Fleur de sel
16 tablespoons (8 ounces) unsalted butter, cut
    into pats

1. Keeping the husks attached, peel them back in sections on each ear of corn, and remove the silk. Cover the exposed corn with the husk.
   Soak the corn in cold water for 5 to 10 minutes.
2. Preheat one grate of a well-oiled charcoal or gas grill to medium-high and another to high.
3. Place the cilantro, lime juice, garlic, salt, and pepper in a small food processor or in a blender and pulse to combine. With the machine running, slowly drizzle in the oils. Alternately the pesto can be combined by hand. Set aside.

4. Place the corn, still covered by the husk, on the medium-high grate. Cook for 3 minutes, turn to the other side, and cook for 3 minutes.
   Remove from the grill, peel back the husk, return to the high grate to mark and lightly char the corn on all sides, turning and jockeying between medium and high as needed for 5 to 7 minutes total.
5. Remove the corn from the grill and brush generously with the pesto. Squeeze lime over the ears and sprinkle with fleur de sel. Serve with any remaining limes, and pats of butter on the side.

GRILLED FENNEL WITH SMOKED TOMATOES AND OLIVES

SERVES 8

For this one, I combined some classic Mediterranean ingredients, and let the cooker do the rest. The fennel gets grilled so it picks up some lovely flavors, and the tomatoes are smoked, for a totally subtle but awesome extra dimension of flavor. The combination—the sweet fennel, tangy tomatoes, and salty olives—make a dream team with veal or lamb, but this dish can make a meal in itself if you spoon it over couscous.

8 ounces black and green Cerignola olives
½ cup loosely packed basil leaves

Tomatoes
3 garlic cloves, peeled, halved, germ removed, and grated on a Microplane grater
1 teaspoon fresh thyme leaves
1 tablespoon extra virgin olive oil
1 teaspoon kosher salt
1 teaspoon freshly ground coarse black pepper
4 ripe plum tomatoes

Fennel
4 medium to large fennel bulbs, about 12 ounces each
4 garlic cloves pressed and pureed, or grated on a Microplane grater
¼ cup extra virgin olive oil
½ teaspoon kosher salt
½ teaspoon coarsely ground fresh black pepper

About 2 tablespoons high-quality, aged balsamic vinegar
About 2 tablespoons extra virgin olive oil
Fleur de sel

1. Preheat an indirect barbecue with a drip pan and fruitwood (preferably apple), a ceramic cooker with deflector plate and fruitwood (preferably apple), or a charcoal or gas grill with a box or packet of fruitwood (preferably apple) to 325°F.

2. For each of the olives, cut the flesh from the two opposite sides of the olive and then cut those pieces in half lengthwise. Cut the flesh from the two remaining sides. Discard the pit. You will have about ¾ cup of olive pieces. Set aside.

   Working with a few basil leaves at a time, stack the leaves, roll them together into a cylinder shape, and then cut across to make ¼-inch ribbon-like strips (chiffonade). Set aside.

3. Combine the garlic, thyme, olive oil, salt, and pepper in a medium bowl.

   Cut the tomatoes in half lengthwise. Over a small bowl, squeeze each half to remove the seeds. Strain, discard the seeds, and reserve the liquid. Toss the tomato halves in the medium bowl with the oil mixture, being sure the garlic is equally distributed.

4. Place the tomatoes, cut side up, on a grilling or other rack and place in the cooker to cook for 30 minutes.

5. Meanwhile, if not using a grill to smoke the tomatoes, preheat a charcoal or gas grill to medium-high and prepare the fennel.

   Cut the fennel bulbs across at the top to remove the fronds. Trim ½ cup of the fronds and reserve for garnish.

   Trim the bottoms of each bulb, keeping the full bulb intact. Remove any hard exterior leaves. Cut each bulb lengthwise into ½-inch wedges.

   Combine the garlic, olive oil, salt, and pepper in a medium bowl.

   Toss the fennel wedges in the medium bowl with the oil mixture, being sure the garlic is equally dispersed.

6. During the last 10 to 15 minutes of smoking the tomatoes, grill the fennel over medium-high for 3 minutes on each of the 3 sides. The fennel should be well marked and tender when pierced. If necessary, move the pieces over indirect heat or jockey over the direct heat until tender.

7. In a large bowl, combine the fennel, tomatoes, olives, and basil. (If either the tomatoes or the fennel finish slightly earlier, place in the bowl and cover loosely with foil to keep warm.)

   Transfer the vegetables to a serving platter and drizzle with the balsamic vinegar, olive oil, and reserved tomato water. Sprinkle with fleur de sel, and garnish with the reserved fennel fronds.

CHARRED EGGPLANT PUREE WITH YOGURT AND GARLIC

MAKES ABOUT 4 CUPS

I can't stop collecting cookbooks. Sometimes, when I'm flipping through one I haven't looked at in a while, I come across a technique so simple and logical that I'll drop everything to try it. Take this trick for cooking with eggplant: Don't peel it, cut it, and salt it—just toss the whole thing on the grill. The skin gets charred and picks up a nice bitterness, which I temper with yogurt, and the flesh gets really smoky, which I ramp up with cumin. I'd eat it with almost any red meat, but I especially love it with my Moroccan-inspired lamb recipes (see pages 222, 228, and 242).

1 cup full-fat yogurt, preferably Greek
3 teaspoons kosher salt
10 garlic cloves, peeled
2 teaspoons crushed hot red pepper flakes
2 teaspoons finely ground fresh black pepper

2 teaspoons ground cumin
2 tablespoons extra virgin olive oil

8 baby Italian eggplants, or 2 to 3 large
    eggplants

1. Line a fine-mesh strainer with a piece of dampened cheesecloth and place over a bowl.

    Combine the yogurt and 1 teaspoon of the salt. Place in the strainer and refrigerate for 2 hours to drain.

2. Preheat a well-oiled charcoal or gas grill to high, keeping one area off for indirect cooking.

3. Lay two sheets of heavy-duty aluminum foil, each about 6 inches square, on top of each other, and fold up the sides, creating a bowl shape with a rounded base about 3 inches across. Place the garlic, red pepper flakes, black pepper, cumin, the remaining 2 teaspoons of the salt, and the olive oil in the bowl. Fold over the sides to create a packet.

4. Place the packet on the indirect area and cook until the garlic is softened, about 20 minutes.

    Meanwhile, after about 10 minutes, lay the eggplant directly on the high grates. Grill, turning every couple of minutes, until the eggplant is well marked and extremely soft, indicating the flesh is well cooked.

    Remove the garlic packet and the eggplant from the grill. Set the garlic packet aside. Place the eggplant in a large bowl. Cover the top with plastic wrap, and let rest for 15 minutes.

5. Scrape the flesh from all of the eggplant into the bowl of a food processor or a large bowl with an immersion/stick blender. It is OK if there is some char. There should be 2½ to 3 cups of eggplant.

    Unwrap the garlic from the packet. Add the garlic, but not all of the spices to the eggplant. Process until smooth. Taste the mixture, and add additional seasoning from the packet, as needed. If it is still warm, let cool to room temperature.

6. Add the yogurt and process until smooth.

7. Transfer to a serving bowl and serve at room temperature, or refrigerate until cold.

ARTICHOKES BASTED WITH ANCHOVY BUTTER

Even if you don't like anchovies, you've got to give this a try. First of all, you can't beat freshly steamed artichokes—nibbling the flesh from the little leaves, gobbling the tender heart. And the insanely good anchovy butter has absolutely no relation to the too-salty fish you may have had once at a takeout pizza joint. Instead, oil-packed anchovies contribute this subtle sea-salty punch that you just can't get from anything else.

Seasoned Butter

8 tablespoons (4 ounces) unsalted butter, softened

4 salted anchovy fillets, rinsed, and finely chopped

2 garlic cloves, peeled, halved, germ removed, and grated on a Microplane grater

1 teaspoon kosher salt

1 teaspoon finely ground fresh black pepper

1 tablespoon freshly squeezed lemon juice

8 medium globe artichokes, 10 to 12 ounces each

3 to 4 lemons, halved and seeds removed

Kosher salt, for salting the water

About ¼ cup canola or vegetable oil

About ¼ cup coarsely chopped flat-leaf parsley

Fleur de sel

1. Preheat all grates of a well-oiled charcoal or gas grill to high.

2. Combine all of the butter ingredients together and set aside.

3. Cut off the thorny ends of the artichokes with scissors and then cut the artichokes lengthwise in half. Rub the cut sides of the artichokes with a lemon half and place, cut side down, on a sheet pan. Add enough lightly salted water, 2 to 3 cups, to come ¼ inch up the sides of the artichokes.

   Place the pan with the artichokes directly on the grate, reduce the heat to medium-high if you can (those cooking on coals won't be able to, and must monitor the water level especially closely), close the lid, and cook, adding water as needed to maintain the level at ¼ inch. Cook until tender when pierced with a paring knife, about 30 minutes.

4. Carefully remove the pan from the grill. Using a spoon, scoop the fuzzy choke from each of the halves. Transfer the cleaned halves to a new sheet pan.

   Using your hands or a brush, evenly, but lightly, coat both sides of the artichokes with canola oil.

5. Place the artichokes, cut side down, on the grate and grill until well marked and lightly charred, 2 to 3 minutes. Flip and repeat on the second side, grilling for 2 to 3 minutes.

   While still cut side up, place about ½ tablespoon of butter in each of the cavities and allow it to melt.

   Squeeze lemon juice over the top and sprinkle with parsley and fleur de sel.

6. Remove the artichokes from the grill and arrange on a serving platter.

ROASTED MARINATED PEPPERS

There are a thousand and one recipes for this easy staple of outdoor cooking, and it feels like I've tried all of them. But none quite match up to this one. After you've charred the peppers on the grill, you just pop them in a resealable plastic bag until you can slide the skins right off. Then you submerge them in a mixture of olive oil, vinegar, and garlic until they pick up a bit of tang. They're amazing on their own, piled on Griddled and Grilled Italian Sausages (see page 60), or tossed with my Paella (see page 289). These will last a week in the fridge, but I bet you'll finish them before then.

8 red bell peppers
¼ cup thinly sliced garlic
¼ cup thinly sliced shallots
1 tablespoon fleur de sel
1 teaspoon finely or coarsely ground fresh
    black pepper
¼ cup red wine vinegar

½ cup extra virgin olive oil
2 tablespoons coarsely chopped flat-leaf
    parsley

1. To blister the peppers, place over an open flame or directly on the coals. Turn to grill on all sides until the skin is completely blackened. Immediately transfer to a large resealable plastic bag or place in a large bowl and cover the top with plastic wrap to seal. Let sit for 30 minutes, or until cool enough to handle.

   Working with one pepper at a time, transfer to a work surface. Remove the skin, stem, and seeds. It's OK if some bits of char remain, that will add great flavor.

(The peppers are used at this point when making Paella, page 289.)

   Cut the peppers into 2-inch strips and toss with the garlic, shallots, fleur de sel, pepper, and vinegar. Let sit at room temperature for at least 1 hour, or up to 4 hours to allow the flavors to develop.

2. Toss with the olive oil and parsley just before serving.

BEETS ON
A BED OF SALT

Boil them if you must, but this method is even easier and gives you unbelievably sweet beets. The barbecue concentrates the flavor and even adds a touch of smoke, the perfect accent for the sweetness of the beets. All they need is a simple dressing and some crunchy walnuts.

8 large, tennis-ball-size beets
5 to 6 cups kosher salt, 1¾ to 2 pounds

Dressing
½ cup red wine vinegar
¼ cup thinly sliced shallots
2 tablespoons freshly squeezed lemon juice
Kosher salt
Finely ground fresh black pepper

1 cup extra virgin olive oil
¼ cup roughly chopped dill, large stems
    removed

2 tablespoons walnut oil
¼ cup toasted walnuts, roughly chopped
Fleur de sel

1. Preheat an indirect barbecue with a drip pan and fruitwood or hardwood, a ceramic cooker with deflector plate and fruitwood or hardwood, or a charcoal or gas grill with a box or packet of fruitwood or hardwood to 350°F.

2. Scrub the beets well to remove all dirt. Keep the root end intact and trim the beet greens to within ½ inch of the beet top.

3. In a pan that will hold the beets in an even layer without touching (a 9 × 9-inch square or a 10-inch skillet works well), pour in the salt. There should be about a 1-inch layer. The amount of salt will vary based on the size of the pan you are using.

   Nestle the beets, root side down, in the salt, adding additional salt as needed to create a bed to keep the beets upright.

4. Place the beets in the cooker and bake until completely tender when pierced with a paring knife, 2½ to 3 hours.

5. Remove the beets from the cooker and let cool slightly.

6. Meanwhile, in a large bowl, combine the vinegar, shallots, and lemon juice. Season with salt and pepper and let sit at room temperature for at least 15 minutes while you peel the beets.

7. When cool enough to handle, peel the beets, using a paper towel or wearing latex gloves to avoid staining your hands. Cut into ½-inch wedges.

   Stir the olive oil and the dill into the shallot mixture. Add the beets and toss to coat.

8. Transfer the beets to a serving bowl. Drizzle with the walnut oil, top with the walnuts, and sprinkle with fleur de sel.

MELTING GARLIC

MAKES 2 CUPS

There's a reason I call it "melting" and not "roasted" garlic: Some people just lop off the top of the bulb and stick it in the cooker, but I take the time to peel each one and cook them slowly, immersed in olive oil, until they're so soft that they almost liquefy when you touch them with a fork. The pulpy mass you end up with has this rich, almost creamy texture and a deep, mellow garlic flavor. Spread it on toast with some of the garlic-infused oil and serve with any meat that comes off the grill.

TIP: Garlic peels easily if you allow it to soak in hot tap water for 10 minutes.

2 tablespoons kosher salt
3 cups extra virgin olive oil

2 cups peeled garlic cloves, from 4 to 5 heads
2 thyme sprigs
One 4- to 5-inch rosemary sprig
1 teaspoon crushed hot red pepper flakes

1. Preheat an indirect barbecue with a drip pan and fruitwood or hardwood, a ceramic cooker with deflector plate and fruitwood or hardwood, or a charcoal or gas grill with a box or packet of fruitwood or hardwood to 250°F.

2. In a small bowl whisk together the salt and the oil.
   Put the garlic cloves into a medium saucepan with the thyme, rosemary, and pepper flakes. Pour over the oil.

3. Place in the cooker and cook until the garlic is tender and easily pierced with a fork, about 3 hours.

HARD SMOKED EGGS

When I worked in French kitchens, we used to infuse eggs with all kinds of fancy stuff, like cheese and truffles, but before my friend Marc Farris, BBQ TV, clued me in to this cool way to cook eggs, I had never infused them with smoke. It's insanely easy: Boil them a bit and then throw them in the smoker for about 45 minutes. Believe me, nothing makes a better egg salad than these babies.

1 dozen large eggs in a cardboard carton
   (save the carton)
1 tablespoon kosher salt
2 tablespoons finely chopped chives
2 tablespoons thinly sliced scallions, white
   and green portions

1 teaspoon freshly squeezed lemon juice
1 teaspoon celery salt
¼ cup to 6 tablespoons extra virgin olive oil

1. Preheat an indirect barbecue with a drip pan and hardwood (preferably hickory or oak), a ceramic cooker with deflector plate and hardwood (preferably hickory or oak), or a charcoal or gas grill with a box or packet of hardwood (preferably hickory or oak) to 225°F.
2. Place the eggs in a saucepan that will hold them in an even layer.

   Pour in just enough water to cover and stir in the salt.

   Place over high heat and bring to a boil. Cover and remove from the heat. Let sit, covered, for 12 minutes.

   Remove the lid and put the eggs under cold running water for 5 minutes.
3. Remove the eggs from the water.

   Roll each egg on the table to crack the shell. The shell should remain intact, but be cracked. Set the eggs back in the carton.
4. Place the carton of eggs with the top open in the cooker for 1 hour.
5. Meanwhile, in a small bowl toss the chives and scallions with the lemon juice, followed by the celery salt.
6. Remove the eggs from the cooker.

   When cool enough to handle, but still warm, peel the eggs.

   Cut the eggs in half lengthwise and arrange on a plate. Drizzle with olive oil and sprinkle with the chive mixture.

BAKED BEANS

SERVES 8

One of the MVPs of barbecue sides, baked beans started out as a food of convenience, a simple dish you could cook over the campfire. I've seen them and made them all sorts of different ways, but always return to this one: I trick them out with three different kinds of beans, add plenty of bacon, and leave them uncovered in the barbecue, so they pick up tons of smoky flavor. The key is not to make them too sweet, so I make sure the deep, dark molasses and brown sugar are balanced by some tang from my barbecue sauce and apple cider vinegar. These are showstopping as is, but add Burnt Ends with Melting Garlic (see page 173) or any other chopped pork or beef barbecue for that matter, and they become almost a meal on their own.

TIP: These beans are all about convenience. You can put them in an active cooker with whatever else you are making as long as the temperature is above 225°F and below 325°F. Just note that the baked beans will get more caramelized when cooked in a hotter cooker.

1 green bell pepper
1 sweet white onion
6 garlic cloves, peeled
1 tablespoon kosher salt
1½ cups APL BBQ Sauce (page 362), or your favorite barbecue sauce
¾ cup unsulfured blackstrap molasses
¾ cup firmly packed dark brown sugar
6 tablespoons apple cider vinegar
One 15-ounce can black beans, rinsed
One 15-ounce can red kidney beans, rinsed
One 15-ounce can vegetarian baked beans, lightly rinsed

5 slices thick-cut bacon

¼ recipe Burnt Ends with Melting Garlic (page 173), warm (optional)

1. Grate the bell pepper on a box grater. Place in a clean towel and squeeze over the sink to extract all of the juices. Place the dried out pepper in a large bowl. Repeat with the onion.

    Create a paste of garlic by chopping the garlic and gradually working in the salt and then rubbing the mixture against the cutting board with the broad side of the knife. Add to the bowl.

    Stir in the BBQ sauce, molasses, sugar, vinegar, and all of the beans.

    Pour into a baking dish or disposable aluminum pan, preferably a 13½ × 9⅝ × 2¾-inch lasagna pan.

    Lay the strips of bacon, lengthwise, on top.

2. Place the pan into the active smoker or ceramic cooker, ranging from 225°F to 325°F.

    Bring the beans to a simmer, bubbling steadily, and cook for at least 1 hour, preferably 2. The top of the beans and the bacon should be nicely caramelized, giving the beans a smoky flavor.

3. Stir in the burnt ends, if using, and serve.

NEW POTATOES WITH OLD BAY AND DILL

SERVES 8

At the Food Network's South Beach Wine & Food Festival, some chefs and I gathered for an impromptu barbecue. We had new potatoes, but only a few bottles of water—not nearly enough to boil them. So I packed them in a foil parcel and used the ingredients we had on hand. And, man, they were so good that they've become one of my barbecue mainstays.

2 pounds thin-skinned, golf ball–size new potatoes, as similar in size as possible, scrubbed well

8 tablespoons (4 ounces) unsalted butter, cut into ½-inch cubes

1 tablespoon Old Bay Seasoning (see Sources page 378)

1 teaspoon crushed hot red pepper flakes

5 thyme sprigs

¾ cup dill sprigs, large stems removed, about 10 sprigs

1 tablespoon coarsely ground fresh black pepper

1 cup water

Dijon mustard
Fleur de sel

1. Lay two sheets of heavy-duty aluminum foil, each 16 to 18 inches long, on top of each other, and fold up the sides, creating a bowl shape with a rounded base about 9 inches across.

   Place the potatoes in the foil bowl. At this point, they should be in a snug even layer. Top with the butter, Old Bay, pepper flakes, thyme, ½ cup of the dill, and black pepper. Pour in the water. Gather the sides of the foil bowl, bringing them together to create a sealed rounded packet about 6 to 7 inches across.

2. Place directly on hot coals and cook for 20 to 30 minutes or cook in a 350°F barbecue for about 1 hour to 1 hour 15 minutes, or until tender when pierced with a paring knife.

3. Carefully open the packet and transfer the potatoes to a serving bowl, removing the cooked herbs.

   Garnish with the reserved ¼ cup of dill. Serve with the mustard and fleur de sel on the side.

MASHED SWEET POTATOES WITH BANANA AND BROWN SUGAR

SERVES 8

I know what you're thinking. Bananas? Trust me. It's a little trick I picked up from my nights in the kitchen at the famous Le Cirque, in Manhattan. I don't always reveal my secret ingredient, and most people can't put their fingers on what exactly makes this sweet potato recipe so good. But everyone loves them. Of course, some heavy cream, butter, and brown sugar doesn't hurt.

8 sweet potatoes or large yams, each about 10 ounces
About 3 tablespoons kosher salt, plus additional as needed
1 banana, with a 2-inch slit cut into the peel

8 tablespoons (4 ounces) unsalted butter
2 cups heavy cream
1 cinnamon stick
¼ cup firmly packed light brown sugar
1 teaspoon finely ground fresh black pepper, plus additional as needed

1. Wash each of the potatoes well, poke holes into them with a fork, rub each with about 1 teaspoon of salt, and wrap with heavy-duty aluminum foil.
2. Place directly on hot coals and cook for about 20 minutes, or cook in a 350°F barbecue for about 50 minutes, or until tender when pierced with a paring knife. At the same time, cook the banana in the peel until blackened, about 15 minutes.
3. Carefully take the potatoes out of the foil and scoop the flesh out from the skin into a large bowl. Cover with foil. Scoop the flesh out of the banana into a separate bowl.

Increase the temperature to high.

4. Place a small roasting pan or deep baking dish with high sides that can take the direct flame (a 13 × 9-inch baking dish with a 15-cup capacity is ideal) over the heat and let heat up for 5 minutes.

Add the butter and let melt. Add the cream, cinnamon stick, brown sugar, potatoes, banana, 1 teaspoon of salt, and 1 teaspoon of pepper. Using a potato masher, mash the potatoes and banana, and stir to combine.

Season to taste with additional salt and pepper as needed.

KALE WITH BACON

SERVES 8

Hearty greens with bacon is a classic Southern combination, but this one's a little different. Typically, the bacon cooks with the greens, so they pick up its smoky, porky flavor. I do something similar here, using the bacon fat to cook the kale, but I also make sure to add some crispy bacon at the end.

2 pounds kale, about 4 bunches
One 3 × 6-inch piece of slab bacon, cut into
   ½-inch cubes
2 to 3 tablespoons extra virgin olive oil
12 garlic cloves, thinly sliced
¼ cup fresh marjoram leaves

2 tablespoons fresh thyme leaves
Kosher salt
Coarsely ground fresh black pepper
3 cups water
¼ cup finely chopped chives

1. Preheat all grates of a well-oiled charcoal or gas grill to high.
2. Cut the leaves off the ribs of kale and discard the ribs. Make sure the kale is well dried.
3. Place a small roasting pan or deep baking dish with high sides that can take a direct flame on the grate (a 9-×13-inch baking dish with a 15-cup capacity is ideal). Close the lid, and let heat up about 5 minutes.

   Pour 2 tablespoons of the oil into the pan and then add the bacon. Cook until crisp, turning to brown all sides, about 10 minutes. Remove the bacon from the pan, cover to keep warm, and set aside.

   Add the garlic slices to the pan. Pour in additional oil only as needed to lightly coat the garlic. Cook, stirring occasionally until the garlic is light golden, 3 to 5 minutes. Add the marjoram and the thyme, and stir just to wilt.

   Begin adding the kale in batches, seasoning with salt and pepper and stirring to coat as it wilts down, about 5 minutes.

   Pour in the water.

   Keeping the temperature at 325°F, cook the kale until tender and until the majority of the liquid has evaporated from the pan, about 20 minutes.

   Toss the bacon with the kale.
4. Transfer to a serving bowl and sprinkle with chives.

APPLESAUCE

This is the best applesauce your pork chops will ever meet, and it'll become a staple at your barbecue. All you do is mix the ingredients, wrap them in foil, stick the bundle on the grill, and forget about it for 20 minutes. While the apples are steaming and melting along with the sugar, and cinnamon, you can tend to your meat or just kick back with a beer.

6 apples, preferably Granny Smith
1 cinnamon stick
1 cup apple juice

½ cup firmly packed light brown sugar, plus additional as needed
2 tablespoons apple cider vinegar

1. Preheat one grate of a charcoal or gas grill to medium.
2. Grate the apples on a box grater over a medium bowl. You will need about 4½ cups of grated apples. The apples should be used right away.

   Lay two sheets of heavy-duty aluminum foil, each 16 to 18 inches long, on top of each other, and fold up the sides, creating a bowl shape with a rounded base about 9 inches across.

   Pour the apples, all of their juice, the cinnamon stick, and apple juice into the foil bowl. Gather the sides of the foil bowl, bringing them together to create a sealed, rounded packet about 6 to 7 inches across.

3. Place the packet on the grate and cook for 20 minutes.
4. Carefully remove from the grill, open, and pour into the bowl of a food processor, or into a bowl if using an immersion/stick blender. Add the sugar and vinegar and blend until smooth. Season to taste with additional sugar and vinegar as needed.
5. Pour the applesauce into a storage container or a serving bowl and cover with plastic wrap. Refrigerate until cold, about 2 hours, or preferably overnight.
6. Serve cold or at room temperature.

APRICOT COMPOTE

My wife, Fleur, is to blame for this utterly addictive dish, which my mother-in-law also makes me as a treat. In this recipe, I tone down the sugar a bit and turn it into more of a condiment for savory stuff like barbecued pork or chicken instead of a spread for toast.

2 pounds fresh apricots, halved and pitted 1 cup granulated sugar	½ cup water

1. Preheat one grate of a charcoal or gas grill to medium.
2. Toss the apricots in the sugar.

   Lay two sheets of heavy-duty aluminum foil, each 16 to 18 inches long, on top of each other, and fold up the sides, creating a bowl shape with a rounded base about 9 inches across.

   Place the sugared apricots in the foil bowl. Pour in the water. Gather the sides of the bowl, bringing them together to create a sealed, rounded packet about 6 to 7 inches across.
3. Place on a grate over medium heat, or on coals that are at medium, and cook for 30 minutes. The fruit should be tender, but still in whole pieces. For a more sauce-like consistency, continue to cook for an additional 10 to 20 minutes.
4. Carefully open the packet and transfer to a serving bowl. Refrigerate until cold.
5. The compote can be served cold or at room temperature.

DRESSED ARUGULA

What pickled ginger is to sushi, this zippy salad should be to barbecue. Tangy, well-dressed greens act as a foil for all that meaty richness. I like arugula's peppery bite and its body, which can stand up to lots of lemon juice without wilting. I usually just serve this in a bowl, but man, does it make a killer topping for a sandwich of my Crisp and Unctuous Pork Belly (page 100) and homemade Applesauce (see page 345).

8 cups baby arugula
⅓ cup thinly sliced red onion
¼ cup flat-leaf parsley leaves
Zest (grated on a Microplane grater) and
    juice of 1 lemon
2 tablespoons extra virgin olive oil

1 tablespoon red wine vinegar
1 teaspoon thinly sliced serrano chile
    (optional)
½ teaspoon fleur de sel
½ teaspoon freshly ground coarse black
    pepper

1. In a serving bowl, toss together the arugula, onion, and parsley.
2. In a small bowl combine the lemon zest and juice, olive oil, vinegar, chile, if using, fleur de sel, and pepper.
3. Drizzle the dressing into the bowl of arugula and, using your hands, toss to coat the greens.
    Serve immediately.

MARINATED TOMATOES

A lot of people say that the refrigerator is the enemy of tomatoes. But somehow, this no-cook side proves that there's at least one exception to that rule. Not only that, I swear that the cold makes them even better, so I usually eat them right out of the fridge. Sometimes, just for fun, I'll stack the pieces up to re-create the shape of a tomato, but you certainly don't have to.

6 vine-ripened beefsteak tomatoes (see Note), 8 to 9 ounces each
½ cup sherry vinegar, plus additional as needed
½ cup extra virgin olive oil, plus additional for drizzling
¼ cup minced shallots

6 tablespoons finely chopped chives
1 tablespoon fleur de sel, plus additional for seasoning
1 teaspoon finely ground fresh black pepper, plus additional for seasoning

1. Core the tomatoes and then slice horizontally as thinly as possible, ideally ⅛ inch thick.
   Combine the vinegar, oil, shallots, ¼ cup of the chives, fleur de sel, and pepper.
   Line a half sheet pan with plastic wrap.
   Lay the tomato slices on the sheet pan, overlapping slightly as needed.
   Drizzle the oil mixture evenly over the tomatoes, making sure that the shallots and chives are evenly distributed.
   Refrigerate for at least 3 hours, or up to 24.
2. Remove from the refrigerator. Arrange the tomatoes on a serving tray, reserving the marinade and any residual liquid, if desired.
   The residual liquid can be made into a dressing, adding additional vinegar, salt, and pepper to taste.

Drizzle olive oil and dressing over the tomatoes and sprinkle with the remaining 2 tablespoons of chives.

NOTE: If you're feeling ambitious and would like to add a little fire-roasted flavor to the tomatoes and give them a more melting texture, you can first blister the whole tomatoes on the grill.

Fill a large bowl with ice water and have it near the grill. Then, working with one tomato at a time, pierce the end with a fork to create a secure handle for turning the tomato. Place over a direct flame or medium-high to high heat and rotate every 15 to 20 seconds; the skin may split slightly.

Immediately transfer the tomatoes to the ice water and let sit in the water until chilled, 30 seconds to 1 minute. Remove one at a time and peel off the skin.

CRISP CARROT SALAD WITH CURRANTS

SERVES 8 (ABOUT 12 CUPS)

Here's a no-fuss salad that tastes so fresh and delicious. The carrots stay crunchy, but not too crunchy, and every bite brings a burst of flavor: tangy currants, the tingle of chile powder, and the acidic bite of red wine vinegar. You might not see this in the barbecue shacks of the South, but it can share my table with pulled pork or brisket any time.

¼ cup finely chopped shallots
1 teaspoon grated fresh ginger
¼ cup red wine vinegar
2 tablespoons freshly squeezed lemon juice
2 teaspoons kosher salt
1 teaspoon cayenne pepper
1 teaspoon mild chile powder, preferably Chimayo (see Sources page 378), Ancho, or Hatch

1 teaspoon turmeric
¼ cup Zante currants
¼ cup boiling water
3 pounds carrots (about 12 large), peeled
¼ to ½ cup extra virgin olive oil
¼ cup coarsely chopped chives

1. Combine the shallots, ginger, vinegar, lemon juice, salt, cayenne, chile powder, and turmeric in a bowl large enough to hold the carrots. Let sit at room temperature for 10 minutes to allow the flavors to develop.

2. Place the currants in a small bowl, pour over the water, and let sit for 10 minutes to plump. Drain and discard the water.

    It is preferable that the carrots be thinly sliced on a Japanese mandoline (see Sources page 378) and then cut across into matchsticks. They can also be grated through a large grate using a food processor or box grater. You will need about 12 cups.

3. Add the carrots and the currants to the dressing and toss to coat.

    Drizzle in ¼ cup of the oil and the chives and toss again. Add additional oil as needed to coat the carrots.

CHOPPED SALAD

What a fantastic barbecue side: It's juicy, crunchy, and bright enough to provide delicious relief even from your richest dishes, and substantial enough to stand in for starchy sides like potatoes. I add a ton of marjoram and dill, but chives and basil taste amazing, too.

½ cup finely chopped red onions

¼ cup water

½ cup red wine vinegar

2 teaspoons kosher salt, plus additional as needed

2 teaspoons coarsely ground fresh black pepper, plus additional as needed

½ to 1 cup extra virgin olive oil

1 large head iceberg lettuce, cut into ½-inch pieces, 6 to 8 cups

1 cup Roasted Marinated Peppers (page 331), cut into ½-inch pieces

½ cup pitted green olives, such as Cerignola, halved

½ cup pitted black olives, such as Cerignola, halved

1 cup haricots verts, cut into 1-inch pieces

1 cup English cucumber, peeled and cut into ½-inch pieces

2 tablespoons fresh marjoram leaves

¼ cup flat-leaf parsley leaves

¼ cup coarsely chopped dill, large stems removed

1. In a small bowl, combine the onions, water, vinegar, salt, and pepper. Let sit at room temperature for 5 minutes to allow the flavors to develop.

    Add ½ cup of the oil to the vinegar mixture. Add additional to taste.

2. In a large bowl, combine the lettuce, roasted peppers, olives, haricots verts, cucumber, and herbs. Toss with enough dressing to coat, and season to taste with additional salt and pepper. Serve any remaining dressing on the side.

COLESLAW

Come on, what's barbecue without coleslaw? I can never seem to make enough of this side, which disappears so quickly from the table. It adds texture and flavor to pulled pork sandwiches. It makes a perfect partner for grilled chicken. To me, this is the iconic version of slaw—tangy and crunchy as well as creamy and sweet.

3 pounds green cabbage, cored and finely shredded
1½ pounds red cabbage, cored and finely shredded
¼ cup granulated sugar

Dressing
1 teaspoon caraway seeds
1 teaspoon celery seeds
½ cup water
1 cup mayonnaise
½ cup heavy cream
1 tablespoon granulated sugar
⅓ cup minced red onion
2 garlic cloves, grated on a Microplane grater

3 tablespoons apple cider vinegar
1 tablespoon freshly squeezed lemon juice
1 teaspoon kosher salt, plus additional for seasoning as needed
½ teaspoon cayenne pepper, plus additional as needed
½ teaspoon finely ground fresh black pepper, plus additional as needed

1 large carrot, coarsely shredded, about 1¼ cups
1 large Granny Smith apple, peeled and cut into ¼-inch matchsticks, about 1½ cups
¼ cup coarsely chopped flat-leaf parsley

1. Place the green and red cabbage in a large bowl and toss with the sugar.
2. Place the caraway and celery seeds in a small dry skillet over medium-high heat until fragrant, about 20 seconds. Remove from the heat, pour in the water, and let cool completely.

   Combine all of the remaining dressing ingredients in a blender or in a bowl using an immersion/stick blender. Pour in the seeds and their liquid and blend until smooth.
3. In a large bowl toss to combine the carrot, apple, and parsley with the cabbage. Pour in the dressing gradually, tossing to combine; you may not need all of the dressing. Season to taste with additional salt and black pepper.

POTATO SALAD

SERVES 8 (ABOUT 8 CUPS)

Creamy potato salad screams summertime. And since you don't want to spend a stunning summer day inside, I make it easy to make this one on the barbecue. The secret to its flavor? Pop open a can of chipotle chiles in adobo, and add some to the dressing. I don't add enough to make this dish spicy, but just the right amount so that the smoky flavor comes through in each bite.

3 pounds thin-skinned, golf ball–size or slightly larger new potatoes, scrubbed well
1½ cups water
1½ tablespoons kosher salt
⅓ cup apple cider vinegar
⅓ cup extra virgin olive oil
¼ cup minced shallots
¼ cup flat-leaf parsley
1¼ cups finely diced celery

Dressing
¾ cup mayonnaise
6 tablespoons heavy cream
1½ tablespoons finely chopped sweet white onion
1 garlic clove, peeled, halved, germ removed, and grated on a Microplane grater
¾ tablespoon chipotle in adobo, any excess sauce wiped off
3 tablespoons apple cider vinegar
1 teaspoon kosher salt
1 teaspoon finely ground fresh black pepper
3 tablespoons canola or vegetable oil

¼ cup finely chopped scallions, white and green portions
¼ cup minced chives
Fleur de sel
Coarsely ground fresh black pepper

1. Preheat one grate of a charcoal or gas grill to high.
2. Lay two sheets of heavy-duty aluminum foil, each 16 to 18 inches long, on top of each other, and fold up the sides, creating a bowl shape with a rounded base about 9 inches across.

   Place the potatoes in the foil bowl. At this point, they should be in a snug even layer. Add the water and salt. Gather the sides of the bowl, bringing them together to create a sealed, rounded packet about 6 to 7 inches across.
3. Place the packet on the grate and cook for 20 to 30 minutes, or until the potatoes are tender when pierced with a knife. (Alternately the potatoes can be boiled on the stovetop in salted water.)
4. Remove from the heat and cool slightly.

   Combine the vinegar, oil, shallots, parsley, and celery in a large bowl.

   While still warm, but cool enough to handle, cut the potatoes in half and toss in the oil mixture. Set aside to let cool completely.
5. Combine the mayonnaise, cream, onion, garlic, chipotle, vinegar, salt, and pepper in a blender, or in a bowl using an immersion/stick blender. Blend until completely smooth and slightly aerated, about 3 minutes. With the blender running, slowly add the canola oil and again blend until smooth.
6. Using a light folding motion, add about one-quarter of the dressing and half of the scallions and chives to the potatoes. Then add enough dressing to coat the potatoes, and stir in the remaining scallions and chives; you may not use all of the dressing. Season to taste with fleur de sel and pepper.

   Transfer to a serving bowl for a neater presentation.

PASTA SALAD

SERVES 8 (ABOUT 11^1/2 CUPS)

Ah, the final member of the classic cold salad trio, and one of the best make-ahead sides out there: Somehow, it's even better the next day. I use twisted pasta like gemelli or fusilli, because it traps just the right amount of dressing. To add texture and extra bursts of flavor, I add crunchy chopped bell peppers, grape tomatoes, and red onions.

2 red bell peppers, cut into thin strips about the length of the pasta

1 green bell pepper, cut into thin strips about the length of the pasta

1/4 cup thinly sliced red onion

1 1/2 cups grape tomatoes, halved

2 tablespoons finely chopped scallions, white and green portions

10 medium to large basil leaves

2 tablespoons minced chives

1 tablespoon coarsely chopped fresh marjoram leaves

1/4 cup extra virgin olive oil

2 tablespoons sherry vinegar

1 pound gemelli, or other twisted pasta

Dressing

3/4 cup mayonnaise

6 tablespoons heavy cream

1 1/2 tablespoons finely chopped sweet white onion

1 garlic clove, peeled, halved, germ removed, and grated on a Microplane grater

3/4 tablespoon chipotle in adobo, any excess sauce wiped off

3 tablespoons apple cider vinegar

1 teaspoon kosher salt

1 teaspoon finely ground fresh black pepper

3 tablespoons canola or vegetable oil

Fleur de sel

Coarsely ground freash black pepper

2 tablespoons minced chives

1. Combine the red and green bell peppers, onion, tomatoes, scallions, basil, chives, marjoram, olive oil, and vinegar in a large bowl.

   Cook the pasta in salted water, according to the manufacturer's instructions, until al dente.

   Drain the pasta and immediately toss with the pepper mixture. Spread out on a baking sheet and let cool completely, about 30 minutes.

2. Combine the mayonnaise, cream, onion, garlic, chipotle, vinegar, salt, and pepper in a blender, or in a bowl using an immersion/stick blender. Blend until completely smooth and slightly aerated, about 3 minutes. With the blender running, slowly add the canola oil and blend again until smooth.

3. Place the pasta mixture in a large bowl.

   Using a light folding motion, add about one-quarter of the dressing and half of the chives to the pasta. Then add enough dressing to coat the pasta and stir in the remaining chives; you may not use all of the dressing. Season to taste with fleur de sel and black pepper.

4. Transfer to a serving bowl for a neater presentation.

Herb Bundle
(page 365)

BASIC
RECIPES

APL BBQ SAUCE

After years of sampling and experimenting, I've come up with what I consider the ultimate base sauce, the perfect balance of sweet, salty, and tangy that I think best complements barbecue. The serious depth of flavor comes from first sweating onion, bell pepper, and garlic before moving on to the spices and later transitioning into those beloved concentrated ingredients, like mustard, ketchup, apricot preserves, and molasses. A last-minute blast of heat, texture, and tang comes from grated jalapeño and green apple. I tweak it a bit here and there—adding some honey or hot sauce or vinegar, depending on what I'm cooking—but the foundation is all here.

½ cup canola or vegetable oil

5 garlic cloves, peeled and coarsely chopped

1 medium sweet white onion, coarsely chopped

1 green bell pepper, coarsely chopped

2 teaspoons kosher salt, plus additional as needed

¼ cup bourbon

3 tablespoons chili powder

1 tablespoon coarsely ground fresh black pepper

¼ teaspoon ground allspice, plus additional for seasoning

¼ teaspoon ground cloves, plus additional for seasoning

1 cup firmly packed dark brown sugar

2 cups water

2 cups ketchup

½ cup unsulfured blackstrap molasses

½ cup prepared yellow mustard

½ cup apple cider vinegar, plus additional as needed

2 teaspoons hot sauce

½ cup apricot preserves

1 jalapeño chile, grated on a Microplane grater, stopping before the seeds

½ Granny Smith apple, grated on a Microplane grater

Pour the oil in a large saucepan and place over medium heat until it starts to shimmer. Stir in the garlic, onion, bell pepper, and salt. Cook, stirring occasionally until the vegetables have softened, about 10 minutes.

Pour in the bourbon and cook until the alcohol has cooked off, about 5 minutes. There will no longer be the strong smell of alcohol.

Combine the chili powder, black pepper, allspice, and cloves and add to the pan. Cook, stirring continuously, until fragrant, about 3 minutes.

Stir in the brown sugar, water, ketchup, molasses, mustard, vinegar, hot sauce, and preserves. Bring the mixture to a boil, stirring occasionally to be sure nothing sticks to the bottom and burns. Reduce to a simmer. Continue to simmer, stirring often, until thickened, about 45 minutes.

Add the jalapeño and apple. At this point the sauce can be left chunky or blended in a blender (blend in small batches since it will be hot), or in a bowl using an immersion/stick blender until smooth.

Season to taste with additional allspice, cloves, salt, and vinegar to taste.

APPLE JUICE SPRAY

A mixture of apple juice and water, this spray takes no time to make. But although it's simple, it truly makes a difference in your final product. Not only does it encourage the development of that gorgeous sheen on the outside of your barbecue—the diluted apple juice is just sweet enough to caramelize but not so sugary that it easily burns—but it also cools down the meat's surface, so the outside doesn't get too dark before the inside is sufficiently cooked.

1 cup unsweetened apple juice
1 cup water

Combine the water and juice and place in a spray bottle.

NOTE: For Apricot Spray, substitute apricot nectar for apple juice.

HERB BUNDLE

Sure, you *could* use a brush or mini mop to baste your meat with compound butter. But come on, how cool does it look to use an herb bundle instead? OK, that's only one reason I do it. Besides looking cool, using your bundle to baste lets you slowly, steadily, and subtly layer on the aromatic oils in those herbs. And it means that there's no skanky old brush threatening to contribute off-flavors to your meat. When I'm done basting, sometimes I chop up the warm, toasty herbs, mix them with a bit of melted butter, and slather the mixture on my cutting board. That way, any meat I'm slicing will pick up all its fabulous flavors.

1 bunch fresh herb(s), such as thyme, sage, or rosemary, or any combination

Using kitchen twine, tie the bunch to the end of a wooden kitchen spoon or a dowel. This will make it easier to use as a brush for basting.

COMPOUND BUTTER

MAKES ABOUT 1 POUND

If you've read my recipes, you'll notice that I have a thing for compound butter. That's because it's a killer way of adding color and flavor. It's unbelievably easy to make, it's great to prepare ahead, and it stands up well to freezing (you can even use it right out of the freezer). I brush it on meats as they cook, sometimes using a bundle of herbs, and spread it on my cutting board when I'm slicing meat that comes off the grill, so that some hangs on to each slice.

1 pound (4 sticks) unsalted butter, softened at room temperature
¼ cup finely chopped flat-leaf parsley
2 tablespoons finely chopped shallots
1 garlic clove, peeled, halved, germ removed, and grated on a Microplane grater
Zest of 1 lemon, grated on a Microplane grater
2 teaspoons finely ground fresh black pepper
2 teaspoons kosher salt

Combine all of the ingredients in a medium bowl, pressing down on the butter slightly to smooth and to evenly incorporate the other ingredients.

Lay out a piece of plastic wrap about 18 inches long. Place the butter in the center of the plastic and spread into a rough log shape that is about 1½ inches in diameter. Fold up the plastic from the edge closest to you and use it as a guide to roll the plastic into a smooth log.

Wrap the log tightly in the plastic wrap, twisting the ends to compact the log slightly. Wrap in a second sheet of plastic wrap, if necessary. Tightly wrapped, the butter can be refrigerated for 1 week, or frozen for up to 1 month.

FRESH AND DRIED BREAD CRUMBS

MAKES ABOUT 2 CUPS

Store-bought bread crumbs in a box are a sad substitute for bread crumbs you can make yourself in no time.

3 cups country-style white bread, preferably one day old
1 tablespoon extra virgin olive oil

For fresh bread crumbs: Cut the crusts from the bread and discard. Cut the remaining bread into 1-inch cubes. Place in a food processor and process until coarsely ground.

For dried bread crumbs: Toss the fresh bread crumbs with the olive oil.

Heat a large cast-iron skillet over medium-low to medium heat (either on the stovetop or on the grate) and toast, stirring often, until golden, about 10 minutes.

BLUE CHEESE DRESSING

MAKES ABOUT 3 CUPS

Fabulous with Buffalo wings or spooned generously over a wedge of iceberg lettuce, blue cheese dressing is a steakhouse classic. However you use it, this version is so much better than bottled.

1 cup crumbled blue cheese (about 4 ounces, if starting with a block)

1½ cups mayonnaise

6 tablespoons white wine vinegar

1½ to 2 tablespoons granulated sugar

¼ cup heavy cream

2 tablespoons finely chopped chives

Combine the cheese, mayonnaise, vinegar, 1½ tablespoons of the sugar, and the cream. Add additional sugar to taste. Stir in the chives.

Refrigerate for at least 2 hours, but preferably overnight for the flavors to develop.

YOGURT SAUCE

Also known as *tzatziki,* this Greek sauce is an amazing counterpoint to the sort of big, bold flavors you get when you're cooking outdoors. Its cooling, tangy flavors match up beautifully with char and toasty spices. I especially love it with lamb.

1½ cups whole-milk yogurt, preferably Greek
1½ teaspoons kosher salt
½ cup thinly sliced seedless cucumber
1 tablespoon coarsely chopped fresh dill
1½ tablespoons coarsely chopped mint
1 tablespoon coarsely chopped flat-leaf parsley
1 to 2 garlic cloves, peeled, halved, germ removed, and grated on a Microplane grater
1½ tablespoons extra virgin olive oil
Zest of ½ lemon, grated on a Microplane grater
1 tablespoon freshly squeezed lemon juice
1 teaspoon freshly ground black pepper

Line a fine-mesh strainer with a piece of dampened cheesecloth and place over a bowl.

Combine the yogurt and 1 teaspoon of the salt and place in the strainer. Refrigerate for 2 hours to drain.

Meanwhile, 30 minutes before the yogurt finishes draining, toss the cucumbers with the remaining ½ teaspoon of the salt and let sit in an even layer, at room temperature, for 30 minutes.

Place the yogurt into a food processor or into a clean bowl.

Place the cucumbers in a clean towel and squeeze over the sink to extract all of the juices. Add to the yogurt with all of the remaining ingredients, beginning with 1 clove of garlic and adding additional to taste.

Process to blend in the food processor, or in the bowl using an immersion/stick blender. Blend until smooth.

The sauce can be served at this point, but preferably refrigerate it for 24 hours to allow the flavors to develop.

AMPED-UP COCKTAIL SAUCE

MAKES ABOUT 2¹/2 CUPS

Another far-superior substitute to its bottle equivalent, this cocktail sauce is revved up with plenty of lemon juice, bottled horseradish, and an equal amount of the nose-clearing fresh kind. I can't imagine serving anything else with cool, plump cocktail shrimp.

TIP: Fresh horseradish is available in many markets and is worth seeking out. If you can't find it, the sauce won't have that extra punch, but it'll still have great flavor. Use additional bottled horseradish to taste.

2 cups ketchup
2 tablespoons freshly grated horseradish root (see Note)
2 tablespoons high-quality bottled horseradish
2 tablespoons freshly squeezed lemon juice
1½ tablespoons Worcestershire sauce
1 tablespoon hot sauce
2 medium shallots, peeled, and grated on a Microplane grater

Stir together all of the ingredients in a medium bowl and refrigerate for at least 2 hours, but preferably overnight for the flavors to develop.

HERB SAUCE

Like pesto, this is an extremely effective and delicious herb-delivery system. But since I combine several different fresh herbs and don't add any nuts or cheese, you get this light, bright, unbelievably lively sauce that blows most pestos out of the water. I spoon this on my Pounded Boneless Chicken Breasts (page 254), but you'll find lots of other uses for it.

½ cup water
½ cup flat-leaf parsley leaves
¼ cup coarsely chopped chives
¼ cup fresh tarragon leaves
¼ cup fresh dill, large pieces of stem removed
¼ cup small fresh basil leaves (or large leaves roughly torn)
¼ cup coarsely chopped scallions, white and green portions
1 tablespoon coarsely chopped shallot
Zest of 1 lemon, grated on a Microplane grater
1 serrano, Thai Bird, or other small hot chile of choice, thinly sliced and seeds removed
1 tablespoon kosher salt, plus additional as needed
1 teaspoon finely ground fresh black pepper, plus additional as needed
1 to 1½ cups extra virgin olive oil

Combine the water, parsley, chives, tarragon, dill, basil, scallions, shallot, lemon zest, chile, salt, and pepper in a food processor. Begin by pulsing to incorporate and then blend until smooth, scraping the sides down as needed, until a smooth puree forms.

With the processor running, slowly add 1 cup of olive oil. Add additional oil as needed to reach a sauce consistency.

Season to taste with salt and pepper.

ASIAN DIPPING SAUCE

MAKES ABOUT 2 CUPS

I pack my little juicy Asian Pork Meatball Skewers (page 55), and this dipping sauce is all about echoing those flavors and adding a spark. Which is exactly what funky fish sauce, lime juice, rice wine vinegar, and chiles provide. It's also an excellent addition to my Vietnamese-inspired pork chops (page 49).

½ cup hot water
½ cup fish sauce
¼ cup freshly squeezed lime juice
4 garlic cloves, peeled, halved, germ removed, and grated on a Microplane grater
1 tablespoon rice wine vinegar
1 tablespoon chile paste, preferably Sriracha or sambal
1 tablespoon granulated sugar
2 small hot chiles, preferably Thai bird, sliced into rounds, seeds removed
¼ cup finely grated carrot

Combine the water, fish sauce, lime juice, garlic, vinegar, chile paste, and sugar in a blender, or in a medium bowl with an immersion/stick blender. Blend until smooth. Stir in the chiles and carrots.

GARLICKY HERB VINAIGRETTE

MAKES ABOUT 2¾ CUPS

In Argentina, people treat this condiment, also called chimichurri sauce, like we treat ketchup—they put it on *everything*, especially steak. Taste it, and you'll immediately see why.

½ cup red wine vinegar
¼ cup freshly squeezed lemon juice
¼ cup finely chopped shallot
6 garlic cloves, peeled, germ removed, and grated on a Microplane grater
1 small hot chile, preferably Thai Bird or serrano
1 tablespoon kosher salt, plus additional as needed
1 teaspoon pimentón (see Sources page 378), or other smoked paprika
1 teaspoon dried oregano, preferably Mexican
1 teaspoon finely ground fresh black pepper
½ teaspoon ground cumin
1 cup coarsely chopped flat-leaf parsley
½ cup coarsely chopped cilantro
1 cup extra virgin olive oil
½ cup finely chopped tomato

Combine the vinegar, lemon juice, shallot, garlic, chile, salt, paprika, oregano, black pepper, and cumin in a medium bowl. Let sit for 10 minutes for the flavors to develop.

At this point, the additional ingredients added should be pulsed in a bowl using an immersion/stick blender or in a small food processor or blended with a mortar and pestle. The sauce should be well combined, but there will still be visible pieces of the herbs and tomato.

Add the parsley and cilantro, pulsing or blending to combine. Slowly pour in the oil, keeping the herbs in pieces, but allowing the oil to partially emulsify in the mixture.

Either blend or stir in the tomatoes, and season to taste with salt.

SCIENCE:
AN INTERVIEW WITH
DAVE ARNOLD

When you cook a lot, you start to take certain things for granted. You notice meat sticking to your grill grates, so you take measures to prevent it. Your pork shoulder comes out luscious even though its internal temperature clocks in well above what you shoot for with your pork chops, so you keep doing what you're doing. You rarely ask yourself why these things happen, but doing so can give you a deeper understanding of the cooking process and, in the long run, improve your food.

When everyday questions require thoughtful, precise answers, you turn to folks who spend their time thinking about the science that underlies, well, just about everything—people like Dave Arnold. A few years ago, he created, and now runs, the illustrious French Culinary Institute's program on culinary technology. He pretty much plays around with high-tech gadgets with culinary applications, and runs cool experiments that occasionally call into question some of our most deeply held assumptions about cooking. Not a bad job, huh? So I asked him to elaborate on some common phenomena in the world of outdoor cooking.

ADAM PERRY LANG: When I grill, I cook meat so that its internal temperature is around 120°F to 165°F, depending on the cut and type of meat, of course. But when I'm cooking Southern barbecue, the internal temperature goes way above that. I'm talking 190°F-plus! Why do you think it comes out moist and delicious and not dry and tough?

DAVE ARNOLD: You're right, by the standards of rare, medium rare, and well-done, barbecue seems incredibly overcooked. But when you keep meat at barbecue's relatively low temperatures for a long time, you start breaking down the meat's collagen, a type of connective tissue composed of three helixes of gelatin. When the internal temperature reaches a certain level, which is well above what we think of

as "well-done," the collagen breaks apart into gelatin. And gelatin has an unctuous, moist mouthfeel that we like, because it holds on to water in a way that muscle proteins do not.

APL: When I'm barbecuing and my meat's internal temperature hits about 163° F, it stops going up for a good three hours. Any idea why?

DA: This might be when the collagen in the meat is breaking down into gelatin. There's a theory that when things are changing states, there is a temperature plateau. Perhaps the most famous example is when ice becomes water. Ice is a crystal structure, and breaking it apart to turn it into water consumes energy. Heat is a type of energy. So instead of seeing a steady rise in temperature as ice becomes water, the temperature stays level until the transformation from solid to liquid is complete. Something analogous might be happening as collagen breaks down into gelatin. This reaction takes energy, and the heat in the barbecue is relatively low, so the temperature can't rise until the reaction is finished.

APL: What is your take on meat sticking to a grill or any cooking surface for that matter?

DA: Here's the theory: Most cooking surfaces are porous: that is, they have holes or gaps on a microscopic level and even sometimes on a macroscopic level (you can actually see these as dots on some aluminum pans). When meat touches this hot surface, it begins to give up moisture, which contains soluble proteins. These proteins hit the surface, denature, coagulate, and lock into these pores like Velcro.

But there's another theory that suggests sticking has to do with hydrogen bonds and van der Waals interactions happening between the proteins and the cooking surface. Don't worry about the details. Just know that once you cook the proteins long enough to sufficiently modify their structures, then they no longer have the same affinity for adhesion with the surface and they release. That's probably why you hear the advice that you shouldn't move or flip your meat right after you put it on the grill.

APL: What's going on when you're searing meat? You're not really "sealing in the juices," right? And while we're on the subject, what the heck makes something "juicy"?

DA: Let me start by saying, no, you're definitely not sealing in any liquid. Harold McGee [the brilliant author of *On Food and Cooking*, which explores the science of the kitchen] dispelled this myth. In fact, he explains that you're actually expelling moisture when you sear—that's why your pan sizzles.

APL: So why do we sear meat and why does meat with a brown crust often seem juicier than meat without this crust?

DA: Well, uncooked meat doesn't taste like much, but when you apply heat, something cool happens—an incredibly complex reaction between proteins, amino acids, and reducing sugars (like glucose) in the meat produces hundreds of new compounds. Called the Maillard Reaction, but more commonly known as "browning," this is where a lot of the flavor we associate with meat comes from. (It's also referred to as caramelization, though I have to add that technically, caramelization refers to a breakdown of sugar, like sucrose.) Because it, along with the breakdown of proteins into amino acids and the breakdown of fat, produces such awesome flavor, we salivate when we eat it, creating the perception that the meat is "juicier." Juiciness, by the way, does not hinge only on the amount of liquid that meat contains. It's a sensation produced by multiple factors—including external ones (like saliva production) and fat, which provides lubrication—that all add up to how the meat feels in your mouth.

APL: Brining (basically, submerging meat in a mixture of salt and water) can do wonders for pork and chicken. I like to imagine an army of tiny cooks traveling deep into a chop or breast with their miniature tools and pumping flavor and water into each cell. But what's really going on when you brine?

DA: This may sound counterintuitive, but bear with me. When meat is brined, it first loses water. Nature hates to have a higher concentration of one thing (like, say, lots of salt in water) and a lower concentration of another (no salt in water), so in striving for equilibrium, water inside the cells of the meat heads out into the brine to decrease the concentration of salt. But the salt in the brine increases the ability of the proteins in the meat to trap and hold water, even at high temperatures, which more than compensates for the water loss. This provides a sort of buffer against drying out the meat by overcooking it. After a while, as some of the salt permeates the meat and there becomes a higher concentration of salt inside than out, the meat cells take in some of that brine water along with any tasty things you've used to flavor it.

APL: It's relatively common knowledge that to prevent food-borne illness due to a few nasty bacteria, you should make sure your meat doesn't spend too long in the so-called temperature danger zone (between 40°F and 140°F). So the idea of cooking meat for a long time at a low temperature—a trademark of Southern barbecue—makes some people nervous. Can you provide some comfort?

DA: Sure. First of all, let me just make clear that it's not as if the bacteria are fine and dandy and then all of a sudden the temperature hits 140°F and they all die. They do not die at once and they do not die instantly. In fact, salmonella, E. coli, and other bacteria that can cause food-borne illness actually start dying around 52° C (125.6°F), or at least stop growing. Second, bacteria don't all of a sudden start growing when the temperature hits the danger zone. There's a lag period: Even when the temperature hits the zone, the bacteria takes awhile to start multiplying.

Another important point: The inside of meat is relatively sterile—its surface is where the bacteria resides. (Note, though, that bacteria can be introduced with a thermometer that hasn't been sanitized or during the grinding process, when the outside of the meat is mixed with the inside.) So even barbecue's relatively low heat (say, 225°F, to use an example on the lower end) is hot enough to kill the surface bacteria. In addition, the inside of the meat, which doesn't contain as much scary stuff, reaches a high temperature (around 190°F) that could kill just about anything bad. Finally, as with many traditional cooking methods, lots of layers of safety have been built into barbecue: Smoke, salt, and spices all have antimicrobial properties.

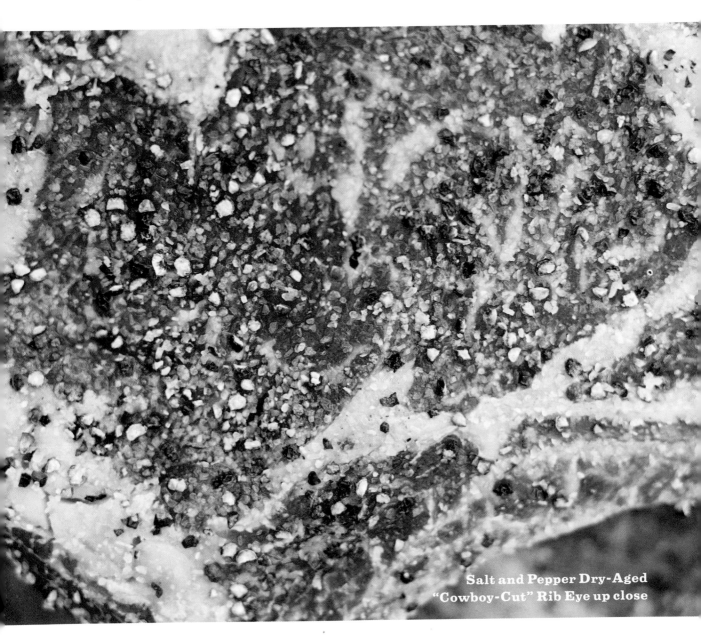

Salt and Pepper Dry-Aged "Cowboy-Cut" Rib Eye up close

Sources

B&G
www.bgfoods.com
Ac'cent Flavor Enhancer

BBQ Forum
www.bbqforum.com
An informative barbecue blog

Bell and Evans
www.bellandevans.com
Air-chilled chicken

The Big Green Egg
www.biggreenegg.com
Ceramic cookers and accessories

Cookshack
www.cookshack.com
Fast Eddy's pellet-fired smokers, wood, pellets, and outdoor-cooking accessories

Da Gift Baskets & Bags
www.dagiftbasket.com
A variety of chile powders, including Chimayo and green Hatch, and other herbs and spices such as Mexican oregano, many kinds of dried chiles, and annato seeds

Eat Wild
www.eatwild.com
A great resource for finding local grass-fed meat, eggs, and dairy products

Falls Mill
www.fallsmill.com
Stone-ground cornmeal

Frank's Red Hot
www.franksredhot.com
Hot cayenne pepper sauce

Goya Foods
www.goya.com
Goya Sazón Azafrán, fruit nectars, seasonings, and other Spanish, Mexican, and Hispanic products

Hawgeyes BBQ
www.hawgeyesbbq.com
Bear paws, chicken sitters, grilling baskets, heatproof gloves, injecting syringes, meat pounders, instant-read and remote thermometers, a variety of fruit and hardwoods, and other grilling and barbecue supplies

The Home Depot
(or your local hardware store)
www.homedepot.com
Firebricks and foam-backed tape

ImportFood
www.importfood.com
Maggi Seasoning, Thai basil, and other Asian products

Koch Equipment
www.kochequipment.com
Butchery supplies and other industrial equipment

JB Prince
www.jbprince.com
Kitchen supplies, including sheet pans and Silpats

La Caja China
www.lacajachina.com
Caja China cookers and accessories

La Cense Beef
www.lacensebeef.com
Grass-fed beef

La Tienda
www.latienda.com
Bomba rice, chorizo, pimentón, saffron, paella pans, and other Spanish products

Le Creuset
www.lecreuset.com
Two-burner, cast-iron reversible grill / griddle

McCormick Spices
www.mccormick.com
Montreal Steak Seasoning, Old Bay Seasoning, and a variety of other spice blends

Microplane
www.microplane.com
The best zester out there

Naked Whiz
www.nakedwhiz.com
Recommendations for and reviews of specific brands of charcoal

Niman Ranch
www.nimanranch.com
All-natural beef, lamb, pork, and poultry

Old Hickory Pits
www.oldhickorypits.com
Smokers, cookers, and accessories

Penzeys Spices
www.penzeys.com
An amazing variety of spices

Reynolds
www.reynoldswrap.com
Bags, plastic and foil wrap, and other cooking supplies

SpitJack
www.spitjack.com
Spits and accessories

Sur La Table
www.surlatable.com
Kitchen supplies, including grill presses

Viking
www.vikingrange.com
Grills, ceramic cookers, and accessories

Weber
www.weber.com
Grills and accessories

Williams-Sonoma
www.williamssonoma.com
Kitchen supplies, including meatloaf pans

Zatarain's
www.zatarains.com
Crab-boil spice mix and other New Orleans-inspired products

Acknowledgments

I could fill another book just with the names of all the people I want to thank. If it were possible, I'd include every home cook who has ever fired up his or her barbecue. But because space is tight, here it goes:

I'd like to thank my mom and dad, Jane and Paul Lang, for setting such a great example, for giving me unconditional support throughout my career, for giving me the courage and love to start cooking professionally and follow my dreams.

My father, Fred Perry, who enjoys cooking as much as I do, and who spoiled me with his amazing Sunday breakfasts when I was a kid.

JJ Goode, probably the most talented food writer I know, whom I was blessed to work with, a true master at untangling my thoughts and doing justice to my culinary obsessions.

Amy Vogler, my "wing-girl," the glue that held this book project together, who proved that there is definitely someone just as obsessive as I am about detail, precision, and perfection.

My partners Bob and Richard Gans, for what we created together at Daisy May's.

Jeff Cicio, my brother, friend, and spiritual advisor, and the rest of the team at Daisy May's, whose hard work gave me the ability to go out, explore, and write such a book.

Lisa Queen, my tremendously skilled book agent and a great friend, who believed in my vision and helped to make it a reality.

Will Schwalbe, the angel who first approached me to write a book and had enough faith in me to take time out of his busy schedule to help me do it right.

Ellen Archer, Kristin Kiser, Will Balliett, Brendan Duffy, Phil Rose, Shubhani Sarkar, Linda Prather, Marie Coolman, Allison McGeehon, Sarah Rucker, Maha Khalil, and Mike Rotondo.

David Loftus, my incredible photographer, for his friendship and his magician-like ability to make food come to life.

Cyd and Tim McDowell, Megan Hedgpeth, and Nicole Ganas, who with their effort, patience, and styling helped make the book's photos look so amazing.

John "Smoke" Markus, for being an incredible friend and brother in smoke, and for allowing us to shoot photos at his gorgeous property in the Hudson Valley.

Nick Mautone and his family, for their friendship and for letting us into their lovely home for the Hamptons beach photos.

John Tarpoff, my Beef Sensei and a great life mentor who is always walking the walk.

Everyone at Niman Ranch, who are truly living the gospel and proving that amazing meat and animal welfare go hand in hand.

Al Doering, Dan Barber, Jerry Davenport, and Dave Arnold, for their wisdom, which contributed so much to the depth of this book.

Mario Batali, the Zen master of chef coolness, who invited me to be his partner at Carnevino and share what I love to do best.

Rachael Ray, for inspiring me with her sincere friendship and incredible work ethic, not to mention those incredible dinners at her house.

Jamie Oliver, a kick-ass chef, business partner, and one of my closest friends, who not only inspires me in the kitchen, but who has also shown me what it means to be charitable and how rewarding it is to give.

Daniel Boulud, the chef who taught me what it means to be one, and to never give up or underestimate how much you can achieve.

David Waltuck, who taught me that you don't have to yell to be a great chef.

Sottha Khunn, whose humility and discipline have shaped the way I approach cooking.

Mike Tucker of Hawgeyesbbq.com, the go-to guy for anything new, old, and fun in the world of BBQ products—a great fishing buddy, too.

Ray Basso, the founder of BBQforum.com, for tying together the BBQ community, which I'm so proud to be part of.

William Kriegel at Le Cense Beef, for showing me that American grass-fed beef can be incredible.

Jimmy Kimmel, for helping me name this book and for being a great cooking buddy who is as insane and passionate about food as I am.

Jeff Bennet and Colin Rosenbaum, for saving the day with the helicopter and lending a hand when one was really needed.

Scott Solasz of Master Purveyors, for letting me into his meat mecca in the Bronx and introducing me to and teaching me the world of old-school beef.

Mark Pastore and Pat LaFrieda, two unbelievable guys who preach the meat gospel and are responsible for some of the most unbelievable meat in New York City.

Fred Carl and his company, Viking Range, for his support and use of their equipment.

Everyone on the BBQ circuit, because they inspire me every time I start up my barbecue.

My wife, Fleur, who has been with me every step of the way, tolerating my very-late-night work sessions and many spontaneous "I just have to go" culinary explorations.

My children, Max and Noa, for teaching me what true inspiration really means.

Index

eggs, hard smoked, 337
equipment, 8–9

F

fajita-style marinated flank
    steak, 143–44
Farm Bill, 3
Farris, Marc, 108, 337
fat, 33
    in beef, 114–15, 118–19
    in pork, 36–37
fennel, grilled, with smoked
    tomatoes and olives,
    324–25
firebricks, 9
fire extinguisher, 8
flanken-style riblets, 188–89
flank steak, fajita-style mari-
    nated, 143–44
flare-ups, 5, 10–12
flatiron steaks marinated in
    red wine, 150–51
flavor:
    building of, 5, 25–30
    direct grilling and, 10
foil, 9
French Culinary Institute, 375
frozen meat, 39
fuel, 8

G

garlic:
    bacon-wrapped skinless
        drumsticks with sage and,
        271–72
    charred eggplant puree with
        yogurt and, 326–27
    crispy suckling pig with
        spicy sweet-sour glaze,
        92–95
    glazed pork loin with
        cilantro and, 71–72

hanger steak with thyme,
    crushed red pepper and,
    148–49
herb studded cracked lamb
    short loin, 235–36
herb vinaigrette, 373
-honey glaze, tri-tip with,
    146–47
and jalapeño dressing, pork
    T-bone with, 44–45
marinated skirt steak with
    cilantro and, 141–42
melting, 335
melting, burnt ends with,
    173–74
picnic shoulder marinated
    in citrus, cumin and,
    77–79
slivered, lamb blade chops
    with marjoram and,
    230–31
slivered, pounded veal
    round with oregano and,
    154–55
slivered and melting, long
    cook beef shank with,
    191–92
Texas toast, 312
veal rib chops with thyme,
    sage and, 152–53
garlic salt, chuck roast crusted
    with instant coffee and,
    183–84
gas grills, 10, 13
German deli-style top round of
    beef, 182–83
glazes, 5, 30
gloves, 9
grater, microplane, 8–9
grates, 8, 12
griddle, 9, 12
grill basket, 9

grill brush, 8
grill press, 9
grills:
    calibrating, 15
    ceramic cookers, 14
    direct, 9–12
    gas, 10, 13
    indirect cookers, 12–13
    maintenance of, 17
    temperature control and,
        15–16
Guerra, Roberto, 92

H

ham:
    smoked "baked," 106–7
    steak glazed with dark
        brown sugar, 51
hanger steak with thyme,
    crushed red pepper, and
    garlic, 148–49
herb:
    bundle, 5, 365
    sauce, 371
    vinaigrette, garlicky, 373
honey:
    baby back pork ribs glazed
        with, 63–64
    -garlic glaze, tri-tip with,
        146–47
    -glazed spatchcocked
        chicken, 266–67
    -glazed whole turkey breast,
        298–99
    lamb shanks, Moroccan-
        spiced, 222–23
    orange blossom, lamb
        tenderloins glazed
        with thyme and,
        206–7
hormones, 114, 116–17
hot wings, 274–75

I

indirect cooking, 12–13
    with ceramic cookers, 14
Italian sausages with peppers
    and onions, griddled and
    grilled, 60–61

J

jalapeño:
    and garlic dressing, pork
        T-bone with, 44–45
    grated, marinated boneless
        lamb loin with marjoram
        and, 216–18
jars and containers, 8
jerk drumsticks, 282–83

K

kale with bacon, 344
kebabs:
    Asian pork meatball skewers,
        55–56
    lamb, 212–13
knives, 9

L

lamb, 198–246
    blade chops with slivered
        garlic and marjoram, 230–31
    boneless butterflied leg of,
        219–21
    butterflying, 221
    chops, double, inferno, 201–2
    chops, pounded, with
        seasoned bread crumbs,
        204–5
    gaminess in, 198
    grain finished vs. grass
        finished, 198
    gyro, smoked, 245–46
    kebabs, 212–13
    leg of, boned, rolled, and
        tied, 232–33

loin, marinated boneless,
    with grated jalapeño and
    marjoram, 216–18
marbling in, 198, 199
rack of, crusted with grain
    mustard and chili powder,
    225–26
selecting, 199
shanks, Moroccan-spiced
    honey, 222–23
shanks, quick-cook sliceable,
    209–10
short loin, herb studded
    cracked, 235–36
six-hour leg of, "mechoui,"
    228–29
spit-roasted spring, 239–40
stew, Moroccan, 242–43
T-bones with lemon, mint,
    and oregano, 214–15
tenderloins glazed with
    orange blossom honey
    and thyme, 206–7
Le Cirque, 1, 343
lemon, lamb T-bones with
    mint, oregano and, 214–15
Lilly, Chris, 82
lime:
    crispy suckling pig with
        spicy sweet-sour glaze,
        92–95
    picnic shoulder marinated
        in citrus, garlic, and
        cumin, 77–79
livers, smoked chicken, 292–93

M

marinades, 25–26
marjoram:
    chopped salad, 353
    lamb blade chops with
        slivered garlic and, 230–31
    marinated boneless lamb

loin with grated jalapeño
    and, 216–18
McGee, Harold, 376
meat:
    collagen in, 24, 31, 36, 117, 375
    doneness of, 24–25
    fat in, see fat
    frozen, 39
    juiciness of, 33, 376
    searing, 376
    sticking to cooking surface,
        375–76
    wrapping of, 5, 31, 33
meatball skewers, Asian pork,
    55–56
meat pounder, 9
"mechoui," six-hour leg of
    lamb, 228–29
mint:
    lamb T-bones with lemon,
        oregano and, 214–15
    yogurt sauce, 369
Moroccan:
    charred eggplant puree
        with yogurt and garlic,
        326–27
    lamb stew, 242–43
    six-hour leg of lamb
        "mechoui," 228–29
    -spiced honey lamb shanks,
        222–23
mustard:
    boneless rib roast with
        pepper and, 180–81
    grain, rack of lamb crusted
        with chili powder and,
        225–26
myths, barbecue, 5, 33

N

New Mexican chile pork stew,
    110–11
notepad, 8